HEY, DON' REMEMI

WWII memories of Lancaster
and Martin Marauder operations

100, 12 & 626 Squadrons, RAF & 12 Squadron SAAF

by

Alan H Alcock

Copyrighted Material
First Print Edition, 2012

Copyright © Alan H Alcock 2012

Alan H Alcock has asserted his right under the Copyright, Designs and Patents Act 1988 to be identified as author of this work.
All rights reserved.
This book is a work of non-fiction based on the life, experiences and recollections of the author. The author has stated that to the best of his recollection the contents of this book are true. In a small number of instances, names have been changed to protect the privacy of those who may still be living.
Every effort has been made to obtain the necessary permissions with reference to copyright material, both illustrative and quoted. The author apologises for any omissions in this respect and will be pleased to make the appropriate acknowledgements in any future edition. All photographs & illustrations are from the author's collection.
No part of this publication may be reproduced, stored in a retrieval system, or transmitted, in any form or by any means, electronic, mechanical, photocopying, recording or otherwise, without the prior permission of the author.

The Author at home on leave from Italy, 11 January 1946.

This book is dedicated to my family and friends.

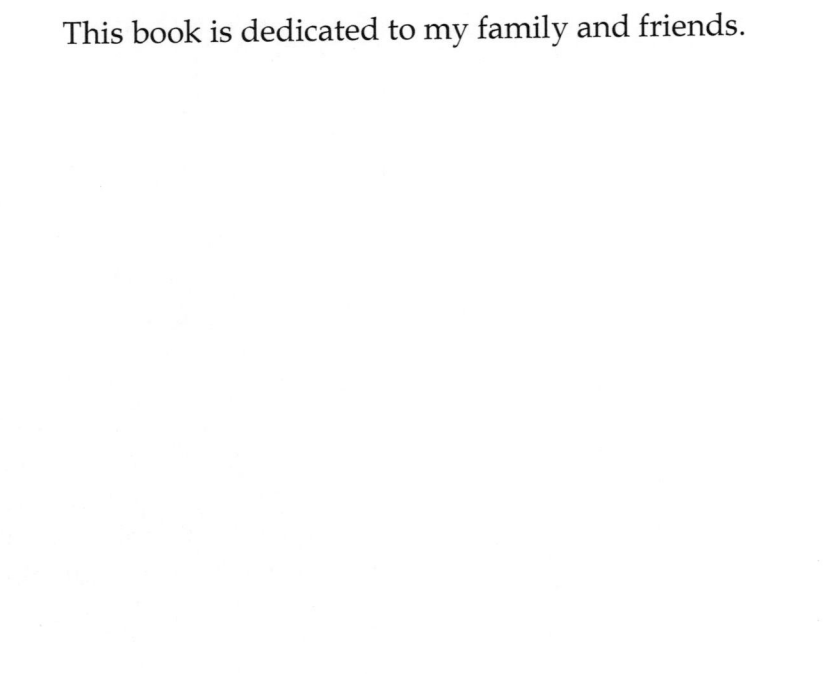

Preface

In late 1941 I volunteered for aircrew duties with the R.A.F. My reasons for doing so were three-fold: I wanted to fly, I preferred air-force blue to khaki, and something akin to patriotism stirred in my breast. However, I soon found that there was very little pleasure to be had as a "rookie" airman, so I worked hard and qualified as a sergeant air gunner. I became a rear-gunner, a member of an operational crew of a Lancaster bomber. We flew from Waltham, in Lincolnshire, with 100 Squadron, and later from Wickenby, also in Lincolnshire, with 12 Squadron.

From then on my life was all "ups and downs", becoming increasingly fraught with danger as, in 1943, R.A.F. Bomber Command concentrated its efforts on the Ruhr, Hamburg and Berlin. I flew on fourteen "ops" to the Ruhr, two to Hamburg and one to Peenemunde, which was described at "briefing" as a "Radio Location Research Plant" but which was, in reality, where the Germans were developing their V weapons. My first visit to the dreaded "Big City" (Berlin) followed, in August 1943. It was a second operation over Berlin, in November 1943, which completed my "first tour" of 30 operations.

My crew and I qualified for seven days leave, which, for me, was extended because I fell ill. Perhaps that head cold saved my life. On my return to my squadron I found that my crew, with a replacement rear gunner, had failed to return from Berlin. Five of the crew are buried in Berlin war cemetery and two have no known grave.

With my first tour of operations completed, I was posted away from my bomber squadron. I became an instructor for a short period, flying in Avro Anson aircraft. Then, in Spring 1944, I became attached to the South African Air Force, flying in American-built B26 Martin Marauder aircraft in support of the 8th Army in Italy.

As it had been in the night sky over Germany, death was never far away. My squadron suffered grievous losses over the northern-Italian city of Udine in December 1944. In March 1945, my Maruader, "N" for "Nemesis" was shot down, crash-landing on an Italian beach. We, the members of the crew, all managed to survive.

By the end of the war I had flown on 49 operations on my "second tour" and had reached the rank of Flying Officer. Surplus to requirements, as were most aircrew, my non-flying career in the R.A.F. commenced. I was given three roles to choose from: viz, War Graves, Intelligence or Transport. I opted for Transport and became a train conducting officer, visiting Italy, Austria, Switzerland and France before my "de-mob" in 1946.

I think I should say a little about my intentions with regard to this book. The book is not intended as a history; there are several excellent histories of R.A.F. Bomber Command available. It is intended to set down my memories of what life was like back then, in air crew training and on operations. I hope, therefore, it is of interest to readers who want to know more about what life was really like at that time.

I have divided the book into three parts. In part one, are my recollections of life in aircrew training in wartime Britain of 1941 and 1942. In part two, are my detailed recollections of my operations over Germany with R.A.F. Bomber Command in 1943. Part three covers my brief time as an instructor, my operations with the South African Air Force in Italy in 1944 and 1945 and then my spell as a train conducting officer lasting through to 1946.

I hope you will appreciate that whilst some memories are still crystal clear to me, others grow dimmer or may have been confused. Any factual errors are my own.

Finally, I would like to thank friends and family for their help with the making of this book.

Alan H Alcock
Lincolnshire, November 2012

Table of Contents

PART ONE	1
"Jankers"	2
A Case of Mistaken Identity	8
The High-Born Ladies	15
Air and Other Experiences	22
Home-Coming For A Hero	31
A Trip To Jerusalem	37
In the Deep Mid-Winter	52
"DTs"	60
PART TWO	66
Chocks Away	67
CREW ROSTER: - MAY - JULY, 1943	69
01 TARGET FOR TONIGHT: - DORTMUND.	71
02 TARGET FOR TONIGHT: - DUISBURG.	82
03 TARGET FOR TONIGHT: - BOCHUM.	83
04 TARGET FOR TONIGHT: - DUSSELDORF.	90
05 TARGET FOR TONIGHT: - ESSEN.	92
06 TARGET FOR TONIGHT: - DUSSELDORF.	97
07 TARGET FOR TONIGHT: - BOCHUM.	99
08 TARGET FOR TONIGHT: - OBERHAUSEN.	102
09 TARGET FOR TONIGHT: - COLOGNE.	106

10 TARGET FOR TONIGHT: - KREFELD.	110
11 TARGET FOR TONIGHT: - WUPPERTAL.	112
12 TARGET FOR TONIGHT: - GELSENKIRCHEN.	114
13 TARGET FOR TONIGHT: - COLOGNE.	119
14 TARGET FOR TONIGHT: - GELSENKIRCHEN.	124
15 TARGET FOR TONIGHT: - TURIN.	128
16 TARGET FOR TONIGHT: - HAMBURG.	130
17 TARGET FOR TONIGHT: - HAMBURG.	132
CREW ROSTER: - AUGUST TO NOVEMBER, 1943	138
18 TARGET FOR TONIGHT: - NUREMBURG.	140
19 TARGET FOR TONIGHT: - MILAN.	143
20 TARGET FOR TONIGHT: - PEENEMUNDE.	148
21 TARGET FOR TONIGHT: - LEVERKUSEN.	150
22 TARGET FOR TONIGHT: - BERLIN.	152
23 TARGET FOR TONIGHT: - MUNCHEN GLADBACH / RHEYDT.	158
24 TARGET FOR TONIGHT: - MANNHEIM-LUDWIGSHAFEN.	165
25 TARGET FOR TONIGHT: - MUNICH.	168
26 TARGET FOR TONIGHT: - KASSEL.	169
27 TARGET FOR TONIGHT: - STUTTGART.	172
28 TARGET FOR TONIGHT: - LEIPZIG.	175
29 TARGET FOR TONIGHT: - DUSSELDORF.	178
CREW ROSTER: - 18/19 NOVEMBER, 1943	181
30 TARGET FOR TONIGHT: - BERLIN.	184
LEAVE	188
CREW ROSTER: - 2/3 DECEMBER, 1943	192

PART THREE	193
New Boots for Old	194
See Naples and...	202
Shoe Shine Boy	213
A Bitter Tale	218
Dario	225
A Second Tour of Operations.	230
That Thin Blue Band	233
Papal Blessing	238
Yet More Operations.	249
"Nemesis"	251
An Itchy Tale	263
Hitch-Hike	267
Farewells all Round.	271
Padre's Pint	277
The Blanket	279
Mammas Mia	287
Alano in Milano	290
The Swiss Lieutenant's Woman	298
APPENDICES	
Papal Blessing - The Aftermath	304
R.I.P.	309
Gunnery Combat Report	312
Glossary	315

HEY, DON'T YOU REMEMBER?
You called me Al

PART ONE

"Getting Some Service In"

Chapter One

"Jankers"

(Mid-Winter 1941)

I have been an airman, second class, for some time now, and the weird and wonderful things I'm finding out about myself never cease to amaze me.

Recently a corporal - who would have looked more at home in S.S. uniform than R.A.F. blue - set alarm bells ringing in my mind over the validity of my parents' marriage, and yesterday a drill sergeant informed me, as I marched proudly past him, that my bearing bore all the characteristics of a pregnant duck.

Turning left or right, never before a problem, even to my simple mind, is beyond my comprehension when such an order is suddenly barked at me, and when I'm told to pull my stomach in and stick my chest out the opposite invariably happens.

I have also discovered that field service caps, airmen for the use of, refuse to stay put on brilliantined hair, and uniforms fit where they touch. When hair styling is mentioned, short back and sides implies that if you get on parade looking like a convict you'll pass muster, and a close shave means just that - not just a near miss.

It would also appear that the rifle I sometimes carry for drill purposes is not meant to be dropped from frozen fingers onto the crushed snow that covers Blackpool promenade!

Blackpool, my present "home". Ah, what memories the name conjures up! The *"Pleasure Beach"*, where not so long ago my brother threw balls at coconuts to win a coconut! Candy floss, a light fluffy mass of spun sugar my mother claimed would be the ruination of my teeth. Rock, with "Blackpool" running all through it. Toffee apples and milk shakes. Side-shows on the *"Golden Mile"* displaying a two-headed sheep, manikins, the tallest man in the world and a bearded lady. Bacon and eggs with fried bread for breakfast, roast beef and Yorkshire pud for lunch - or dinner as we called our midday meal - all served up by a landlady anxious to please. Slot machines on the piers. *"What the Butler Saw"*, which wasn't much. Saucy young lasses from Lancashire cotton towns, primping on the prom. My father on the firm sand, sweating profusely as he chased a beach ball into the sea. Mum, fair, fat and well over forty straining the canvas of a deck chair. My sister, scolding me for spitting, chewing gum, picking my nose and calling her "four-eyes"; that same sister who earlier in the year had berated me when I had returned from Birmingham having passed a stringent aircrew medical: - 'Have you no thought for your parents?' 'Have they not suffered enough, having lost one son already?' 'Why are you deliberately tempting fate by volunteering to fly in an aeroplane?'

Blackpool! Ugh, the reality! A bitterly cold wind, forever blowing. No money in my pocket. Wartime rations. The never ending one-pause-two of square-bashing on vast stretches of snow covered promenade. Blackpool! Burtons, no longer full of natty suits, but overflowing instead with airmen striving to get acquainted with dots and dashes invented by a Mr. Morse. Lectures at the *"Winter Gardens"*. Milk bars turned into guard-rooms, and land-ladies providing as few of life's creature-comforts as possible for the airmen freezing under their roofs.

And it is in a milk bar metamorphosed into a guard room that I am at this precise moment. Here I have spent the evenings of this past week doing "jankers", which is yet another of the never ending procession of new words and sayings that have entered my vocabulary. "You've had it", for instance, which appears to mean "I can't get it", and "Erk", which describes what I am - a rookie, an A.C. plonk. "Blackouts" are not just streets shrouded in darkness they are also Waaf knickers, items of underwear I've often thought about but not yet seen. "Cheesed off" means fed up, disgruntled, and "bulsh" is "spit and polish". If I get excited, I'm "flapping". "Gen" is information, and if I boast I'm a "line shooter".

But back to "jankers", which is something you get if you break rules, and the rule I have broken is that my cap should adorn my head at all times, even when fetching fish and chips! Two very unsympathetic R.A.F. policemen had stressed the point when I'd returned to my billet late one evening, and they'd promptly slapped me on a charge. So here I am, a "jankers wallah"!

The crime committed was to my mind a trivial one, the punishment dished out quite unfair. Nevertheless, for the past seven evenings, I have cleaned Lee-Enfield rifles and scrubbed floors. The rifles are ancient. Dating from the time Kitchener got his finger out they are used solely for drill purposes, consequently their barrels gleam with inner cleanliness. The N.C.O. in charge of me, a morose sergeant with "regular" written all over him, has, however, insisted that my punishment be carried out to the letter. Therefore from time to time he's tapped ash from a smouldering "*Wild Woodbine*" cigarette into a rifle barrel before depositing the rest onto the floor.

'Call this rifle clean, airman?' has been followed with, 'This floor's bloody filthy, get down on your 'ands an' knees an' clean it proper.'

To restore rifle barrels to their pristine condition has been easy but cleaning the floor has proved to be rather difficult. A mucky rag and dirty water from a red painted bucket with "FIRE" emblazoned on its side being my only cleaning utensils.

This evening, my last on "jankers", has seen a slight variation of the silly routine. A corporal, a buddy no doubt of the sergeant, paid him a visit. He not only added his quota of ash to the rifle barrels, he also filthied the floor with spent chewing gum, snow from his greatcoat and slush from his boots. An occasional ejection of saliva from his pursed lips increased the contents of the fire bucket, the accuracy of his aim bearing eloquent testimony to a misspent youth spent in spittoon-equipped pubs.

At 21.00 hours my punishment comes to a welcome end, and I'm preparing to leave the guard room with what might be termed "unseemly haste" when a thunderous shout of, 'Airman!' brings me to an abrupt halt.

'Y, y, yes, sarge,' I stammer, fearing the worst.

'You don't want to be put on another charge, do you?'

'Why no, no of course not, sarge, er, sir.'

'Then you'd better put this on yer 'ead.'

'Oh! Thank you sir,' I cry, catching my service cap which he's thrown at me.

'An' stop callin' me sir, I'm not a ruddy officer! And less of the sarge, I'm sergeant to the likes of you!'

I distance myself as quickly as I can from the three-striped bully. Hunger gnaws at my insides. Hurrying along, cap held very firmly to my head, I turn a corner and find myself outside the fish and chip shop that had been instrumental in my having to do "jankers". I do not pause but press on regardless for I know that in my billet, which is but a short distance away, a "delight" awaits me - a parcel, carefully wrapped in stout brown paper tied firmly with string, sent to me by the best mum in the world. It will, I know, be full of goodies that will help me forget the misery of "jankers".

I reach my not so "home from home" and note, with some surprise, that our landlady is graciously allowing the rest of the billetees the unheard of luxury of electric light. My raised eyebrows soon return to their normal position however for the illumination is merely filtering through a glass panel that separates her lounge from the room occupied by her "guests".

After leaping up the stairs, two steps at a time, I fling open my bedroom door and whoop with joy at the sight of the parcel which sits on a small cabinet by the side of my bed. The sound strangles in my throat however for what had once been a cornucopia of gastronomic delights is now a thing of shreds and tatters. All that remains is torn wrapping paper, knotted string and crumbs! An inedible collection that mocks me as it lies there, surrounded by the droppings of mice or possibly the excreta of rats.

'Damn! Damn! Damn!' I say, out loud.

Why hadn't I put the parcel in a safer place? I had, after all, had sufficient warning of the presence of vermin. Tears fill my eyes, but it is not the emptiness of my stomach that upsets me, it's the knowledge that my parents will have "gone without", will have given up their own meagre rations for my sake. With my misery turning to anger I charge downstairs, determined to "have it out" with my landlady but she is not at home.

'Gone to the flicks,' someone says.

'We ought to get this blasted billet closed!' I remonstrate, but I'm talking to myself, for my comrades in arms are paying no heed to my belly-aching. They are not interested in what has happened to my parcel, their minds are full of "five card tricks" and "pontoon", as one of their number deals from a grubby deck of cards.

I bid them a caustic, 'Good-night,' and if anyone replies I don't hear him.

Wearily I mount the stairs just one step at a time, and pause to relieve myself in the lavatory which is situated on a landing between floors. A chill wind vibrates the piece of cardboard that covers a broken window pane. I shiver, and come to the conclusion that a winter wind is indeed not so unkind as man's ingratitude.

Stretching out on my bed I snuggle under a rough blanket and curl my lip at the thought of sergeants, corporals, landladies, rodents, about-turns and dropped rifles. My belly rumbles.

I dream fitfully of "civvy street", sausage and mash, cheese on toast, egg and chips, kate and sydney pie and a fruit cake taller than Blackpool Tower.

Chapter Two

A Case of Mistaken Identity

(Early Spring 1942)

'Do you think we'll ever make an airman of him, corporal?' the station warrant officer growls.

'I doubt it, sir,' sighs the junior N.C.O, positioning himself once more in front of me before repeating a barrage of drill instructions that are already a confused jumble in my mixed up mind: 'Attention!' 'Slope Arms!' 'Present Arms!'

The commands mingle with, 'Stand at ease!' 'Easy!' 'By the left, quick march!' 'Airman, halt!' I'm dizzy with orders created aeons ago to ensure that an airman's life is one of sheer misery. Little do they care, these two sadists, that my body aches with fatigue, and I doubt they'd show any signs of remorse if my arms were to fall off.

'Why is he waving his rifle about, corporal?'

'I've no idea, sir.'

'Are you deaf lad, or that thick you can't understand the simplest of orders? You are being spoken to in your native tongue, aren't you? Not Swahili, double-Dutch, or Welsh!' The S.W.O. removes his handlebar moustache from in front of my face, and I sigh with relief when his beery breath no longer fills my lungs. 'Try again, corporal.'

The two striped one does as he is instructed but my attempt to present arms turns into a disaster of the first magnitude.

'Did you order the airman to ground arms?' the S.W.O. asks.

'No sir, I did not!'

'Then why is his rifle lying on the deck?'

'I don't know sir, but I'll do my best to find out. Airman, why have you placed your rifle on the ground?'

I stand mute, ill at ease, wretched in my awkwardness.

'Well airman?' the S.W.O. questions, fingering his moustache. 'Um, I've got an idea, corporal, maybe we should transfer this one to the W.A.A.F. He does, after all, act more like a wench than a bloke, and it would certainly get him out of our hair.'

Transfer me to the W.A.A.F.! What a wonderful idea, one of the best I've heard in many a long day.

Buoyed up with hope I recall with pleasure the events of yesterday when it had been my duty to rouse from their sleep - at five in the morning - airwomen who worked in the cookhouse. One of the young ladies had sat up reluctantly in her bed when I'd shouted, 'Wakey wakey!' After rubbing her eyes and telling me in no uncertain terms what I could do with myself she'd searched for a packet of cigarettes, and by doing so had inadvertently revealed part of her shapely bosom.

'Yes, please,' I implore under my breath. 'Transfer me to the Waaf.'

'I asked you a question, airman. Why is your rifle lying on the ground?'

'I dropped it.'

'"Dropped it!" "Dropped it!" Airmen have been shot for less!'

'Yes corporal, sorry corporal.' I apologise, stooping to pick up the offending weapon.

'Attention! Did I give you an order to retrieve the rifle?'

'N, n, no, corporal,' I reply, straightening up with alacrity.

The S.W.O. walks to and fro, shaking his head from side to side. Twiddling his moustache he takes a small silver box from his pocket and helps himself to a pinch of snuff. As he sniffs I am overcome with the desire to sneeze. My nose twitches.

'You're not finding this amusing are you, airman? Is that a smile on your face?'

'N, n, no, sir.'

'I do believe he thinks that dropping his rifle is something to laugh about, corporal.' Suddenly the face is once again only inches from my own. 'Now listen, airman, and listen good! Because of leave and sickness I've no one but you to put on guard duty so for the next two hours you will be guarding, with your life if needs be, the main road into this camp. And for gawd's sake stand still while I'm talking to you! The security of the Central Flying School of His Majesty's Royal Air Force will be in your hands and your hands alone. Do you understand? Oh, take him away, corporal.'

A quick march brings us to a sentry box with its attendant barrier.

'Now listen, airman,' says the corporal, imitating his superior. 'Your duty for the next two hours will be to inspect the identity cards, passes, papers and such like of anyone who tries to enter this camp. Don't raise the barrier until you are absolutely certain that the visitor is a friend, not a foe. You would recognise the enemy I suppose? Hitler for instance?'

'Oh yes, yes of course I would, corporal.' The S.W.O.'s face looms large in my imagination.

'An' Goerin', an' Goebbels, an' Mussolini?'

'Yes.'

'An' them what's on our side like the King an' the Prime Minister?'

'Why?' I ask in surprise. 'Do they come here?'

'Anybody who's anybody comes here airman, so be warned! If you let me down, if you make a balls up of this guard duty, I'll see to it personally that the S.W.O. has your guts for garters. An' I'll make sure that the rest of your time in the Royal Air Force is spent peelin' spuds an' whitewashin' coal!'

He then goes on to talk about pennants flying from the bonnets of cars and which officers are entitled to a present arms, but the words fail to reach my ears for at that precise moment a Spitfire chooses to beat up the camp.

'Who, which ones?' I shout, but he is gone, and I'm left alone with my awesome responsibilities.

R.A.F. Upavon, the camp I am guarding with my life, is to the best of my knowledge situated on the vast open space that is Salisbury Plain. Somewhere to the north is Marlborough a town I visited recently as it dozed peacefully in the sunshine of a Sunday afternoon, and not far away is Avebury, where silent stones speak eloquently of the past. To the south, beyond Netheravon, is Stonehenge and then Salisbury, with its splendid cathedral. The city also has a cinema where last week-end I saw Errol Flynn in a flick called, "*They Died with Their Boots On*".

Boots! I glance down at my own and hope that the title of the film will not prove prophetic, for I'm quite sure the S.W.O. will terminate my existence if I give him the slightest cause.

The sun has got his hat on and he's come out to play with rays so bright that I'm forced to shield my eyes with my free hand as I search the surrounding countryside. I have no cause for concern however, for nothing mechanical is on the move. Overall there hangs a sun-drenched stillness. A peace disturbed only by the occasional flight of a bird, the buzz of a bee, and the fluttering by of a lonely butterfly.

'Attention!' I shout, as boredom takes over. 'Forward, quick march. Left, right, left, right. Airman, halt!' I follow my commands then scan the horizon where I find that all is quiet, and not only on the Western Front.

Rapidly becoming cheesed off I affix bayonet to rifle and rout a horde of imaginary Krauts who are attacking the camp. The enemy scatters in all directions but my joy is short lived, for as I wipe the sweat of victory from my brow a small cloud of dust appears on the horizon.

'Now don't get uptight,' I tell myself but my stomach churns and ignores the order when I realize that the dust is being thrown up by a motor car. I peer anxiously through half closed eyes but am unable to tell if there is a pennant on display.

Phew, I'm sweating now, regretting the routing of the pretend enemy.

'Come on, pull yourself together. Follow the corporal's instructions because if you don't it will be "good-bye" to flying duties, and "hello" to never ending heaps of coal and mountains of unpeeled spuds.'

Suddenly the vehicle is upon me.

'Halt,' I order, a good two seconds after the car has come to a stop.

Sweat and sunshine combine to reduce my vision to almost nil, and when I attempt unsuccessfully to inspect a document thrust at me by the driver the faint aroma of cigar smoke reaches my nostrils. I peer into the back of the vehicle and dimly make out a cherubic face, well-tailored suit and smouldering Havana.

Ye Gods! It's him! It's Winston! Heaven help me! What sort of a salute does a Prime Minister warrant?

The document disappears, the car window closes, and an impatient toot on the horn brings me to my senses. I raise the barrier and to my surprise a chubby hand acknowledges my belated "present arms".

Rooted to the spot I feel quite sick when I realise that not only had I failed to properly inspect the proffered document, I had also failed to ask for identification of any sort!

Wiping toil, sweat and tears but as yet no blood from my brow, I lean my rifle against the sentry box and seat myself inside the wooden structure. Gradually, as something akin to rational thinking takes over, my fears subside. Someone as important as Winston would surely have had an escort of sorts, and lots of balding middle-aged men wear black jackets and pin-striped trousers. Yet the man had been smoking a cigar! I dab at my face with a grubby handkerchief and know one thing for sure - it wasn't Hitler in the back of the car. He'll be in the sergeants' mess sniffing snuff and guzzling beer!

My thoughts are interrupted by the arrival of the corporal with an airman in tow who is to relieve me of my duties. A "comic opera" changing of the guard ceremony ensues, and at its conclusion I am free to return to the main camp, where, as I place my rifle in the rack provided, I'm informed that the S.W.O. wants to see me "at the double".

Oh, heck! So it had been the "great man"! Which means that my guts will soon be garters! I straighten my tie, adjust my cap, clear my throat and knock on the door of Adolf's office.

'Come in!'

I do as ordered and come smartly to attention in front of a large desk behind which the great man sits.

'Alcock?' he questions, without bothering to look up.

'Yes sir,' I answer, my knees developing Saint Vitus's dance.

'I've news for you, airman.'

Oh, no! Not eternal potato white-washing and everlasting coal peeling!

'Your posting's come through,' he grunts, before adding with considerable relish, 'I'm pleased to say.'

Hardly able to conceal my delight at hearing such wonderful news I stand and gape until he finally dismisses me from his presence. I mumble my thanks, perform an almost military-like about turn, and march from the room with a smile on my face that a Cheshire Cat would be proud of. I'm about to open the door when a further grunt stops me in my tracks.

'Oh, one other thing, airman. The C.O.'s tailor has arrived from London and he's asked me to convey his thanks for the "present arms" you gave him. Come to think of it I should thank you as well. You put him in such a good mood he gave me a cigar, and he's never done that before!'

Chapter Three

The High-Born Ladies

(Summer 1942)

London! The very name conjures up a tingle of excitement, an inner thrill. Not that I'm foolish enough to have expected the streets to be paved with gold but I am young enough, and of a sufficiently impressionable nature, to marvel at the thought that I am part of the hustle and bustle of the world's most famous, most cosmopolitan city. London! The capital of Britain and the British Empire!

I am billeted in St John's Wood, an area of the city which appears to be comprised mostly of modern, medium-rise buildings, and the flat is about a cricket-ball's throw away from that hallowed shrine - Lords.

Yesterday, I was issued with a piece of white cloth which did wonders for my ego. Today, I have marched tall with the cloth adorning my service cap, for this "white flash" as it is called proclaims to the world that I have been accepted for aircrew training - which means that my long cherished ambition to fly could soon be realised.

What a wonderful day it is! God's in his heaven and all's well with a Wellington bomber as, with engines on song, it plays hide and seek with puffy white clouds dancing carefree in an azure sky. Ahead of me lies Regents Park.

My pulse quickens as I march towards the entrance, and there's a spring in my step as I visualise myself up there in that not so wild blue yonder. I reflect also but more soberly, that the wild animals evacuated from the zoo - to make way for we human animals in air-force blue - were better trained than I, and that before I manage to get airborne an awful lot of "gen" will have to be absorbed.

I respond to a command and together with my fellow "white-flashers" wheel smartly to the left to enter a former animal house that has become a dining hall.

'D'you fancy coming into town tonight?' a handsome looking airman asks as he seats himself beside me.

'Town?' I query, feeling, and no doubt sounding, rather puzzled.

'Yeah! Good old London town.'

'I can't. I haven't got a pass.'

'You don't need a pass,' he laughs. 'All you need is a head for heights. As soon as it's reasonably dark I'll be off down the fire escape and away. I've done it for two nights on the trot. It's a piece of cake. How about it?'

'No, I don't think so,' I say, shaking my head.

'It's dead easy,' he confides, moving closer. 'In no time at all you are in Baker Street, then its Oxford Street I think they call it, and hey presto, Marble Arch! You should have been with me last night, I couldn't move for dames! I picked up a Scottish lass and boy was she some red-hot Momma! She had better physical attributes than Ava Gardner! And you don't have to worry about the service police, they'll be busy sorting out drunks and stopping fights. What d'you say?'

I weigh in my mind the prospect of London night life against doing a spot of "jankers" were I to get caught, and "jankers" outweighs the imagined joys.

'No thanks,' I say, making my desire to hit the sack at an early hour my excuse for not accompanying him.

'I know a joint where the strippers are out of this world,' he says, persuasively. 'And when the shows over they'll do most anything for a chap in uniform. If you're short of a bob or two, no sweat, I'll stake you.'

The thought of a night on the town at little or no cost to myself gradually tips the balance scales of my mind; and later in the day as I sit in the stand at Lords half listening to a poison gas lecture I agree to accompany my new found friend on his nocturnal jaunt. I doze and romantic thoughts of sweet scented young ladies oust unpleasant, imaginary odours of garlic smelling *di-chloro-di-ethyl sulphide*, better known as mustard gas, from my mind.

'Crystals,' I hear the instructor say, and when there's talk of talk of tear gas and something that ends in, '…arsine,' my own thoughts crystallise and I imagine myself slowly descending, eyes tight shut, the fire escape at the rear of the flat - something which, a few hours later, I manage to achieve.

He knows his London does my mentor but his timing is way-out, and our furtive trot to Marble Arch has taken longer than he estimated.

I'm gazing in awe at the famous landmark when he informs me, with a smack of his lips, that we are close to a pub that serves the best "mild" in town.

'I don't drink beer,' I say, rather feebly.

'Streuth! You're a case you are, you could have told me before now.' And with that he is gone leaving me standing on my own, with very little money and even less courage, in the heart of the mighty metropolis.

I wander aimlessly and eventually find myself in the comparative quiet of Bayswater Road.

My earlier joie de vivre has disappeared and fears crowd in on me. What will happen if I get caught? How do I find my way back to the St John's Wood area? Will the fire escape still be extended on my return? I remonstrate with myself for being so weak willed, so easily led. Will I never learn? Only a fool would have agreed to engage in such a crazy enterprise. An aircraft stooges overhead but now the sound of its engines fills me with trepidation not joy, realising as I do that if I am picked up by the service police my flying career could well fly out of the window. I continue to castigate myself for being such a bloody fool, for not having the courage of my convictions.

I must get back to the flat, but how? I undertake a thorough search of the contents of my battledress pockets and find that I might well have enough cash to pay for a taxi, but when one slows to a stop - with headlights dimmed and screened - the driver ignores my outstretched hand.

I'm puzzled, but soon discover the reason for his total lack of interest in me when an elegantly clad female emerges from the shadows. Gliding forward on her high-heeled shoes she joins a male passenger already seated in the rear of the vehicle.

Being rather naïve I do not realise what is going on until the taxi returns a while later to discharge no doubt satisfied passengers - the man sexually, the woman financially. I'm intrigued! Bayswater Road is full of sex and sin, and, as I traverse its length, taxis are stopping and starting with considerable regularity.

I'm fascinated! Then, when another vehicle slows and I turn to witness more of the game, I find it is not a taxi but a three-ton truck. Seated inside is a collection of dejected looking airmen, all of whom have "white flashes" in their caps.

'Get in,' snaps a corporal, after he has satisfied himself that I am not legitimately viewing these "sights of London".

Obeying the order I find myself seated opposite my "friend", and in the available half-light I see that he is but a pale shadow of his former cock-sure self.

"Jankers"! I hadn't known the meaning of the word! Trying to run at the double along the tarmac surface of the zoo's outer circle I realise that the scrubbing of dirty floors and cleaning of rifle barrels in Blackpool had been heaven, compared to the hell of the present.
'Pick those feet up,' a warrant officer yells.
'Close ranks,' snarls a flight sergeant.
'Left, right, left, right,' yells a corporal.
I don't know how much more of this inhuman treatment I can take as, in the searing heat of this mid-summer day, I lurch past the warrant officer for what must be the fiftieth time; and when his mouth opens wide to bellow yet another order it occurs to me that the zoo authorities have failed to transfer all of their gorillas to Whipsnade.
'Bastard,' hisses my "comrade", as he pants by my side.
'That makes two of you,' I snap, knowing that but for this man's hair-brained scheme I would be in the N.A.A.F.I. sipping a cool lemonade and doing my best to avoid breaking my teeth on a rock bun.
'Stop talking in the ranks,' snarls the flight sergeant.
'Left, right, left, right,' squeals the pip-squeak of a corporal.
Staggering along I recall that people in the Middle Ages were quite often pressed to death. Was theirs a worse fate I wonder than the one I'm suffering now? For I too am being pressed to death, under a full-pack surmounted by a steel helmet. The temperature is in the high seventies yet I've been forced to don greatcoat, scarf, gloves and balaclava. My gas-mask case bobs up and down on my chest and the rifle I carry has a bayonet affixed. Bathed in sweat, I have red-hot coals for feet and my mouth craves water.

Ahead of me an airman, exhausted by heat and cruelty, collapses. The warrant officer shows no compassion, merely orders the rest of us to pick up our feet as the body is dragged away.

'Close ranks,' roars the flight sergeant.

'Left, right, left, right,' cries the corporal.

Then, quite suddenly, our tormentors tire of their sport and we are dismissed.

Staggering to the safe haven of my flat I divest myself of all equipment and indulge in the sheer luxury of an ice cold shower bath.

From a nearby room a voice croons, 'I don't want to join the Air force, I don't want to go to war, I'd rather hang around Piccadilly Underground, living on the earnings of a high-born lady.'

And he'd be living in luxury if last night's goings on in Bayswater Road were anything to go by I reckon.

I towel myself dry and join the chorus of raised voices that are attempting to silence the would-be Bing.

'Belt-up!'

'Put a sock in it.'

'Wrap-up!'

There are other suggestions but not the sort heard in polite society.

Later the perpetrator of my misery joins me. To my utter annoyance I see that he's in excellent shape physically.

'How are they?' he asks, casting a quizzical glance at my bruised feet and fallen arches.

'Sore, ruddy sore, thanks to you. And that goes for my back, shoulders and most other parts. I doubt I'll ever walk properly again!'

'What a pity,' he drawls, lighting up a cigarette. 'If you were game I was going to suggest we have a night out on the town!'

The Author, sporting his "White Flash".

Chapter Four

Air and Other Experiences

(Early Autumn 1942)

Being short of cannon fodder the Air Crew Selection Board at St John's Wood decided that I should be an Air Gunner, and I have, therefore, joined a group of airmen who, like me, will soon be on the way to a Gunnery School somewhere in Wales.

One of the chaps mentions a place name I've never heard of.

'Lan, where?' I ask.

'It sounded like "Landrog".

'How do you spell it?'

'IT'

'Oops, I asked for that!'

'Sorry. Landrog, I suppose.'

'It is pronounced Thlanduroch, and spelt L l a n d w ro g,' says a know-all, spelling the name out for us.

'Is it now! And where is it?'

'In Wales, of course. It could hardly be anywhere else with a name like that!'

'And what is it?'

'An Air-gunners and Observers advanced flying unit. Number nine, I think.'

'Nine, eh?' someone quips. 'Just what the doctor ordered!'

'I don't understand. Is that some sort of joke or other?'

'No, according to my father there was a pill, or something similar, that was handed out by M.O.s in the '14 -'18 bash called a number nine. It cured just about everything, or so he said.'

'So it's not a joke?'

And neither is a flying unit! I think to myself. It's for real. I can hardly believe it! I'm going to be flying at long, long last!

Someone produces a map of North Wales and my eyes follow in the wake of a finger as it sails down the Menai Strait.

'Are you sure it's not Valley?' one of the chaps asks, pointing at Anglesey.

'Quite sure, that would be far too easy to spell. Look, there it is, not far from Caernarfon which has a whopping great castle.'

'And there's a whopping great bay too over which we will be doing our flying training.'

Flying training! I find it hard to believe that in the not too distant future I might well be making some sort of contribution to the war effort, a war that has managed to get along without my help for nearly three years. A war that has Winston Churchill in Moscow visiting Uncle Joe Stalin, the S.S. in Warsaw making life hell for the Jews, and Stalingrad refusing to capitulate to Hitler's Wehrmacht. There is also an air force bod with lots of scrambled egg on the peak of his cap, a certain Arthur Harris, who is threatening to scourge the Third Reich from end to end.

The airstrip at Llandwrog is situated to the south-west of Caernarfon, and what's impressed me most are the tales of doom and gloom I've heard. Clapped-out Whitley bombers were in use until quite recently, and last year two of them collided when one tried to take off as the other was landing.

'Seventeen killed,' my informant said grimly, before going on to tell me that accidents were commonplace. 'You can't expect anything else in an area of high mountains and sea. There are lots of aircraft out there in the bay you know, and still more scattered about Snowdonia.'

So it is with mixed feelings that I am about to lift off from terra firma for the first time in my life. The aircraft in which I am to undertake this hazardous and daring enterprise is a Mark IV Bristol Blenheim. Numbered 6356 she is due to become unstuck at 13.55 hours, this 9th day of September, 1942.

Wearing a flying helmet and parachute harness over my battledress, I crouch inside a fuselage that I feel sure wasn't designed to accommodate three would-be aircrew and an instructor.

The aircraft taxies to its take off point, and when the pilot opens up the throttles butterflies perform circuits and bumps in my stomach. I brace myself and expect the worst.

Slowly at first but with ever increasing speed, the Blenheim - powered by two Bristol Mercury radial engines - moves forward. Then, after a final bump, it lifts off and becomes airborne!

The feeling of elation that engulfs me is short lived, being quickly replaced by one of horror when a heavy thud reverberates through the aircraft. The fear quickly subsides however when I realise that the noise was caused by the undercarriage folding into its housing.

My instructor, a flight sergeant sporting an air-gunner's brevet, gives me a thumbs-up.

I crawl along the fuselage but my attempt to climb into the gun turret proves to be more difficult than when I had practised the manoeuvre on the ground. Reaching upwards I accidentally depress the lever which raises and lowers the seat and find myself suspended in mid-air.

The instructor, who has without doubt seen it all before, is soon by my side. Shaking his head he assists me, and with a wisdom born of experience holds firmly onto the seat until I have elevated myself into the Perspex dome of the gun turret.

For a few moments I sit with eyes tight shut but when the pilot banks the aircraft gently to port I open them and see below me stone walls, fields, trees, and in the distance a house. Another turn and I am staring down at hedgerows, gates, more fields, cows and a group of Land Girls who appear to be waving up at me. Everything is in miniature, and for a few wondrous moments I am back with the farmyard toys of my childhood.

A drop in altitude, which I blame on an "air-pocket", brings me back to the present. With ever increasing confidence I inspect the Browning machine guns, eye the reflector sight and partly rotate the turret. Suddenly the aircraft is no longer flying over land but over a wide expanse of water. Calm and peaceful, Caernarfon Bay has white horses trotting gracefully on its waves.

Somewhat gingerly I elevate and depress the guns, check the ammunition feed and rotate the turret to its full extent. An imaginary German fighter aircraft attacks from out of the sun but it is no match for me and I soon consign it to a watery grave. I am thoroughly enjoying myself now but the fun comes to an end when a hand tugs at my battle-dress trousers. Reluctantly, I lower the seat and drop awkwardly to the floor of the aircraft.

'Why didn't you plug your inter-com into its socket?' yells the flight sergeant, lifting the flap of my flying-helmet.

'Oh! I'm sorry, flight,' I shout, glancing down at the "jack" and cursing myself for making such an elementary mistake.

But my chagrin is short lived, being replaced by a feeling of joy when I realise that I am truly airborne, and showing no signs of air sickness which would have put an end to my flying career. I'm overjoyed. I want to stay up here in the sky for ever and ever. Yet, at the same time, I'm anxious to get down on the deck in order to record this all important first flight in my pristine *"Air Gunners and Observers Flying Log Book"*.

The weeks following my inaugural flight have been crammed with flying. Air firing at a drogue pulled by a Martinet aircraft has seen me averaging 17 hits from every 200 rounds fired, but whether that's good, bad, or just plain indifferent "shooting" I've no idea, and no one has seen fit to enlighten me.

Non-flying hours have been spent learning the rudiments of air-gunnery - from what action I should take if a machine gun stops firing to what I should do if an attack comes from the beam, or the quarter, or underneath astern. Deflection and bullet trajectory is no longer a mystery, and the dismantling and re-assembling of a breech-block without having a part left over at the end has been achieved.

The shapes of enemy aircraft have become familiar to me. I can now recognise, from all angles, Junkers 88's, Me 109s and 110s, and Fw190's. I have also familiarised myself with Flying Forts, Halifaxes, Whitleys, Wellingtons, Stirlings, Spitfires, Manchesters and Hurricanes, for it is not the done thing to shoot at a "friendly" kite, though I have on occasion done just that using a cine-camera gun.

For light relief I was taken late one night - with a few of the other chaps - to a desolate spot, where I climbed into a Frazer-Nash gun turret and gave vent to my feelings by blasting away with four machine guns at illuminated caricatures of Adolf H. and Benito M. The area was not called *"Hell's Mouth"* for nothing!

Having on two occasions in the recent past learned to my cost that disobeying orders can result in an unpleasant spell of "jankers", I've obtained a pass from a clerk in the orderly room that enables me to travel "legitimately" to Caernarfon.

I take a bus into the town and make for the castle, the building of which I've been informed was undertaken in the thirteenth century by King Edward the First.

A wall of impenetrable thickness greets me, and I feel like an attacking warrior of old must have felt for all gates and entrances are barred. With a feeling of disappointment I wander towards the quay where a three-masted ship lies at anchor. I inspect the barque and sense that I am not alone.

'Splendid isn't she, but then anything to do with the sea is splendid,' a female voice informs me.

Startled by this unexpected intrusion I turn to find that the speaker is inspecting me closely.

'You fly in aeroplanes I suppose,' she says. 'I wouldn't if I was a man, I would find a ship and sail the seven seas.'

The lady is wearing a swagger suit and I am reminded of a similar outfit in green, worn by my sister in the mid nineteen-thirties. This ensemble, however, is overall grey, as grey as the sky, the water, and the walls of the immense fortress dominating the town.

'He gained a world, or was it a word? I'm never too sure these days. He gave that world its greatest, er...?' The lady stamps her foot. 'Oh never mind, I'm sure it will come to me, it usually does. Sail on, sail on.'

I search for some means of escape from this strange creature who, with a wave of a hand, appears to be inviting a seagull to join us. The bird, after giving the lady a "head on one side" enquiring look, hovers uncertainly then makes a perfect two point landing on a capstan.

'Pity the sailor that has wandered, or was it the bird that wandered? Hurry him home and let him come no more to the sea, no, the ocean, or is it sea? I have such trouble remembering these days, and, the pity of it is, most of my books remain in London.'

For a moment or two the rambling voice is stilled and the ensuing quiet is disturbed only by the cries of sea birds. Then, following vague inaudible mutterings, my companion proclaims, 'Stevenson I think, or is it Longfellow?'

The gull gives me glance which seems to suggest that I should be supplying an answer but I am unable to do so, and what is more I have no wish to for I have had enough of this woman. I attempt to move away but a hand restrains me.

'Are you a lover of poetry?' Without giving me the chance to reply she decides that I am not, preferring instead to play Patience.

'Patience!' I cry, sounding incredulous.

'Now, let me see. What is it that the tide does? Rise? Fall? Both, I suppose, but I'm not sure. I live near to Dinas with mummy, she prefers it to London. It is safer of course but there is nothing here apart from the wonderfully firm sands and breathtaking views, Snowdonia, and the Nevin Rivals. But it is the sea that cries out, the wonderful ships, the sea, no, no. Ah! What mystery!'

'I really must be going,' I say, shivering under my greatcoat.

The mysterious-one teeters towards the edge of the quay and stares into the murky waters below. The gull, hoping perhaps that some stale bread or other titbit might come its way, marks time with its feet.

'I forgive you for not liking poetry.' The lady steps back and brushes my cheek with ice-cold fingers. 'Patience, that's the pastime for you.'

'Patience!' I cry, recoiling from her touch.

'Now! Now! Patience is not to be spurned. High Court judges get great comfort from it, and I know at least one Bishop who excels at "*Uncle Walter*".'

I shake my head. There's no doubt about it, one of us is round the bend and I'm alright Jack!

Undeterred, the lady rambles on. 'Oh dear, my memory is failing me again. Are two packs of cards required for "*Caledonian*"? And as for "*Rosamund's Bower*", who knows? I suppose the lonely sky really is where someone like you would fly down to the sea. I must go down again, I must, I must.'

'Yes, and I must be going too.'

'You are about to leave me, for we are like ships which pass in the night.'

'Yes, yes, that's exactly what we are,' I agree, making good my escape.

To my relief I find the bus for Llandwrog is about to depart. I clamber aboard, find a vacant seat, rub away condensation that has clouded the window pane and peer outside. At first I can see nothing but then as the mist shifts momentarily and the vehicle moves closer to where I had been standing I see a seagull, lonely and forlorn, atop a capstan. There is no sign of the lady in grey.

The following day, having joyfully brought my feet together, I stand stiffly to attention. This is one parade I am happy to be on, knowing as I do that by the time I'm dismissed I shall have become a sergeant, with three stripes on my arm and a flying brevet on my battledress blouse. I thrill when my name is called, throw up a smart salute after the C.O. has presented me with my new rank and insignia, then hasten to my billet where I get busy with needle and thread.

One of the lads brings out the tackle he would normally use for applying blacking to his boots, but on this occasion it is his pristine three stripes and not his footwear that gets brushed. Before long they have acquired the dullness of apparent old age. He is delighted with the result for he has no desire to look like a rookie sergeant.

He offers the brush to me but I shake my head. I am as proud of my new rank as I know my father will be of me when tomorrow he greets me at the start of the week's leave I've been granted.

Later, with sleep eluding me, I realise that my insomnia is not entirely due to the excitement of the passing-out parade; for when I try counting sheep my mind conjures up instead a female figure clad in a grey swagger suit. Barely visible, surrounded by a swirling mist, she stands motionless. Atop a nearby capstan, no longer lonely and forlorn, stands a seagull.

Chapter Five

Home-Coming For A Hero

(Late-Autumn 1942)

Seventeen across. "Lacking all force and vitality". Eight letters. The word starts with an "M" and I've got an "I" and a "B" in the middle, with a "D" at the end. Er, um, ah yes, of course, "Moribund"!

And if ever a cross-word clue correctly describes my current state it is most certainly seventeen across. Yet, as I lay my newspaper aside and in spite of my lethargy, a feeling of elation steals over me for never before have I completed a cross-word puzzle! For the first time in my life I've triumphed over those little black and white squares. I mentally notch up the achievement, and with a self-satisfied smile creasing my features attempt to survey my fellow travellers. But this proves to be well-nigh impossible, for in the sickly yellowish light that fitfully illumines the compartment of the railway carriage we share, their features are rather blurred.

Indistinct human beings they may be but this hasn't stopped them from bellyaching. Unscheduled halts and long delays at blacked-out stations have been greeted with cries of disgust, hoots of derision, tut-tuts and much moaning.

Tired of the non-stop criticism I have sought relief by attempting to read the various notices that adorn the walls of the compartment, in particular one dog-eared poster that instructs passengers as to what they should do in an air-raid. There are six items listed and I sincerely hope that I do not have to perform any of them, especially the last which suggests that passengers should lie on the floor - something I would find rather difficult to do because my right wrist is encased in plaster.

I glance down and smile at the comments that adorn the stiff white covering. "Get well soon, Jenny." "Love Mandy, parachute section." "Plastered again," appears twice, and an open-mouthed lip-sticked kiss from someone called Thelma has got smudged. I turn my arm over and discover "Regards Adolf", "Kilroy signed here" and "Press-on rewardless, Steve".

A cloth-capped chap seated directly opposite has indicated for some time his desire to converse with me but thus far I have managed to ignore his overtures.

Another passenger, holding aloft a newspaper, attempts to derive maximum benefit from the small electric light bulb above his head. Occasionally he is obliged to use his free hand to brush crumbs from his lap, crumbs that have dropped from the sandwiches being eaten by his neighbour. These obviously tasty morsels consist of egg and lettuce, and we have been informed on several occasions by the consumer that the egg has come from one of his chickens and the lettuce from his allotment.

Jolly good show, I think to myself. What a patriotic fellow.

I do my best to read the back page of the suspended newspaper, and when it is held still further aloft I see that it contains reports of soccer matches.

Huh! Soccer! It is because of soccer that I am here in this wretched railway carriage, and I grimace when I recall the incident responsible for my present predicament.

We, the air-crew NCOs of number 28 Operational Training Unit, had challenged the officer types to a game of soccer, and a right shower they turned out to be - excusing their pathetic performance by stating a preference for the oval ball. The score at half-time was 6-0 in our favour, and I had just celebrated the resumption of play by scoring a goal which completed my hat-trick, when a burly character - who would have been more at home in a rugger scrum - floored me in the most ungentlemanly fashion. After dumping me unceremoniously on the turf this immovable object of an officer had picked me up, shaken me as if I were a rag doll, and announced that as I quite obviously wasn't hurt the game should continue. But I was hurt, and the cracking noise that had been heard the length and breadth of the pitch signified that my wrist was in some way damaged.

After spending a couple of days in hospital I returned to camp to find that I had been granted two weeks sick leave, something which proved to me that the proverb "Every cloud has a silver lining" held a certain amount of truth.

So here I am, en route to fourteen-days home cooking.

The civilian sitting opposite inspects me yet again. His eyes travel slowly down from my "flying-wing" and sergeant's stripes to the plaster encasing my wrist, and he can contain himself no longer. 'Looks like you caught a packet, sergeant,' he observes.

I do not reply, merely indicate with a nod of my head that he is correct in his assumption. To disillusion him would be too much fag.

An elderly gent sitting to the left of the speaker pats an empty sleeve that is folded neatly into his jacket pocket. 'Lost this at Ypres,' he says proudly, 'and a brother on the Somme.'

'You did, Jack, you certainly did,' someone agrees.

'Must be hell going over the top night after night,' continues the one-armed old soldier.

Over the top indeed! I smile to myself, intrigued by this use of trench-warfare phraseology in relation to the night bombing of Germany.

The other passengers, who up to now have been castigating the railway company desist, and I am now the centre of attention. Questions are fired from all sides and opinions expressed with scant regard for the careless talk that costs lives.

'Twenty-one bombers lost the other night,' I am informed as I search the luggage rack for a listening Adolf, and under my seat for an ear-trumpeted Hermann.

'I certainly admire you chaps,' says the sandwich-eater, who is also searching but only for a crumb that has settled in one of his trouser turn-ups. 'The way you press on regardless of fighters and flak. Like you say, Jack, it must be hell on earth, or hell in the sky more like.' He laughs at his own remark but no-one else is amused.

'Is it true that the flak is sometimes thick enough to walk on?' the man who first spoke to me asks.

I smile, and the grimace appears to be taken as confirmation by the questioner.

What he does not realise is that the grim humour I display is due to my thinking that if the flak barrage was as intense as the questions being fired at me, then I'm quite sure I would be able to walk on it, though I doubt I'd want to climb out of an aircraft to prove it!

Come on train! Get a move on! I inwardly urge, as questions increase in number and the pain in my wrist worsens. I want to get home, where I know a warm welcome awaits.

A piece of lettuce drops to the compartment floor as the "*Dig for Victory*" man helps himself to yet another sandwich. The sight of it lying there makes me realise just how hungry I am, having had nothing to eat since leaving camp.

The train slows. The babble of conversation subsides and an air of expectancy fills the compartment. One of the passengers inches up a window-blind. At first he shakes his head but when the train stops, only to start and stop again, he shouts, 'I think it's Etruria. Yes it is, it's Etruria.'

I rest my arm in my lap. Despite the unpleasant twinges emanating from the area of the fracture I'm over the moon. My station is the next scheduled stop.

'You'll be a "Tail-End Charlie" I shouldn't wonder,' says the man seated opposite.

And you shouldn't wonder, I think to myself.

The "14-18" veteran is nodding his approval of me. 'You've got the worst position in a bomber.' he confides.

I smile at him, then drop my eyes demurely when a chorus of approval greets his words.

'Give it 'em back a hundred fold,' says the sandwich man. 'I only wish I was young enough to join you.'

'They started it!' cries the look-out whose position at the window is I feel no less vital to the rest of the passengers than that of a rear-gunner to his pilot. 'Knock 'ell out of 'em lad, they deserve all they get when you think what they've done to some of our cities.'

'The salt of the earth, that's what you bomber boys are,' opines another, but he fails to offer me a congratulatory cigarette as he lights one up for himself.

I squirm in my seat, inhale second hand *Wild Woodbine* smoke, and give vent to a huge sigh of relief when the look-out shouts, 'Longport, it's Longport.'

I rise and raise my left arm but desist when several pairs of willing hands reach out for my kitbag. Smiling my thanks I stand and watch as it is taken down from the rack.

The train comes slowly to a halt. After some careful negotiating I step onto the platform where I'm overjoyed to find my father waits to greet me. We embrace with difficulty. Then, as the train pulls slowly out of the station, I attempt to bid farewell to my erstwhile travelling companions. My words, however, are drowned by a barrage of instructions.

'Drop one on Adolf for me.'

'Give' 'em some stick.'

'Save one for Lord Haw Haw'.

The engine, determined not to be outdone, issues its own toot of praise. As the last carriage disappears I turn to my father. 'You would hardly credit it, Dad,' I laugh. 'For someone who has yet to go on a bombing raid over enemy territory, for someone who hasn't fired a shot in anger, I'm quite a hero!'

Chapter Six

A Trip To Jerusalem

(Early Winter 1942)

Tommy Jackson and I have recently become members of the same crew based at No. 28 O.T.U., Wymeswold, near Loughborough, and before long we expect to continue our flying training in clapped-out Wellington bombers.

Our "skipper" chose the two of us, together with a navigator and wireless-op, at the airfield a few days ago and now, because of some urgent family business, he's been granted compassionate leave, or passionate leave as Tom calls it. This break in our training means that our bomb aimer and I have a couple of days free from duty, so we have obtained S.O.P.'s and hitch-hiked our way to Nottingham. S.O.P., short for "Sleeping Out Pass", being yet another part of the strange lingo and multitude of initials to which I am gradually becoming accustomed.

There's no doubt about it the R.A.F. has concocted a language very much its own. "Wizard", "three-pointer", "Tail-End Charlie", and "split-arse turn" are all in common usage, and most everyone seems to know the words of the saucy songs sung whenever and wherever airmen and airwomen congregate.

One of the most popular of these ditties, sung to the tune of the well-known tango "*Jealousy*", is all about a sleeping out pass.

Tom and I have duly admired the pleasing features of the city's young ladies, who according to the natives are the prettiest in the country, and we are now queuing to see another beauty - Miss Vivien Leigh - in *"Gone with the Wind"*.

We had toyed with the idea of seeing Frederick March in *"One Foot in Heaven"* but changed our minds. With "operations" over enemy territory looming, we feel that we may have one foot in there already - or in that other place!

An unhappy looking young lady occupies the cinema's ticket kiosk. Speaking through a nose as red as her sweater she rebukes Tom when he politely requests two tickets at reduced price, a concession usually granted to members of H.M.F. in uniform.

'No reductions,' she says, snottily.

'Two at half-a-crown then,' says Tom, pushing five shillings towards the grille.

'No seats,' sniffs the girl. 'We're full up in the two and sixes.'

'How about the three bobs?'

'D'you want to sit together?'

'Of course we do.'

'Nothing together in the three shillings.'

'Well where we can sit together then?'

'Four an' nines.'

'Four shillings and ninepence! Four and nine! That's daylight robbery! I've never paid more than a couple of bob to go to the flicks.'

'Suit yourself,' sneezes the cashier.

The queue of people that has formed is becoming restless. I pretend I'm not with this bolshie sergeant and turn instead to admire a pin-up of Lana Turner filling her sweater

'Very well,' Tom growls, taking a grubby looking ten shilling note from his wallet. 'Two four and nines and the film had better be bloody worth it!'

'There's no need for language. I'm not here to be sworn at!' the cashier cries, sniffing into a tiny lace hanky. 'And you'd better close your wallet before any more fly out.'

'Any more what?' asks Tom, grabbing the sixpence change and walking straight into the trap she has set for him.

'Moths,' she says, with a triumphant snort that sprays germs all over the ten shilling note. 'Oh! Now look what you've made me do!'

'Cheeky so and so,' moans Tom, and he's still carrying on as we take our seats in the blacked out cinema.

After baking in the heat of the upper circle and basking for hours in the Technicolor glow of the American Deep South, Tom and I have made certain of a night's lodgings by booking two beds at the Y.M.C.A. We have filled our stomachs at a classy eating joint called "Nan's Café", and are now attempting to put large coloured balls into tiny pockets.

Judging from our lack of success it would appear that neither of us has misspent his youth, for we have been at the snooker table an hour and have yet to finish a frame.

Most of my score has been presented to me by my generous opponent, and the white ball is so stressed by Tom's lack of finesse that it has made at least three attempts to escape. On the last occasion it jumped clean off the table and was later discovered cowering behind a radiator.

'It'll never take the place of pocket billiards,' Tom comments drily, as we make way for two lip-curling civilians.

'Where to now?' I ask, laughing at his prophecy.

He smacks his lips. 'I don't know but I could certainly chew a pint. How about you?'

'No thanks.'

'Oh yes, of course, I keep forgetting you're teetotal. You could have a bottle of pop, couldn't you?'

A barman at the inn which stands at the foot of Castle Rock, a hostelry that boasts the intriguing name of *"Ye Olde Trip To Jerusalem"*, suffers from verbal diarrhoea.

He has told us on several occasions that the "*Trip*" is the oldest pub in England, that it is part of a collection of caves used as air raid shelters, and he's now repeating his tale of how the Crusaders met here before leaving for the Holy Land.

What he does not realise is that Tom and I are not in the mood for ancient history, being far more interested in two modern misses seated at a nearby table.

'I don't...' says Tom, but I cut him short.

'Please don't say it.'

'Say what?'

'That you don't like the one I'm getting.'

'I was going to say that I don't go much for brunettes. Being a gentleman, I naturally prefer blondes.'

'Oops!' I apologise. 'Please accept my most humble.'

'Oh heck, don't hang your head like that Al, even in fun. You'll frighten 'em off.'

And the young ladies are most certainly not over the moon when we invade their privacy; in fact the brunette gives me a quite disdainful look when I attempt to "chat her up". Tom, however, is soon getting along quite famously, which for me proves the point that blondes do not prefer gentlemen.

'And where are you stationed, sergeant?'

'Eh! Pardon?' I ask, taken aback by the question.

'Where are you stationed. What sort of aircraft do you fly in?'

Really! Talk about careless talk! If she's a spy then by gosh she's a forthright one!

I inspect her closely, and decide that, though she's attractive enough to be a modern day Mata Hari, she certainly lacks that lady's subtlety. What will the brazen madam be asking me next I wonder?

'I suppose you operate over Germany most nights?'

I choke, mop up the lemonade I've spilled, and give her a look of utter disbelief. Slowly the corners of her mouth turn up, and before long she's smiling at my obvious discomfort.

'Don't look so worried, I'm not really an enemy agent. I'm A.C.W. Allen and I'm punishing you for not recognising me. Don't be fooled by the "civvies". Like you I'm stationed at Wymeswold. I've looked after you many times in your mess but don't seem to have made much of an impression on you. By the way, how's your wrist?'

'My wrist? You know about that!'

'I ought to! I signed my name on the plaster cast, together with "Get well soon". Now do you remember me?'

'You must be Jenny,' I say in surprise. 'Gosh, don't you look different out of uniform? Is your friend a Waaf too?'

'Mavis? No, she's in the A.T.S. We've known each other for years. We live in the same street but this is the first time our leave has coincided. Your pal doesn't waste much time does he?'

I glance at Tom and find that he has moved in as close as he can to his "target for tonight". From time to time Mavis attempts to free herself but her resistance is only half-hearted.

By her side lies a newspaper, open at a page that displays a large advertisement. 'Hey, look at that,' I say. '"Men over forty-two, feed the men who fly. Cook for the R.A.F. Even if your only claim to cooking means that you've lent a hand in an emergency. Complete the coupon below. Do not seal the envelope. Affix a one penny stamp and send immediately to the Air Ministry".'

'Ah-hah!' cries Jenny, and there's a note of triumph in her voice. 'Maybe you'll stop blaming we waitresses for the quality of the food you get, now that you know it's cooked by inexperienced middle-aged men. Men whose only previous experience in a kitchen was probably due to an emergency!'

Tom is mystified by Jenny's tirade, until I explain that she's a waitress at Wymeswold.

'Well there's a coincidence,' he laughs. 'Small world, ain't it!'

'Yes, and it's also a small mess,' says Jenny, dismayed that Tom too has failed to recognise her.

The drinks flow, and, because we are enjoying ourselves, time flies.

'How are you getting home girls?' asks Tom when "time" is finally called, and the four of us are huddled together for warmth outside the hostelry.

'Shanks's pony,' dithers Mavis.

'May I escort you, Miss?' I ask, doffing my cap before bowing low to Jenny.

'Do you think that's wise?' she asks. 'It's kind of you to offer but we live some distance from here.'

'Who cares,' I cry, adopting a tone of studied nonchalance. 'Pray, take my arm.'

Guided by Mavis we set off through what, for me, are the uncharted wastelands of Nottingham.

My colleague whistles "*Jealousy*" through the gap in his front teeth but when the resultant noise is greeted with howls of derision he breaks into song. 'I daren't tell my mother I'm having another, t'was all over my S.O.P.'

'I don't think Sinatra's got much to worry about.'

'You're right there Jenny,' laughs Mavis, 'nor Bing.'

'If you lot carry on like you're doing, the blithering sleeping out passes will get us all locked up,' I warn, expecting at any moment to feel the arm of the law on my shoulder.

But my companions ignore me, caring not one jot that they are disturbers of the peace.

The air temperature outside an outhouse situated at the bottom of the yard at the rear of Jenny's parents' house is below freezing, and dropping rapidly. Inside the outhouse the temperature is rising dramatically. I stand, awkward, ill at ease, doing my utmost to hide a physical excitement that insists on manifesting itself.

'Steady on,' warns my companion, obviously aware of my condition.

We continue to cuddle and kiss however but when Jenny eventually manages to extricate herself from my octopus-like tentacles she sighs, and then suggests that it is time I departed.

'But, but...' I protest.

'No buts! I'll be back at camp in a few days' time should you wish to see me again.'

'See you again!' I cry hoarsely. 'Of course I want to see you again!'

'But will you recognise me when you do?' she mocks gently. 'I look so different in uniform you know.'

We laugh together, and after one more lingering kiss I find myself hobbling in what I hope is the right direction.

To my relief Tom is waiting for me at the end of the alley. 'Cor, I don't half ache,' he moans.

'You didn't succeed then?'

'Nah! She's a bit of a P.T. is that Mavis. All "come and get me" in the pub but "hands-off" with a vengeance in the wash-house! Did you get anywhere?'

'Does it look like it?' I say, 'just cut me off at the knees and call me tripod.'

Tom comes to a sudden halt. Bending down to tie a shoe-lace he confides, 'I never have, you know.'

'Never have what?'

'You know bloody well what!' he snorts, straightening up.

'Oh that! Good grief, haven't you? You do surprise me.'

Walking by my side Tom is plainly embarrassed in the light of a bombers' moon.

'Hey, d'you want to know something?' I continue.

'What?' My companion's voice is aloof, cold as the night air.

'Neither have I!'

'You're kidding!'

'No honestly, I've never.'

'Never?'

'No,' I shake my head. 'Never.'

'Phew! That's a relief.'

'You know what that makes the two of us?' I laugh. 'In the parlance of our American cousins.'

'No, what?'

'Cock virgins!'

We giggle, happy in our togetherness, overjoyed that we share a physical state we would both dearly love to lose.

The "Y" has a full moon and starry sky for a backdrop. The facade is etched black and neighbouring buildings brood mute, menacing in their silence. Tom places his finger on an ancient looking bell push but it fails to respond to his prompting.

'What time is it?' I whisper.

'Must be way past one o'clock. Why are you whispering?'

'I don't know, why are you? That thing doesn't seem to work. D'you think we should knock?'

'I would if there was a knocker.' Tom shrugs his shoulders, clenches the fingers of his right hand and bangs with his fist on the door. The thud echoes eerily back.

'That was loud enough to awaken the dead,' I laugh uneasily.

'To blazes with the dead, it's the living I'm trying to awaken.'

And he's succeeded for a light has appeared in a window that is inching squeakily upwards.

"Ello, who's that? Who's there? What d'you want?'

'We want to come in,' I shout.

'Come in, at this hour! D'you know what time it is? Clear off and stop makin' such a din.'

'Let us in,' Tom pleads, 'we booked a couple of beds earlier today.'

'Yesterday more like. We're closed. Push off.'

'Please,' I cry, laying on the anguish.

'The place is closed, I tell you. Go away! People are trying to sleep in 'ere.'

'Lucky blighters.' shouts Tom. 'Come on, let us in.'

'Go to 'ell!' The terse instruction is accompanied by the sound of the window inching noisily down. Moments later the light is extinguished.

'So much for the Christian part of the Y.M.C.A.!' I say. 'What do we do now? Go to 'ell like the nice man suggested?'

'I don't know the way!'

'Huh! Some navigator you'd make. Come on.'

Tom gives me a two-fingered sign which he promptly transfers to the "Y" as we set off in search of accommodation. Ere long it becomes quite obvious that our situation is hopeless. The pubs, boarding houses and hotels of Nottingham are locked and bolted against the night. The city is all snores and heavy breathing.

'Show me the way to Mavis's place,

'I'm tired and I want to go to her bed.

'I had lots of pints, hours ago,

'And it's gone right to my... bladder.'

Tom's ruination of "Show me the way to go home" ceases abruptly when he spies a convenient alley.

I stand and wait. An aircraft drones overhead. 'Sounds like a Wimpey,' I say.

'Nah,' disagrees Tom, emerging from the shadow and fastening his flies. 'It's a four-engined job.'

'Why, can you see it?' I ask.

'Of course not, I haven't eaten any carrots lately.'

A crumpled newspaper, stained vinegar brown and reeking of fish and chips, blows in the wind. Tom, however, fails to notice the appetising aroma, engrossed as he is in the night sky. I look at him and smile for standing there, cap askew, arm across his chest, he reminds me of a long dead military person.

'Hey Napoleon,' I joke, 'd'you want to know something?'

'What?'

'We are lost! We are up that famous creek!'

Streets away a clock chimes twice. We walk on aimlessly. Beneath our feet the pavement clouds white with frost. Taking an imaginary dance partner in his arms Tom slides one step forward, two steps back.

'I didn't know you could dance. What are you doing, a slow fox-trot?'

'No, the Tuscana.'

'Never heard of it.'

'Well you have now. Look closely and you'll see that it's based on the Italian way of fighting.'

A poster peeling from its hoarding advertises Famel Syrup. "*Take no risks with coughs and colds,*" it advises, "*Famel Conquers All*".

'Huh! If "*Famel Conquers All*", d'you think it would vanquish my hunger pangs. Hey, what's that over there?'

My eyes follow Tom's outstretched arm and discover something half hidden in the shadow of a building.

'I don't know. What d'you think it is?'

'It looks like one of those tarpaulin covered shacks where long distance lorry drivers can get a cuppa. Come on, let's investigate.'

An icy blast chills my weary bones but the wind responsible offers an apology by kindly lifting the entrance flap into the shack where Tom and I find ourselves in an oasis of warmth, situated we-know-not-where in this blacked-out desert of a city.

Suspended by twisted wire, a flickering oil lamp dangles from an invisible roof. The red end of a cigarette glows from out of the shadows. The smoker lurks, barely visible, behind a counter on which rests an urn, a bowl half full of white sugar that has turned mostly brown, and two glass domes. The latter, in times of peace and plenty, would have contained cakes and other delicacies, now they display a smattering of currants - or are they dead flies?

'Ha!' Tom exclaims triumphantly, his eyes following mine. 'So now we know where they go to in the winter-time!'

'What d'yer want?' a man's voice growls over the singing of a kettle.

'Have you anything to eat?' I ask.

'No!'

'To drink then?'

'Tea.'

'Two cups, please.'

'Mugs,' says the voice, 'an' it'll cost yer a tanner.'

Two chipped enamel mugs are banged down on the counter top. The smoker fills them with a light brown liquid from the urn then adds powdered milk. The disgusting looking result is pushed over the counter and nicotine stained fingers grab the sixpence proffered by Tom. I help myself to sugar and wince as I sip the so-called tea.

Tom too grimaces as he sips. 'I never thought I'd find a brew that could taste worse than the poison they serve at railway stations but, by heck, I have!'

The entrance flap to our classy roadside diner lifts and something enters. I think it is a woman for hidden under a threadbare coat I detect a superficial likeness to the female form. The newcomer blinks and removes a tattered mitten from her right hand. She appears anxious, frightened even, in the yellow ochre glow cast by the paraffin lamp.

Pushing grimy fingers through a mass of matted hair she shuffles, flat-footed, unwashed, dishevelled and unkempt to the counter, where her request for a cup of tea is answered by a curt, 'Bugger off'.

I inspect the lady more closely. Mascara has run in faint rivulets over what remains of a pan-cake make-up, and her mouth is a carmine gash.

'Oh go on Bill, give us a cuppa.'

'You got the money to pay for one? If you ain't, then cart off.'

'Just a cuppa, Bill.'

Mine host ignores the plea, dabbing instead at the counter with a rag more brown in colour than the tea in our mugs.

'Please, Bill.'

'I've told you a million times before an' I'll tell you again. No bloody money, no bloody tea.'

The fierceness in his voice causes the woman to take a step back and in doing so she becomes aware, for the first time it seems, of the presence of Tom and me. She stares at us and as her lips part in an apology for a smile she asks me if I can, 'Spare the price of a cuppa?'

I'm nonplussed. I've never encountered a situation like this before. I glance at Tom for support but none is forthcoming. I'm at a loss for words but the man she calls Bill isn't.

'Get out!' he shouts, pointing to the entrance-cum-exit of the shack.

The unhappy creature stares for a moment into my eyes then transfers her attention to my friend. Getting no response from him she turns and shuffles out into the cold night air.

'I wonder where she's hidden her broom-stick,' quips Tom.

'Forever comin' in 'ere, 'er is, an' 'er's never got no money, well, only sometimes.'

I'm still thirsty, and though the brew is disgusting I push our empty mugs across the counter and request more of the same.

'I s'pose you've got the money to pay for 'em?' Bill growls, with what passes for a grin.

I nod and ask him if he knows of anywhere in the neighbourhood that might provide Tom and I with a night's lodging.

'O'ways comin' in 'ere, 'er is,' he moans, shaking his head from side to side, an action which I assume means that he doesn't know of any such dosshouse.

'Why don't we look for a police-station?' I say, repeating a suggestion I'd made earlier, but Tom is still averse to spending what is left of the night behind bars.

A vehicle, brakes squealing, grinds to a halt outside the shack. A couple of Yanks enter. One of them is a pfc, the other a Negro N.C.O.

'Two coffees bud,' orders the corporal, divesting himself of an enormous pair of driving gloves.

'Ain't got none,' snaps Bill. 'Jus' tea.'

'For Chrisake! I can't stand their goddam tea! Still if there ain't nutton' else, two cups an' make it hot an' snappy.'

After inspecting the lifeless contents of the glass domes the pfc turns to admire a series of smoke rings blown by his cigar-smoking buddy. They rise, these blue rings, ever widening before eventually disappearing into the invisible dark.

'Jeez, Corp. How d'you do that?'

I too am mesmerised, to such an extent that I fail to notice the return of the bane of our host's existence.

'Cuppatea,' she croaks, leaning on the counter.

Bill's surprise at her re-appearance is evidenced by his spilling of the contents as he pushes two mugs of tea towards the Yanks. 'Now look what you've made me do! I thought I'd told you to bugger off. No money, no tea, so get out an' stay out!'

'Please, just a cuppa.'

Leaning across the counter Bill grabs the woman and shakes her so violently she jerks up and down like a puppet on a string. Hurling abuse he flings her across the shack. With shoulders hunched and body shaking she curses him before pausing by the entrance flap to cadge the "price of a cuppa" off the Negro.

'Eh?' he asks, puncturing a newly formed smoke ring with a bejewelled forefinger.

The woman repeats her request.

'Oh!' he guffaws, leaning forward to whisper in her ear. For a moment she appears taken aback by whatever it is he has suggested but after more whispering and tell-tale jingling of coins she gets the message. Without more ado she leaves the shack followed by the Negro who, with a knowing wink, hands his cigar to the pfc.

'Never got no money, only sometimes'. Bill complains bitterly, shaking his head as the pfc tries to emulate his buddy. But the smoke stubbornly refuses to form into rings, and in the end the Yank is left with nothing else to do but to study the flies lying in state in their glass mausoleums.

The entrance flap swings open to admit the corporal who saunters inside adjusting his clothing. He jerks his thumb at the pfc who, with eyes downcast, shuffles self-consciously outside.

'Jeez!' comments the Negro, pulling a face as he drinks his tea. Picking up the cigar, which lies smouldering on the counter, he puts it to his lips and inhales deeply. Then, with due ceremony, he dunks the stub in the sodden tea leaves lying at the bottom of his mug, where it fizzes and dies like a damp squib on bonfire night.

Glancing at his watch he tut-tuts before beating out an impatient eight to the bar rhythm on the top of the counter.

'Aw come on, Himey!' he moans, don't take forever you son of a bitch.'

'You ain't paid me yet,' complains Bill, his arm outstretched and fingers twitching. 'It's a tanner.'

'Is that one of these?' The corporal asks, handing over a shilling.

'It'll do.' There follows a "ching" from the cash machine but no change finds its way into the Negro's pink palm.

'Jeez, is he gonna take all night?'

He is not, for as the corporal executes yet another drum break the pfc returns.

'What took you so long, couldn't you find it? Come on fella, let's take the ozone.'

Donning his gloves the N.C.O. throws a playful punch at his buddy and before long the tea urn is vibrating to the revving of an engine. Brakes are released and then, with tyres protesting, our comrades in arms are gone.

Tom bangs down his mug and affects to throw a left hook. 'Jeez, come on buddy, let's take the air. We've seen it all now!'

He is wrong, however, for the final curtain has yet to fall on the wretched drama we have been witnessing, and the last act sees the return of its "heroine". Her entrance verges on the tragicomical. The court shoe she wears on her left foot has lost its heel. Her mouth is devoid of lipstick.

She shuffles forward and though her gait is unsteady her voice is not.

'Cuppatea, Bill.'

'Bugger off!'

'Come on, let's 'ave a cuppa.' The woman's voice has a confident ring.

'I've told yer, no money, no tea.'

'Who ain't got no money? What's this then?' she snorts triumphantly, placing two shilling pieces on the counter top. 'Nah, give us a cuppa tea!'

'Come on Al!' cries Tom, 'I can't take any more of this. Let's go and find that blue-lamp hotel you've been going on about.'

I glance over my shoulder as we depart. Bill, grabbing at the money with the fingers of his left hand, is sliding a mug of brown coloured liquid over the counter. The night-creature is parking a wad of chewing gum behind her left ear.

Tom affects great tiredness as he slouches by my side.

'Come, come, sergeant!' I reprimand. 'This just won't do! Ah-ten-shun! By the left, quick march! Left, right, left, right, left, right!'

Before long the two of us are marching with commendable precision through the streets of Nottingham. We sing as we go, to the tune of *"Jealousy"*, 'T'was all over my S.O.P. ...'

A cold north-easterly assists us as we march.

I burp, and when Tom releases gas from his nether regions we are truly "gone with the wind".

Chapter Seven

In the Deep Mid-Winter

(Mid-Winter 1942)

Tiny, whose bed space is next to mine, is suffering from a cold in the head, and he's making the most of it. With his large backside thrust close to the only source of heat in our Nissen hut he informs me, for the umpteenth time, that number 28 O.T.U. is the most godforsaken spot on the face of the earth.

'Oh, stop moaning,' I cry, giving my buttons an extra polish. 'I don't know what you expect of a hastily constructed wartime airfield. I'm quite sure Wymeswold is no worse than the rest. Anyway, you should consider yourself extremely fortunate that you managed to fool the M.O., because if you hadn't you'd have been out there with Tom and I clearing snow off the runways.'

'And perishing cold it was too,' says Tom who, like me, is preparing for a visit to Loughborough, where a New Year's Eve dance is to take place in the Town Hall.

'Huh! It's perishin' cold in here,' grieves Tiny.

'That's hardly surprising, for most of the heat from the stove is disappearing up your rear end.'

Eyeing Tom coldly, Tiny gives vent to his feelings with an almighty sneeze.

'Tut, tut,' I mock, 'coughs and sneezes spread diseases?'

Ignoring my jibe Tiny jabs at the coke in the stove with a pull-through that has become a poker. He warms his gloved hands over the resultant red glow. Normally big in stature tonight he is huge, being clad in two of everything in his attempt to keep warm.

'You ready for take-off, Al?' Tom asks, polishing his cap badge to perfection.

'Nearly. What time does the transport depart?'

'In about ten minutes, so there is still time for you to get ready, Tiny,' Tom says. 'Pull your finger out, there's a good lad. I'm sure a couple of beers will help you forget your aches and pains. Surely you don't want to let the New Year in on your own! Come on, climb into your best blue.'

Tiny shakes his head, zips up his flying jacket, and wraps another scarf round his neck.

'Yeah, come on,' I encourage. 'Think of all those popsies you'll be able to trip the light fantastic with!'

'I can't dance, you know I can't.'

'I'm only kidding, you won't have to. There's never much room to dance at a New Year's Eve dance. Did you never see the New Year in at your local hop? Anyway, when it comes to dancing, I'd hardly call Tom or myself budding Fred Astaire's. When Tommy arrives on the dance floor wearing his size tens it's time for all unattached young lasses to hide in the ladies toilet. Come to think of it though, that's nothing to do with him being a lousy dancer!'

'True, very true,' laughs Tom, 'my fame as a great lover always precedes me and tonight will be no exception. Just feed me a couple of pints and I will be all set to de-flower the virgins of Loughborough.'

'There are some then?' I ask, affecting mild surprise before yet again inviting Tiny to join us on our night out.

'No thanks,' he sniffs, curling up on his bed. 'I'll write a couple of letters and have an early night.'

'But it's New Year's Eve,' I protest. 'No one will have an early night tonight!'

'Oh leave him be,' cries Tom, tiring of Tiny's self-pity, 'he's never so happy as when he's miserable.'

The poorly one sneezes several times, and when he's finished Tom leaps up to clutch at floating objects that are both imaginary and invisible.

'What are you doin'?'

'Catching your germs before they infect Al and me,' shouts Tom, depositing pretend micro-organisms into the coke stove.

'Oh clear off, the pair of you.'

'OK, we're off,' I say, giving him a farewell wave. 'While we are away don't forget to take your cold cure tablets on the hour every hour, and your cough medicine in accordance with the instructions on the label.'

A flying-boot flies through the air.

I duck, and it hits the door behind my head.

The exertion brings on another bout of coughs and sneezes during which Tiny moans, 'I wish that Waaf from the parachute section was here, she'd keep me warm.'

'Huh,' I say. 'I thought the heat from the torch you carry for her would have been sufficient.'

'Come on Al!' cries Tom, opening the door to the hut. 'Why does he always call her "that Waaf"? Hasn't the girl got a name?'

'I'm quite sure she has but he's tongue tied in her presence, and he's never summed up the courage to ask her what it is!'

Loughborough Town Hall is full to overflowing. Streamers and balloons swing and sway in time to the music. The dance floor is crowded with servicemen, servicewomen, and a few civilians. Some couples are ignoring warning notices as they attempt to jitterbug. A banner with a strange device hangs over the stage. The letter "Y" has become detached from the message it originally conveyed, and we are now invited to have a "Happy New ear".

A committee room open for the sale of tea and soft drinks is almost empty but the bar next door is doing a roaring trade, dispensing beer that is lukewarm and thin and "shorts" that are exactly that in both quality and quantity.

There isn't even "standing room only" in the "gents", and I laugh when someone remarks that before long we will have to queue to be sick.

After he's swilled down his "pint" Tom and I get in line with the other stags. A number of young ladies are dancing together and their aloof expressions imply that they are "not for splitting", but we chaps know better than that. These superior beings, these ice maidens who are struggling to keep their cool in a hall that has no air-conditioning, will be hoping that tonight will be the night Mr Right will sweep them off their dancing feet. A handsome serviceman perhaps, with something new in the way of chat - not the usual banal drivel of "What's a nice girl like you doing in a place like this", or "Do you come here often?"

'Gosh, that was awful.' Tom's criticism is twofold, directed as it is at both his beer and the band whose wooden tempo has dragged both its own and the dancer's feet through *"The Woodchoppers Ball"*. He inspects the contents of his glass and wonders out loud why he drinks the filthy stuff.

'I know why,' I tell him. 'Without it you wouldn't have the courage to ravage the Loughborough virgins you were telling Tiny about. Hey, look over there, isn't that the Waaf he fancies, the one from the parachute section?'

'So it is, and just look who she's dancing with. It's the blonde-haired beauty of a store-basher I covet! Which reminds me, what happened to your romance with Jenny, the pride of Nottingham?'

I brush away a pretend tear. 'I lost her to a commissioned type.'

'That's the trouble with some buggers, they always pull rank! It puzzles me why Tiny's bird is here, though. Doesn't she know she ought to be in his bed keeping him warm?'

I gaze with admiration at the two beauties in blue. They are certainly proving that a quick-step can be danced properly on a crowded ballroom floor.

'What say we split 'em' Tom suggests.

'D'you think that's a good idea? Are you sure you've consumed enough liquid Dutch-courage to undertake such a bold step?'

'Round ones!' With that terse comment Tom takes my arm and steers me towards the two Waaf. Releasing his hold on me, he transfers his attention to the girl of his dreams but not before he's reminded me to ask Tiny's "girl" what her name is.

The parachute packer is all silk in my arms, and I'm relieved when she adapts her classy dance steps to cater for my clumsy one, two, three, together. We move slowly, for which I'm grateful because it gives me the opportunity to take a good look at my partner. *Um, I'm impressed!* She's Rita Hayworth with a Veronica Lake "peek-a-boo" bang. Tiny's stock rises in my estimation, the lad has taste.

The dance floor is heaving now with happy-go-lucky couples. A soldier, rather the worse for drink, bumps into me causing my left shoe to come into contact with my partner's high heeled feet.

'Damn,' I groan, offering sincere apologies.

The face of the parachute packer betrays no emotion. Her smile remains as fixed as it had been when we'd commenced dancing together.

The music stops, and as I mutter an apologetic, 'Thank you,' my partner withdraws from my clutches and makes good her escape.

Standing alone and forlorn in the middle of the floor I gaze after her, longing for a backward glance of encouragement but it never comes.

I search for Tom. He's not in the "gents", beer queue, or stag line.

Ah! There he is. He's found a niche for himself and his store-basher and they appear to be getting along just fine. Clutched together in a firm embrace, they seem oblivious to the excitement surrounding them.

Depressed, alone in a crowd intent on enjoying itself, I begin to wish I'd stayed in the hut with Tiny. I turn away pretending not to see the Waaf from the parachute section as she glides past enveloped in the arms of a pilot officer. She's glad-eyed now, and he's flushed with expectancy at the thought of what he might achieve later because of his good looks and thin blue band.

To add to my woe the band murders "*Mood Indigo*", and I wince when they fail to finish together. Having cut my jazz teeth on Duke Ellington's peerless seventy-eight-revs-per-minute recording of that moody blues, I can't do with inferior renderings.

Heaven be praised! The midnight hour is at long, long last, upon us! Hooters blow and bells ring.

"1942", in the guise of an emaciated white haired old drunk carrying a scythe exits stage left. "1943", buxom, blonde haired and full of promise, enters stage right. Blowing kisses she is greeted with rapturous applause.

Engulfed in loneliness, I leave the dance floor and make my way to the foyer, where I'm confronted by a snowman who slowly melts and becomes a corporal.

'Gosh!' I cry. 'Is the weather that bad?'

'It certainly is, sarge. Where are you stationed?'

'Wymeswold,' I answer, wondering if I have just divulged a military secret.

'Well I've news for you. The road is impassable, completely blocked with snow. 28 O.T.U. personnel will have to spend the night here, and that's official.'

I return to the festivities. A conga is snaking its way about the dance floor, from whence it slithers upstairs then downstairs past the mayoress's chamber. Balloons that had cascaded earlier from on high are being despatched to oblivion by the red hot tips of cigarettes, and everywhere there is a heaving and a clutching and a shoving. Hands are shaken, strangers lips meet in snatched kisses, and perspiring bodies yearn for each other. Toasts are drunk, and the town hall is filled with forgotten old acquaintances and new resolutions.

The corporal's tale of winter woe and snow drifts slowly through to the dancers, and before long the Wymeswold contingent has gathered in the foyer. They are a sorry looking lot, for the euphoria of "1943" has evaporated, and everywhere early hangovers are in evidence.

An officious-looking civilian accompanied by a wingless-wonder of a flight lieutenant informs us of the state of the roads, and the officer confirms that we shall be spending the night in the town hall.

Blankets appear from out of nowhere, commissioned types are made comfortable in committee room "A", and when a half-hearted attempt to segregate the rest of us into boys and girls comes to nought we are shepherded into a room that had earlier housed cloaks. I seat myself in a leather covered chair that has seen better days, loosen my tie, untie my shoe laces and wrap myself in the blanket I've been issued with. Fitting snug in their picture frames long dead councillors and aldermen stare glassily down, and I'm returning their frosty looks when the lights are extinguished.

I yawn, toss and turn, scratch my head and re-arrange the blanket a dozen times, but no matter how much I try I cannot get comfortable. To make matters worse, irritating nasal sounds emanate from the occupier of the chair to my right. I lean forward and discover that these not so dainty snores are being perpetrated by my erstwhile partner, Tiny's parachute-packing dream of delight.

Oh Tiny, if you could but see her now, I feel sure that the torch you carry would rapidly become extinguished. Dark it may be, but that doesn't stop her nose from shining brighter than any of her buttons. Her lips are no longer cherry red, and her make-up has made off!

I take a furtive look about me, make sure I'm not being observed, then give full reign to my cruel streak by digging her in the ribs. She snorts half-awake and adjusts her position. Slowly her snores subside. Breathing a sigh of relief, I eventually join her in sleep.

'Where have you two been?' asks Tiny, who is still making the most of the cold in his head.

'We couldn't get back,' Tom explains. 'The roads were blocked with snow and have only just been cleared.'

'Did you enjoy yourselves?' From the manner of his asking I get the impression that Tiny couldn't care less If we had or not.

'Sure thing, we had a great time,' Tom says. The blonde lass I fancy from stores was there, so I spent the night with her in a cosy little room in the town hall!'

Tiny sneezes. The ejected spray fizzes as it makes contact with the hot stove.

'What's more,' Tom continues. 'Al had to do the same with that Waaf you dream about from the parachute section!'

'You didn't!' cries Tiny, giving me an unhappy, bleary-eyed look of dismay.

'Oh yes he did,' chortles Tom, turning the knife. 'And he was so busy getting up to things "e 'adn't 'oughter" he never got around to asking her what her name is!'

Chapter Eight

"DTs"

(Spring 1943)

With the New Year's festivities over our flying training started in earnest at Wymeswold, with my sprog pilot seated at the controls of a Wellington bomber. The rest of us, his crew, although thoroughly trained in our flying trades were also comparative rookies, as the small number of flying hours recorded in our log books testified.

Considerable responsibility lay on Skipper's young shoulders, for it was on his ability to handle correctly the vagaries of the twin engine "Wimpey" that our lives depended. Take offs were no problem but landings saw us experiencing more than our fair share of bumps, in a non-stop round of "circuits and bumps". Pressing on regardless we progressed to more advanced activities like "cross-countries", air-firing, practice bombing and a new excitement - night flying. With gunnery, navigation and fighter affiliation also intensifying our training culminated in a series of "bullseyes", exercises carefully formulated to ensure that each member of the crew was fully conversant with his duties.

One "bullseye", which resulted in nearly six hours of night flying, saw us lift off from base to fly over Bedford, London, and Brighton, before returning to Wymeswold. The loss of a Wellington bomber on one of these night exercises exemplified the danger inherent in the war games we were playing, and I was shocked to hear that the aircraft had crashed near my home town.

The early arrival of spring coincided with the successful culmination of our training, and we were posted to number 1656 Conversion Unit, Lindholme, where our crew increased in number from five to seven.

Sergeant Walker, who hails from Liverpool, became our flight engineer, and Sergeant Whitmore our "mid-upper" gunner. The latter has flaming locks so he's an obvious "Ginger" but Walker - who is only eighteen and his boyish looks confirm this - has been given a variety of nicknames: "Johnny", after the whisky; "Scouse", because of his birthplace; "Baby-Face", due to his appearance, and "Syd" after the comic actor.

In the end we took a vote and "Scouse" triumphed.

Our first days of training at Lindholme have been earth bound with each member of the crew concentrating on his own "trade". Yesterday, however, saw a resumption of "circuits and bumps", this time with an extra dimension for there are now four engines to cope with instead of two - hence the necessity of a flight engineer.

Today, a windy Saturday full of blustery April showers, has seen four of us taking off and landing with monotonous regularity in a worn out old Halifax bomber. We have quickly dispensed with the services of a pilot instructor, so Skipper is driving, Nav is in the astrodome, Scouse is keeping an eye on the engine gauges, and I am seated in the rear turret reporting on the proximity of other aircraft in the circuit. After a while I decide that the mid-upper turret would be a better vantage point, so I clamber along the fuselage and continue to search from my new position.

To my surprise, for it has only taken me a couple of minutes to reach and climb into the turret, I find that an engine has been feathered, an operation carried out to reduce wind resistance of the blades of an unserviceable engine to a minimum.

I plug in the inter-com lead in time to hear Skipper reporting the loss of the engine to someone in the control tower. He's given priority to land and the aircraft goes into a long shallow descent, with trees and hedgerows keeping alarmingly close company.

I figure that a three engine landing will hardly be relished by Skipper, he being in sole charge of a heavy bomber for the first time in his R.A.F. career but after several alarming bumps we touchdown.

I sigh with relief, then find, to my surprise, that the aircraft is showing no sign of slowing down. Alarm bells ring in my head and they increase when the control tower recedes into the distance together with hangars, huts, bowsers, a three ton truck and the blood-wagon. A rather confused conversation is taking place over the inter-com, from which I gather that brake pressure, or rather the lack of it, is responsible for our predicament.

The ride, which up to now has been reasonably smooth, gets rough. Branches, stones, and soil whip past the turret. Then, moments before the aircraft lurches to a stop, I see to my surprise a double-decker bus just a short distance away.

Seconds later I am staring up at the tail unit of the bomber. I feel gingerly at a part of my head that has made contact with a gun barrel then scramble as fast as I can to the "conservatory", where I find that the front turret, nose, and engines of the aircraft have come to rest in a muddy ditch.

I release my parachute harness, climb out of the aircraft, and am inspecting the damage done when Skipper joins me.

He gives me a rueful smile and points to the queues of traffic that have formed on either side of the stricken aircraft.

I shake my head and wonder how we've managed to avoid contact with any other form of transport, for we must have crossed the road over which the aircraft fuselage is now hanging. Scouse does his best to retrieve items that are scattered about the ditch and I'm assisting him when the blood-wagon arrives.

Picking up my harness and 'chute I thread my way through a number of stationary vehicles and sense, from the dirty looks directed at me by the occupants, that my crew and I are not the flavour of the month.

After negotiating the traffic jam we are taken to sick quarters where we are examined by the M.O. Pronounced fit for duty we then make for our respective messes.

'Stiff upper lip type, our pilot,' Scouse observes. 'A trifle toffee-nosed but quite comical when he favours us with his shafts of wit.'

'So that's what they are! Tommy calls them "wafts" of something else, and I think his is the more accurate description. Seriously though, he's a pretty unflappable character and one can't ask for more in a pilot.'

'Have you ever listened to the chat that goes on between him and Nav? It's out of this world! Yesterday, Italian opera, this morning it was Spanish dialects!'

'That's what a university education does for you. The only bit of opera I'm familiar with is about a woman with a tiny hand that's frozen, and I only know about her because my father and mother used to listen over and over to a cracked "seventy-eight". As for dialect all I can speak is "Potteries", which isn't surprising because I never got beyond grammar school.'

'I didn't even get that far. I was just a kid when an apprenticeship became available in the docks, and my dad made sure I grabbed it with both hands.'

In the mess we become the centre of attention with lots of the chaps questioning us about our prang.

Tommy Jackson eyes me coldly. 'I don't know, Al,' he says, whistling through the gap in his teeth. 'I've only to leave you for a little while and look what happens. Any injuries?'

'Only to the Halifax.'

'And Skipper's pride, I shouldn't wonder,' laughs Scouse. 'Have you ever wondered why he chose you to be a member of his crew, I can't imagine why he picked me.'

'Your angelic looks maybe?' Tom suggests, 'or were you the only flight engineer not crewed up? I well remember how we became a crew at O.T.U. Al was standing around looking like a spare whatsit at a wedding, so I took pity on him and suggested that we join forces in our search for a pilot. En route we took a lonely looking navigator on board and then we found Skipper who already had a wireless-op in tow. I must admit I was overawed at first by "Sparks", him being a flight sergeant with a tour of ops already under his belt, but he was affable enough and so there we were, hey presto, a crew!'

'What amused me,' I laugh, 'was how quickly the atmosphere changed in that Nissen hut. We'd been herded together with instructions to turn ourselves into crews, and for a while navigators, air gunners, bomb aimers, wop-ags and pilots had wandered about looking like lost souls. Then, suddenly, lots of small groups had formed and erstwhile worried faces were wreathed in smiles. I've never seen so much relief! Everywhere there was back slapping and hand shaking. Talk about a transformation!'

'By the way,' says Tom, 'I don't suppose you know just how un-loved you four are?'

'Why? Because we pranged an expensive four-engined aircraft?'

'Oh no, the air ministry will take care of that. You'll have a bob a week deducted from your pay for the "Duration of the Present Emergency". No, it's your unpopularity with the locals I'm talking about.'

'Locals, what locals?' Scouse asks, as bewildered as I am by Tom's comments.

'The soccer-loving locals. Your blocking of the main road into Doncaster prevented a double-decker full of supporters from getting to a match.'

'Oh yes, I saw that bus,' I say rather lamely, 'just before we pranged. Well, well, so that's why we didn't get the chop, fate had decreed that we were to be almost killed by dirty looks!'

We wander slowly back to the "flights", where we bring our log books up to date.

'D'you think what Tommy says is true,' our flight engineer asks, 'that those football supporters will have missed the match because of our little escapade?'

'I doubt it. He's a bit of a leg puller is our Tom.'

Scouse gives me a peculiar look. 'Are you OK? Your hand is shaking. Are you suffering from delirium tremens?'

'"The shakes"? Me? Huh! Certainly not! I've never had the shakes in my life, and I've most certainly not got them now!'

'Why not! You should have, the prefix letters on that Halifax we've just written off were "DT".'

Oh no, don't tell me we've got another "smart alec" in the crew!

HEY, DON'T YOU REMEMBER?
You called me Al

PART TWO

"Chocks Away"

Operations with
R.A.F. BOMBER COMMAND

Chapter Nine

Chocks Away

(Spring to Winter, 1943)

100 SQUADRON
"Death or Glory"
"Sarang Tebuan Jangan Dijolok"
(Do Not Stir up a Hornet's Nest)

No. 1 Group
R.A.F. BOMBER COMMAND

Waltham, Lincolnshire, England

CREW ROSTER: - OPERATIONS 01 - 15.
MAY - JULY, 1943

R.A.F. F/O D. C. Anset   Pilot (Captain)
R.A.F. Sgt. J. Walker   Flight Engineer
R.A.F. P/O S. C. P. Godfrey   Navigator
R.A.F. Sgt. T. R. Jackson   Bomb Aimer
R.A.F. F/Sgt. H. Allan   Wireless Operator
R.A.F. Sgt. H. W. Whitmore   Mid-Upper Gunner
R.A.F. Sgt. A. H. Alcock   Rear Gunner

100 Squadron, based at Waltham airfield on the outskirts of Grimsby, became my new R.A.F. base from the 21st of April, 1943. My crew and I received only the briefest of handshakes on our arrival, which wasn't surprising for the squadron was in subdued mood having just lost their Commanding Officer and his crew in the night sky over Germany.

Suitably respectful as befitted a brand new crew we listened in awe to the tales of "veterans" who had a few ops recorded in red in their log books, and were open mouthed as well as all ears when our pilot returned from Essen, he having flown there as a "second dickey" - a duty undertaken by new pilots as a sort of baptism of fire.

Three "cross-country" flights saw us familiarizing ourselves with our respective crew positions, and on the first of May we flew an air and acceptance test in a brand new Lancaster. Serial number ED 749, the aircraft had been exhibited to the public in Piccadilly, Manchester, as part of that city's *"Wings for Victory"* effort. Much impressed with the aircraft we made ourselves known to the ground crew on touching down, knowing that our lives in the air would henceforth depend on their skill and devotion to duty.

After recording the flight in my log book a quick calculation showed that in my R.A.F. career to the end of April I had done 84 hours 45 minutes flying by day, and 62 hours 45 minutes by night, and I felt quite smug when Squadron Leader J. R. Manahan, the officer in charge of "B" Flight, verified my entries with his signature.

01 TARGET FOR TONIGHT: - DORTMUND.

Tuesday/Wednesday, 4th/5th May, 1943. There were 596 bombers on the raid, 255 of which were Lancasters. 31 aircraft were lost. This, the largest "Non-1000 Aircraft" raid of the war to date, saw the squadron dispatching 13 aircraft, all of which returned safely to base. Marking of the target by the Pathfinder Force had been spot on at the start of the raid but by the time we arrived it had become somewhat inaccurate. Bad weather resulted in numerous crashes and casualties when the bombers returned to their various bases, but we landed "all in one piece" at Waltham, having been airborne for over five and a half hours.

Earlier, as I left the sergeants' mess for the briefing room, the *"Warsaw Concerto"* from the sound track of the R.K.O. film *"Dangerous Moonlight"* crackled through a loud speaker. The music added to my mounting sense of unease for dangerous moonlight seemed synonymous with fighters and flak, and the feeling turned to fear when I realised that at long last the "real thing" was upon me. There was no escape! Gone were the days and nights of playing at being aircrew with non-stop circuits and landings, practice air firing, bombing exercises, "cross-countries" and "bullseyes". If my Browning machine guns were to be used it would be in deadly earnest. With any luck our aircraft's bombs would destroy real targets in Germany, not practice ones off the North Sea coast. My training days were over. No more would I be flying in twin-engined aircraft like the Blenheim, Whitley or Wellington. The rear turret of a mighty four-engined Lancaster would be my abode from now on. I felt relieved that I had not finished up at a Halifax squadron, having crashed in one of those aircraft when converting to heavy bombers at number 1656 Conversion Unit, Lindholme; and there was another reason for my not liking the Halifax - a very close friend from gunnery school had been killed in one when his aircraft had crashed on take-off.

That first operational briefing saw all seven of my crew seated in a row spouting nervous nonsense, which ceased abruptly when "Groupy" entered with his entourage. Having come smartly to attention we promptly sat down again, a wave of the hand having indicated that we should do so. My eyes, blinking through a haze of cigarette smoke, focussed on a large wall map that had a red ribbon stretching to Dortmund and back. At this juncture various officers took it in turn to give out detailed information vital to the success of the raid. Number of aircraft in the attack, take off time, bombing height, flak and night fighter danger spots, weather, wind speeds, turning points, time over the target and much, much more.

Finally, a, 'Good luck chaps,' and another hand wave brought the briefing to an end.

Pushing my half eaten "pre-op" meal to one side I puffed on a cigarette, glanced at the local rag, chatted non-stop to all and sundry and paid my umpteenth visit to the toilet.

Then, with the waiting over, I made for the locker room to don vest, long johns, two pairs of socks, shirt and various other items which included an electrically heated suit, bulky flying clothes and fur lined boots. Finally, there was the Mae West floatation vest, parachute harness and flying helmet. After stuffing things personal, together with other items not intended for enemy eyes into a locker, I handed the key to a Waaf, and collected my escape kit of maps printed on silk, energy sweets, foreign currency and compass.

I made absolutely sure that I had my lucky locket with me, for superstition loomed larger with every passing minute - something to which a scarf made from a bra and other female undergarments draped around our bomb-aimer's neck testified.

Carrying a parachute in my gauntleted left hand I boarded the crew bus. Driven by a shirt-sleeved Waaf the vehicle contained numerous aircrew clad in similar fashion to myself, and at each dispersal point seven of them alighted beside a waiting aircraft. Soon, far too soon for my liking, it was our crew's turn to disembark, and I found myself gazing upwards into the Lancaster's bomb bay. Some thirty three feet by five feet it contained a 4,000 lb. "cookie", together with smaller bombs and incendiaries in canisters.

Climbing aboard the aircraft in my cumbersome flying kit was not easy, and by the time I had stowed my 'chute outside and seated myself inside the rear turret I was both hot and bothered. There was also a queasy feeling in my stomach which I attributed to the all-pervading stink of oil, grease and metal.

Up front our four Merlin engines roared into life enabling me to switch on the turret controls, plug various items into sockets, check the reflector sight, and muse over what use my .303 bullets would be against the cannon shells of Me109s and Ju88s.

Satisfied that everything in the turret was in working order I knew that my fellow crew members would have carried out their own initial checks. Sparks, our contact with the outside world, would have adjusted his radio, and seated at his table "Nav", surrounded by charts and maps, would be at work on his log. At intervals over the inter-com there was "pilot/flight-engineer speak" relating to throttles, pitch, supercharger, radiator shutters and other "starting-up" procedures.

With chocks removed the aircraft taxied out of dispersal to waddle slowly towards the main runway, where a crowd of station personnel had gathered by the chequered caravan to see us off. There followed a green from the Aldis lamp, a last wave from me to the onlookers, and then at full throttle the aircraft charged down the runway. Slowly the tail lifted, the aircraft came "unstuck", and we climbed away to clear the airfield. With a dull thud the undercarriage retracted, and after circling base Skipper set course and speed for the rendezvous point on the coast.

From that moment on "Nav" kept a constant check on our position in the night sky, with Sparks seated nearby listening in to weather and wind-speed reports. As for me, crouched over four Brownings with my eyes sticking out like "chapel hat-pegs", I was grimly determined to spot any enemy intruder aircraft before they spotted me.

Sudden turbulence caused my heart to flutter but composure was quickly regained when I realised that it was the slipstream of a friendly aircraft that had made our Lancaster rock and sink, something to be expected when one was flying in a gaggle of bombers. With the aircraft's navigation lights extinguished the danger of collision increased with other Halifaxes and Lancasters flying at a similar height to ourselves, while below Stirlings and Wellingtons were "sitting ducks" for any "friendly bombs" that might be jettisoned by aircraft aborting due to some malfunction.

With the English coast a dark and distant memory I searched beneath the aircraft but could see nothing of the cold and inhospitable North Sea. I shivered, whether from fear or the cold I had no idea, but thanks to my electrically-heated suit the feeling soon passed.

'Enemy coast ahead.'

The report had me sitting on the edge of my seat. Bolt upright I waited with considerable apprehension for all hell to break loose. But no din from bursting anti-aircraft shells filled my ears, and the only sound was of someone's voice over the inter-com reporting light flak to port. Sure enough the reported balls of fire had snaked upwards only to fade away below us, but their very presence had me searching the night sky with renewed vigour.

We pressed on into the frightening unknown dark and before long were over Germany.

Bloody Hell, the Third Reich! Now what?

My stomach churned but there was no sign of flak, and the night fighters I saw in the inky dark were figments of my imagination.

What, I wondered as I searched, is happening down there, thousands of feet beneath me?

Had the German equivalent of our own air raid warning sirens wailed? Were the inhabitants of towns and villages hastening to air raid shelters? Worse, from my point of view, were there anti-aircraft guns ready and waiting? Were enemy pilots sitting in the cock-pits of their fighters, itching to take off?

A while later, when Tom our bomb-aimer announced that target indicators were visible, my mind ceased its meandering. Skipper acknowledged the report, his grunt coinciding with red flashes to port which answered one of my queries - yes, the flak gunners were awaiting our arrival.

At this juncture, with his voice betraying the excitement he felt, Tom directed Skipper towards the aiming point. His, 'Bomb doors open,' coincided with a vivid flash of light to starboard.

My God, what was that?

Had a bomber exploded, or was it one of those "scarecrows" experienced aircrew talked about? I trembled, full of apprehension. No longer did I need the warmth provided by my "electric" suit.

Red balls of fire appeared, followed immediately by what sounded like the vague barking of dogs. Something metallic rattled on the fuselage. Mein Gott, had flak got us?

A 'Left, left,' from Tom was followed by a long drawn out, 'steady, steady.'

Searchlights searched, their fingers of light groping for us as more target indicators floated down. On the ground large red areas appeared as fires took hold.

After what seemed an eternity of waiting came the cry, 'Bombs gone,' and from 21,000 feet our own lethal load cascaded into the conflagration below.

More straight and level flying for the photograph, then with bomb doors closed we set course for home.

As we left the target area a drifting veil of stratus failed to obliterate the ever increasing firework display. Target indicators, flares, incendiaries, and flashes from exploding bombs tried to hold my eyes prisoner, but I forced myself to drag them away as I heeded the oft repeated warning – "Rear gunners, don't spend your time looking at the target, if you do it could well be the last thing you'll ever look at!"

An explosion to starboard was followed by a flash of flame which grew and grew as fire consumed a four-engined aircraft. My stomach looped the loop. Suddenly the bomber disintegrated, which meant that no one could have escaped from the flaming coffin. Seven chaps had just died - yet Skipper and Scouse seemed unaware of the horror I had just witnessed as they talked of adjusting throttles and mixture to gain maximum fuel economy.

I searched, then searched again, only to find that the black shape on the Perspex of my turret was a speck of dirt, not a "bird of prey" called a Junkers 88!

Two hours later, chain smoking *"Players Please"*, we all talked at once to an interrogating officer who realised no doubt that the multiple answers he was getting to his every question were from seven over excited "bods" - a crew that had just completed its first operation over Germany.

'How big were the fires?'

'Large, and they were taking hold, visible from miles away.'

'Did you see any bombers shot down?'

'Yes.'

'Searchlights?'

'Yes, loads of 'em, all over the place. There was a great cone of them as we approached the target.'

'Cocoa anyone?' asked the Padre.

Then, when the I.O. indicated that the questioning was over, I rose to my feet and became aware of a W.A.A.F. officer seated at the next table. She was interrogating another crew. "Comely", to say the least, best described her, and for one brief moment the night's events were erased from my mind.

After consuming bacon, two eggs and fried bread, I partook of several cups of sweet tea before retiring to bed "all of a dither". One "op", or mission as the Yanks call them, of my first tour was over and done with. Only twenty-nine to go! I'd broken my duck, and when dawn also broke I awoke from an uneasy sleep that had been filled with gun flashes, pyrotechnics, searchlights and cascading T.I.s. Suddenly, as the sound of four Merlins dinned into my brain, I realised I was no longer dreaming for the aircraft that had roared over the corrugated iron roof of the Nissen hut was without doubt undergoing an air test - in readiness for another visit to Deutschland.

5th May, 1943. The Grimsby Evening Telegraph has headlined the Dortmund raid, calling it a success with bombing well concentrated. Another newspaper reveals that the largest force of four-engined bombers ever sent out by the R.A.F. was used on the raid. I feel rather pleased with myself as I sit and read the reports. For the first time in my life I've been involved in something that has made headlines. I yawn, glance at my watch, and elect to have an early night. The screech of a violin hastens my exit from the mess.

'That was Albert Sandler,' Sparks informs me, as we make for our hut. I nod my head but say nothing - because *"It don't mean a thing (if it ain't got that swing)!"*

6th May, 1943. The weather is poor so no "ops" tonight. We will not be getting the expected visit from Marshal of the Royal Air Force Lord Trenchard either, though I doubt that is because of the weather. We have, however, been visited by an Aussie, Andy Gersekowski by name. He and his crew are on a permanent visit, or until his luck runs out whichever comes first. I mention this because Fred Peake is a member of Andy's crew. Fred, however, is not an Australian, like me he hails from smokey Stoke-on-Trent.

'Up the Potters,' laughed Fred when we first met, 'three cheers for Stan Matthews.'

'Up the Placers,' I replied, but was unable to add anything further because I could not think of anyone famous who had played for Port Vale.

Last week Grimsby Town met an R.A.F. eleven. According to a chap in our mess the R.A.F. side played well together, were superior individually and had had most of the play. Yet Grimsby had triumphed by five goals to one. Funny!

Scouse has let slip that he has a girl friend who lives in Toxteth. On second thoughts I think maybe he is from Toxteth and she is from Anfield, or maybe - oh, what the heck. She's in the A.T.S. and for the past few days we have given voice to the ditty, 'She'll be wearing khaki bloomers when she comes,' whenever he's appeared.

7th May 1943. Local flying today in our very own "Lanc.". With the Lincolnshire Wolds passing prettily beneath me I mused over our squadron's erstwhile "Death or Glory" badge, with its attendant skull and cross-bones.

The motto has already brought forth the obvious quip - 'Never mind the death, bring on the glory' - a comment my fellow crew members will no doubt be repeating many times in the days to come.

9th May, 1943. Tom can't get anyone to go to the flicks with him. The picture he wants to see is on at a cinema in Grimsby. It is an "oldie", like most "pics" shown on Sundays. Called *"The Return of the Frog"* it stars, if that's the right word, Gordon Harker, a Cockney with a jutting lip. Ginger says he saw it years ago, and as it was rubbish then it will hardly have improved with age.   Sparks doesn't think picture palaces should open on Sundays, and Scouse reckons the only films worth seeing are made in Hollywood. My excuse for not going is that I've detested frogs ever since I witnessed the stoning of one when I was a youngster.

10th May, 1943. A surprising number of aircrew have reported sick. Tom, inspecting his fingers for the "shakes", wonders if the chaps have contracted the deadly L.M.F.

11th May, 1943. Formation flying today, enjoyable but a trifle dicey. I kept a careful watch on the Lancs formating too close for comfort to port and starboard, and attempted to moisten my lips with a dry tongue.

My thirst put me in mind of an evening a week or so ago when Tom, together with our mid - upper gunner, had cajoled me into visiting the Ship hotel in Grimsby to partake of an alcoholic beverage.

'Just one half pint of mild,' they had said.

'Does mild really mean mild?' I'd asked.

'Of course it does, you won't know you've had any.'

Oh dear! What would my teetotal father say if he knew that I had partaken of "drink"?

"Mild" was it? Why then, later that night, had my bed spun top like when I closed my eyes? Talk about being under the affluence of incohol!

12th May, 1943. Scouse had me puzzled this morning. For some reason we had got around to talking about civvy-street jobs. What we hoped to do when de-mob came, if we were fortunate enough to survive of course.

'I learned my trade in the Liverpool docks,' he informed me with a smile, 'and I assure you it was really no place for a rosy cheeked, fresh faced, peach bottomed young innocent like myself to be. One morning on the way to work, it was early and just getting light, I dropped a silver threepenny bit but did I bend down to pick it up? Not on your nelly, I kicked it all the way to work!'

I failed to understand what he meant, and still did not comprehend even though he spent a further five minutes explaining why he had remained upright. I was utterly confused, unwilling to believe that a man could do such a thing with a member of his own sex.

Someone in Cleethorpes, a seaside resort not all that far from the airfield, has thought up a couple of slogans for his town's *"Wings for Victory"* week. *"Make Bombers your Buy Word"* and *"They started the Bombing, Give the right reply, Build Bigger Bombers, Blow Berlin Sky-High!"*

The latest met report indicates that the weather is improving, which could mean we will indeed be trying to blow somewhere sky-high ere long - but not Berlin please, not the dreaded "Big City".

02 TARGET FOR TONIGHT: - DUISBURG.

Wednesday/Thursday, 12th/13th, May, 1943. Total number of bombers on the raid: 572, of which 238 were Lancasters. Number of aircraft lost - 34. The marking by P.F.F. was near perfect which resulted in the main force bombing being well concentrated. ED 749 was airborne for 4 hours 30 minutes. All of the squadron's aircraft returned safely to base.

"HELL ON DUISBURG", claimed the Daily Express, before going on to report that we had taken only forty-five minutes to make the greatest raid of the war so far. Half the time of the Cologne 1,000 bomber raid, the previous best. Zero hour was 2 a.m. The first flares and bombs had gone down exactly to time, and by 2.45 the whole area of Duisburg, together with the inland docks of Ruhrort, was covered by dense smoke rising to 10,000 feet.

According to another newspaper the first contingent of over 20,000 Duisburg homeless had been sent to nearby Kaiserburg, pending transfer to Baden and Silesia. The Grimsby Evening Telegraph headlined "Great Inland Port Blasted by 1,500 Tons of Bombs". It also confirmed that the raid was the R.A.F.'s heaviest ever.

Overheard in the mess from a flight-engineer with eyes narrowed to slits Chinese-style.

'Confucius 'e say – "Sergeant who 'ave Waaf on 'illside, 'im not on level".'

With last night's conflagration on the ground and the sky full of flak and searchlights over Duisburg still fresh in my mind, I gave Tommy Jackson a wry smile when he informed me that the Squadron was operating again and our crew was listed to take part. Phew, two nights on the trot!

03 TARGET FOR TONIGHT: - BOCHUM.

Thursday/Friday, 13th/14th May, 1943. Total number of bombers on the raid: - 442, 98 of which were Lancasters. Number of aircraft lost: - 24. The route chosen took us to the Ruhr in a north-easterly direction from the Rhine, between Cologne and Dusseldorf. Take off was at midnight. We bombed the red target indicators at 02.19 hours from 20,000 feet, and were immediately caught by searchlights. Forced to twist and turn for dear life we lost several thousand feet in height but received no damage. The "op" lasted 5 hours.

Ginger voiced similar thoughts to my own when he declared - 'If tonight's goings on are anything to go by we haven't got a snowball in Hell's chance of completing a tour of thirty ops.'

His observation seemed all the more true when we found that our C.O. - Wing Commander McIntyre - had failed to return.

14th May, 1943. Spent time in the mess reading a variety of newspapers. One of them reports a German claim that markers are being used to draw some of our bombing away from target areas. Now there's a thought! Do we go through all that "shock-horror" just to bomb decoys?

There is some good news, however, "Winco" and his crew are safe. They had been forced to crash land at Coltishall because flak near Cologne had rendered two of Lancaster ED 710's engines unserviceable.

'What rotten luck!' observes Scouse, pulling a face as he lays aside a local newspaper. 'Eleven ATS girls including two from Grimsby have been killed. Their hostel in an East Anglian coastal town received direct hits during a sneak raid by F.W. fighter bombers.'

15th May, 1943. Formation flying today followed later by fighter affiliation, our friendly adversary being a Spitfire. Naval Radio Station masts ensure that the airfield is easy to recognise as we approach Waltham but Tom has his own landmarks - the Windmill and the W.A.A.F. site! Ginger has decided that in future he will pee on the tail wheel before take-off. This is common practice with lots of aircrew but why they think such an act will keep them safe in the night sky over Germany I've no idea.

A chap called Sam, a real Lincolnshire "Yellow Belly", is the proprietor of a "pig-wash" cafe in Bull Ring Lane. Tom, who has been known to frequent the place, tells me that Sam has been fined £3 for serving his "delicious grub" after 23.00 hours.

17th May, 1943. We aircrew fly a lot, and so do the rumours that wing their way continually about the airfield. One such tall story has it that because discipline has been very poor of late we are to be punished - with a visit from Vera Lynn.

Hitler is said to chew the carpet when he gets angry, and he's been assassinated again - for the third time in as many weeks!

Handsome "Hairoil" Flynn has committed suicide, they found him in Veronica Lake!

Meanwhile Ginger refuses to comment on a rumour much nearer to base, that he and a nurse from the local hospital have been seen picking wild flowers together in Bradley Woods, wherever they are. I hope she's not afraid of ghosts because Tom reckons the woods have been haunted by a "Black Lady" ever since Wars of the Roses days. Wife of a woodsman who had gone to war, the woman appears to have been raped and then put to death by rampaging soldiers.

A small force of Lancasters has made an attack on three dams that serve the industrial Ruhr. Water rushing down into the valleys has caused wide-spread devastation.

18th May, 1943. A crowd of us went to the loft today to learn about homing pigeons, and their usefulness should a crew get into difficulties
I didn't handle one, I don't care for that sort of bird. Tom, on the other hand, has a great affection for the creatures.

19th May, 1943. Fred Peake looked a bit fraught today. I'm not surprised for his aircraft, piloted as usual by Andy Gersekowski, lost an engine on a mine-laying trip somewhere over the Bay of Biscay.
Overheard in the mess - a merry quip based on the careless talk, "*Be Like Dad, Keep Mum*", poster. 'What did dad say to mum when she told him she was pregnant?' "Oh, that careless stork!"'
Ginger didn't get it until Tom said, slowly and deliberately, 'Care…less…stalk.'
Also overheard in the mess but only at breakfast time, 'Do me a favour, pass me that jar of Ticklers cherry jam'.
This, like Fred's fraught look, isn't surprising, for it is a very tasty jam much enjoyed by we aircrew.

There were far more Waaf than R.A.F. on the late night transport from GY, and most of them seemed familiar with the lyrics of "*Roll Me Over*". One hefty L.A.C.W. was in particularly good voice. Rising unsteadily to her feet she waved her arms above her head and gave out with:

'Now this is number one and the fun has just begun,
'Roll me over, lay me down and do it again.
'Roll me over in the clover, roll me over, lay me down and
'do it again.'

The role of diva proved too much for her, however, for when she reached 'Now this is number two,' she flaked out, well-nigh flattening two of her colleagues as she collapsed on top of them. On the other side of the gang way a bomb-aimer started whistling "*Bless 'em All*", and the chap beside him promptly burst into song using the same melody:

'They say there's a Lanc. just leaving the Ruhr.
'Bound for old Blighty's shore.
'Heavily laden with terrified men,
'All lying down on the floor.'

From the rear a beery voice revealed that:

'Old King Cole was a merry old soul, and a merry old soul was he.
'He called for his Lancs in the middle of the night,
'and he called for his rear-gunners three.'

From the front row came:

'Have you ever been across the sea to Ireland?'

And again from the rear:

'Jesus Christ, it's cold,' said the rear-gunner,
'Corkscrew port like hell,' said the mid-upper,
'Dah-di-di-dah-di-di-dah,' said the wireless-op.'

From somewhere came a snore, from somewhere else the sound of a sloppy kiss. From half under a seat, to the tune of "*These Foolish Things*":

'The faint aroma of a gent's urinal.'

From two rows back a recitation of *"Ten Little Bomber Boys"* was drowned by, 'Any time you're Lambeth way,' which in its turn was interrupted by *"Sweet Violets"*, *"Knees Up Mother Brown"* and *"We're Going to Hang Out the Washing on the Siegfried Line"*.

Ginger, with a snort, awoke from a deep dream of peace. 'I don't care if it rains or freezes,' he mumbled, 'I am safe in the arms of Jeezees.'

'I've got sixpence, jolly, jolly, sixpence,' trilled a greasy nosed Waaf.

'And you weren't bloody worth it,' moaned her male companion.

'Lulu had a baby, she called it Tiny Tim. She took it to the river...'

A soprano, assisted by a contralto, cried 'My eyes are dim I cannot see, I have not brought my specs with me.'

'and threw the bar-steward in.'

'I have not brought my specs with me.'

'We shall go on to the end,' a Churchillian voice growled.

'We are at the end,' bawled the driver. 'Get weaving. Come on, everybody. Out!'

The floods in the Ruhr have extended over fifty miles. Anything standing in their path like railways, bridges and airfields have been swept aside by a great wave of water.

23rd/24th May, 1943. Dortmund was raided again in the early hours but our crew was 'stood down', which enabled me to write home and give my parents the low down on the chaps I fly with. Skipper, in other words my pilot, Flying Officer Anset, is a university type with a fine tenor voice, able to speak it seems in a variety of tongues. He spouts poetry too, at the drop of a hint. Quiet and cultured, Pilot Officer Godfrey is our navigator, he too is a graduate. Wireless-op, Flight Sergeant Allan, is on his second tour of operations, having completed his first tour in twin-engined Whitley bombers, or "flying coffins" as he calls them. I have written previously to my folks about "Scouse" Walker, Tommy Jackson and Harold W. "Ginger" Whitmore but it might interest them to know that Tom says his forebears come from Chile, and when I scoffed he claimed that that country was full of Jacksons. Ginger, the son of a Kentish butcher, hails from Ashford.

My parents know pretty much everything I want them to know about me of course, except that I occupy the coldest spot and most vulnerable position in the aircraft - which makes me a right "Tail-End Charlie". I read what I have written and wonder if the censor will soon be hard at work with his blue pencil. Unsure of what I can, or cannot reveal, I lay the half written letter aside having decided to make another attempt later.

Ginger tells me the Yanks have done a "daylight". The target was a generating plant at Ijmuiden, which is difficult to spell and even harder to pronounce. It seems eleven B-26 Martin Marauder aircraft were involved. They were met by a hail of flak. Ten out of eleven aircraft were lost, and the eleventh only survived because it aborted en route to Holland having developed engine trouble.

I've taken up "shooting". I suppose one could call it a "busman's holiday". Most of my spare time is spent therefore firing a rifle on the 25 yard range, or downing clay pigeons.

Rome Radio, according to the Grimsby Evening Telegraph, has accused Bomber Command of dropping "cough-drops" over Germany. They explode in the mouth when sucked.

So what? I kissed a Waaf last week and when she stuck her tongue in my mouth I almost exploded, but I'm not telling the Telegraph.

Jack Benny was on Forces radio recently. He really makes me laugh. He's so wonderfully mean, and his violin playing is execrable.

24th May. 1943. The recent raid on the dams is still "news", and a cartoon in one of today's papers made me smile.

Dr. Josef Goebbels, holding a microphone, is speaking to the German people about the bombing.

'You are very lucky,' he tells them, 'for never before has fish been so plentiful in the Ruhr Valley.'

04 TARGET FOR TONIGHT: - DUSSELDORF.

Tuesday/Wednesday, 25th/26th May, 1943. Total number of bombers on the raid - 759, of which 323 were Lancasters. Number of aircraft lost: - 27, of which 9 were Lancasters. Two of our squadron's aircraft failed to return. Sdn/Ldr Turgel in LM 320, and the New Zealander Sgt. Moore in W 4998. Dusseldorf was covered by two layers of cloud which resulted in our bombs being scattered over a wide area. We were airborne exactly 5 hours. One newspaper states that this was the biggest ever R.A.F. "bad weather attack", with more than five 4,000 lb. bombs dropped every minute.

I am sure the loss of Turgel and Moore bothers my fellow crew members as much as it does me, but to what extent I have no idea for when it was discussed their demeanour revealed nothing.

The failure of Sdn/Ldr Turgel to return from Dusseldorf means that Skipper is now acting flight commander of "C" flight, and he will remain so until a senior officer returns from leave.

Wing Commander G.P. Gibson, who led the attack on the Ruhr dams, has been awarded the Victoria Cross.

The King and Queen have visited St. Paul's Cathedral where, together with a huge congregation, they gave thanks for the triumph in Africa. Winston Churchill, in Washington, reckons Italy will crack before long, and he's assured the United States that Britain will be by its side in the war against Japan. Anthony Eden, in London, says that Germany will be bombed night and day, day by day, hour by hour. The bombing will be not only be round the clock but also round the map, for Italy will also get its share. Looks like Bomber Command is going to be kept quite busy for the foreseeable future.

If the opportunity arises Ginger and I intend to visit Grimsby because Humphrey and Ingrid are on at the Ritz and Regal in "*Casablanca*". My sister having written, in a recent letter - 'It's a smashing flick, you must see it.'

05 TARGET FOR TONIGHT: - ESSEN.

Thursday/Friday, 27th/28th May, 1943. Total number of bombers on the raid: - 518, of which 274 were Lancasters. Number of aircraft lost: 23, of which 6 were Lancasters. One 100 squadron aircraft failed to return, Flt. Sgt. Townrow and crew flying in ED 821. Cloud over the target meant that sky markers were used. There was an awful lot of off putting heavy flak, probably 105 mm, and searchlights but we managed to bomb the aiming point. We were airborne for 4 hours 30mins.

29th May, 1943. A report from a German source indicates that we inflicted considerable damage on the centre and northern part of Essen. The raid was the heaviest so far on the city. An enormous load of bombs fell on the Krupp arms plant which covers over 800 acres.

Today the King visited nearby Binbrook which is home to 460 squadron. Some of our chaps were bussed over from Waltham to be presented to H.M. The target for tonight was Wuppertal but Flt Lt. Anset and crew were not on the raid, and neither were we amongst the chosen few who had met the King earlier in the day.

Cartoons fill the newspapers and one is in very poor taste. A Lancaster bomber, severely damaged by flak, has broken in two, and the rear gunner as he plummets to earth and certain death says - 'The worst of this job is it's so detached.' I would like to take the cartoonist on a raid, just to prove to him that bombing targets in the Ruhr is no laughing matter.

Sparks says that the "regulars" in a certain pub run a sweep whenever we operate over Germany. The lucky winner is the one whose ticket number coincides with the number of bombers lost! If I had my way I would drop the whole bunch of beer swilling creeps with our next bomb load.

30th May, 1943. Sir Arthur Harris, our Commander-in-Chief, is a shadowy figure known to us as "Butch". In a recent speech at a *"Wings For Victory"* gathering he announced that the bombing Germany has so far received was "chicken-feed", compared to what she is about to get.

3rd to the 10th of June, 1943. A week of "ops" on, "ops" off, due to the inclement weather. I detest this "scrubbing" of operations for it is both frustrating and nerve wracking.

When conditions finally allowed, however, we were able to air test our Lancaster, and as ED 749 flew over Grimsby docks my sight-seeing was interrupted by the sound of Skipper's voice over the inter-com.

'Are you awake, rear gunner?'

'But of course, Skip. Ever vigilant, you know me.'

'Yes, I do. That's why I thought you had nodded off. It must, after all, be very tiring having to fly on "ops" and cope at the same time with the sexual demands of that Waaf of yours.'

'Pardon! What Waaf?' I cried, doing my best to sound indignant.

'Phyllis. That's her name, isn't it?'

'Huh! She's hardly my Waaf.'

'What's her trade? I mean, what does she do, apart from the obvious?'

'She's a met assistant.'

'Does that mean you are familiar with her fronts? I bet you prefer warm ones to cold ones. Is it true love this time do you think?'

Realising that I was being set up, I made no reply.

Then, as he banked the Lancaster to port, Skipper came out with the denouement that his banter had been leading up to. 'And are you going to see-phyllis tonight gunner-rear?'

The rest of the crew found this play on words most amusing. They chortled with glee before adding derisory well-worn comments of their own.

'You should see her, Skipper,' laughed Ginger. 'She has an enormous amount of hair. If you stuck a pole up her backside you could use her as a mop.'

'Her teeth are like the stars, they come out at night,' cried Tom, dredging the bottom of his barrel load of puns. 'And her lips are like petals, bicycle pedals.'

Even Scouse, not normally given to scurrilous jibes, joined in with, 'They call her the camp bike, because everybody rides her.'

I tried to think of something clever to say but when nothing appropriate came to mind I removed a gauntlet and gave the lot of them a two fingered salute.

My Waaf indeed! She was a right nut case, that Phyllis! I had only taken her out on one occasion and my clumsy attempt to kiss her had ended in tears.

Later, when my hand had wandered, she'd pushed me aside and headed post-haste for the Waafery!

There's another *"Wings for Victory"* slogan in the paper to titillate me. This time it is Grimsby's turn with, *"You Bust the Dam Target"*. £500,000! Enough to pay for a squadron of Lancasters and two squadrons of Spitfires.

When Ginger visited Lincoln recently he found a colourful pre-war map of Germany in a dusty old antiquarian book shop. With German Volk in colourful peasant costumes much in evidence, together with their towns and cities, our mid-upper decided that as Deutschland was part and parcel of our current existence we might well be interested in his discovery.

This morning therefore he spread the map out on his bed, elbowed me in the ribs, and cried. 'Look Al, it's no wonder there's so much flak and searchlight activity, see how close together the towns in the Ruhr really are. That's Dortmund there, here's Bochum, Gelsenkirchen and Oberhausen. These docks are Duisburg-Ruhrort. That's Essen with Krupp printed in red, and Krefeld and Munchen Gladbach.'

He moved his finger down the map to Dusseldorf and Cologne, then to the right and upwards before pointing to Wuppertal, Barmen and Elberfeld.

'Who christened it *"The Happy Valley"*?' I asked. 'And how come there's so much green, I thought it was all industrial. They must have planned ahead, you know what thorough blighters the Germans are. I can just imagine a clever monocled Hun fingering his duelling scar and saying as he perused this map, "Ve must ave somver to put unser searchinglights und flak gunz".'

'My geography master said the Ruhr was the equivalent of our Black Country. One huge area of foundries, steel works, chemical plants and coal mines.'

'You must be joking!' cried Tom, inhaling the smoke of a *"Gold Flake"*.

'Why, what d'you mean?' Ginger asked.

'Do you really expect us to believe that you actually went to school?'

'Hey listen to this. It says in this obviously well-informed magazine that the members of a bomber crew are skilled individuals who work together as a team. One of their number, however, never looks forward but always backwards. He is the rear gunner on whose guts, constant alertness and know how the safety of the aircraft and crew depend.'

'Bloody hell! Are you line-shooting line again? Mein Gott, von Cock, you are a bloody show off.'

'What's he reading, *"Comic Cuts"*?'

'Sounds like it. He's right about being backward though.'

Undismayed I scrounge a cigarette off Ginger. 'Have I ever told you about the time I fractured my wrist?'

'Hundreds of times. By the way chaps, have you seen the scribble that's appeared on the shitehouse wall under the "I'd sooner hang around Piccadilly underground" ditty?'

'Are you suggesting it's Al's?'

'Don't be daft.'

'Why?'

'He can't write.'

'Not guilty,' I protest, 'I reckon Kilroy did it, Kilroy does everything. What does it say?'

'It doesn't say anything, it's an equation. "R.A.F. over W.A.A.F. minus FL" equals something or other.'

'What do you mean, something or other?'

'What I say, the rest is smudged.'

Ginger, reading a letter from his father, interrupts with - 'To reduce shock and minimize fear slip a Bob Martin's in Fido's beer.'

'What are you babbling about, you long streak of you know what?'

'Dad thinks our dog's on its last legs, and I'm reminded that he used to say what I've just said when German bombers flew over our house on their way to London.'

'Your dog can talk then?'

'Don't be daft. He just didn't like air raids.'

'Who didn't?'

'Rover. Talk about going crazy. He'd chase his tail and bark like mad.'

'And what did a Bob Martin's do for him?'

'Quietened him down. They were "fit and hysteria" powders. If Pop gave him one when the sirens wailed he'd become calm and would remain so until the "All-Clear" sounded.'

'Any chance of your father sending me one? I'd take it before the bombing run.'

06 TARGET FOR TONIGHT: - DUSSELDORF.

Friday/Saturday, 11th/12th, June, 1943. Total number of bombers on raid: - 783, of which 326 were Lancasters. Number of aircraft lost: - 38, of which 14 were Lancasters.

25 aircraft were put up by the squadron, two of which failed to return. ED 786 piloted by Sdn/Ldr Manahan D.F.C. who had Wing Commander Harrison flying with him as an observer, and ED 976 flown by Sgt. Magill and crew. There was considerable cloud en route, but over the target excellent marking by P.F.F. enabled me to comment later in my log book that the bombing had been concentrated. Extremely heavy flak made life very uncomfortable but ED 749, airborne for 4hrs 55mins, returned unscathed to base.

12th June, 1943. Newspapers litter the mess. One of them states that last night we dropped over 2,000 tons of bombs on Dusseldorf, and another quotes a report from Stockholm that the breaching of the Mohne and Eder dams has resulted in well over 70,000 casualties. There is a warning that the "*Axis*" is getting ready to use poison gas, and an article about Leslie Howard, the film star, who was a passenger in an aircraft flying from Lisbon to Ireland, shot down by the Nazis. I saw Howard in the long-winded "*Gone with the Wind*", and remember a comic remark made at the time about the abnormal length of "G.W.T.W." - that when people left the cinema they had aged so much their relatives could not recognise them.

Since his promotion Skipper's been quite ebullient. He's regaled us with numerous operatic arias, and told us a number of what Ginger calls, "superior varsity jokes". Some have been way over my head but I did understand his "faux pas" tale.

Lord So and So, it seems, allowed his butler to broaden his mind by letting him read from the vast number of books that adorned the library shelves of his stately home. From time to time he would enquire as to what literary progress his "Jeeves" was making.

On one occasion the butler replied that he had come across the expression "faux pas", the meaning of which escaped him.

'Oh, I can explain that quite easily,' cried his Lordship. 'Cast your mind back a couple of weeks to when we entertained the Bishop. You will no doubt recall that he caught his finger on a thorn when strolling with her Ladyship in the rose garden.'

'Yes, I remember it well, my Lord.'

'And later, at dinner, just as you were serving the dessert, her Ladyship turned to the Bishop and asked him if his prick was still throbbing? I said, "My Christ", and you dropped the custard, well that was a faux pas!'

Cartoons about the bombing of the dams still appear. One that brought a smile to my lips showed two middle aged Germans drinking together.

"Beer's gone a bit thin Hans, don't you think," one of them complains, "since that damn dam burst."

I wish the beer at the "*Ship*" in Grimsby would get thinner, if it did I might be able to consume more than half a pint before I get tiddly.

07 TARGET FOR TONIGHT: - BOCHUM.

Saturday/Sunday, 12th/13th, June, 1943. Total number of bombers on raid: - 503, of which 323 were Lancasters. Number of aircraft lost: 24, of which 14 were Lancasters. Twenty of our squadron aircraft were dispatched, one failed to return - W.4989. W/O Dainty D.F.M., and crew. The target area was cloud covered but with the help of "Oboe", a sky marking technique based on radio pulses transmitted from two stations in England, the marking was accurate and intelligence reports indicate that we caused severe damage.

I have saved two specimens of the leaflets we drop over Germany. One of them, which makes reference to Stalingrad, has a photograph of an open-mouthed Adolf Hitler. He appears to be catching flies but is actually haranguing the party faithful. My knowledge of German is only "schoolboy" but from what I can make out the other piece of propaganda is about "Total War", with extracts from Der Angriff and the Volkischer Beobachter. "Bomben auf Coventry" stands out, and there are photographs of that city's damaged buildings and injured civilians. London, on fire, and Liverpool, in ruins, also serve to spell out the message that what British cities and towns have suffered cannot be compared with what happened to Dortmund in 45 minutes of bombing - and what is going to happen to other German towns and cities in the immediate future.

There is an illustration of a Lancaster bomber in the Evening Telegraph, together with words of praise from Hewitts, "Brewers of Fine Ales", who will no doubt have paid for the two column spread. *"We are proud to pay tribute to men of all the Flying Services, and especially to those from North Lincolnshire".*

Wacko, chaps!

I have received a letter from my brother-in-law, an unusual event to say the least.

Most of the content concerns Hitler and his mistakes. How he should have invaded Britain after Dunkirk! Why he should never have left the Libyan campaign to the Italians! That he was mad to have attacked Russia! After such earth-shattering pronouncements my sister's husband will no doubt have returned to his work bench, where some of his colleagues find the time to manufacture Spitfire brooches from pennies!

"Nav", who trained in the United States, tells me they have the largest telescope in the world in that country, at Mount Wilson. It has a reflector one hundred inches across and reveals one million, million stars.

"The bind moggles!" as Tom would say.

Judging from photographs taken of Dusseldorf our visit of the 11th/12th has resulted in the devastation of more than 1,500 acres of the city, the equivalent of nearly two and a half square miles!

I do not like the sound of organs but the opposite can be said of our wireless operator, and Sparks is always delighted when Sandy Macpherson the organist "pulls out the stops" on Forces radio.

Needless to say I am dismayed. Why can't there be more "Swing", with bands like Benny G's, Duke E's, Count B's and Woody H's, filling the air-waves? I'd even settle for a bit of Bert Ambrose!

My erudite pilot informed me yesterday that Tennyson had not only been poet laureate, he was also a native of the county in which we are based. And surprisingly prophetic it seems when it came to flying. Without further ado Skipper had then waxed poetical.

'Saw the heavens filled with commerce, argosies of magic sails,

'Pilots of the purple twilight, dropping down with costly bales,

'Heard the heavens fill with shouting, and there rained a ghastly dew

'From the nations' airy navies, grappling in the central blue.'

08 TARGET FOR TONIGHT: - OBERHAUSEN.

Monday/Tuesday, 14th/15th June, 1943. A Lancaster attack of 197 aircraft from which 17 failed to return - an unsustainable loss of more than 8% of the bomber force. Of the twenty-plus aircraft put up by our Squadron six returned early with various technical troubles, and one failed to return - ED 973, Sgt. Weddell and crew on their first operation. The marking was accurate using "Oboe". There was much searchlight activity together with heavy concentrated flak. We were airborne for 5 hours. Early reports indicate that considerable damage was inflicted on this Ruhr coal and steel centre, which is also a vital transport junction with a population of 192,000.

At interrogation Ginger and I both reckoned we had seen more searchlight activity than on any previous raid.

'An incredible number,' our "mid-upper" had insisted before waxing lyrical. 'In spite of the clouds, they lit up the night sky over the Ruhr from Krefeld in the west to Dortmund in the east.'

Who's been looking at a pretty coloured map of the Ruhr then? I thought, a knowing smile on my lips.

Ginger can be quite profound at times. 'Did you know that lack of rubber can stop more planes taking to the air than the Luftwaffe can ever shoot down?' he asked.

To which Tom, who can be quite crude at times, replied, 'Yeah, and did you know it can result in lots more pregnancies.'

If I ever did covet Phyllis then I don't anymore, for my flighty eye has alighted on a newly arrived mess waitress. A cute-looking lass with an attractive smile she lives, in keeping with apparent Air Force policy, not that many miles away from the airfield. I have twice asked her for a "date" but she always has a reason for turning me down. Washing her hair, learning first-aid, on "late" duty, or writing to friends of whom she appears to have a great number. I have also asked her on several occasions what her name is but to no avail. I've questioned other waitresses but all they do is giggle and act dumb.

On one occasion Tom was seated next to me when she whispered, 'not tonight,' so he promptly christened her "Josephine".

The comment had brought forth an "oldie" from Ginger who hoped for her sake that she was not named Virginia, because if she was and she eventually went out with me we would be calling her Virgin for short but not for long.

So, until I find out what her name actually is, "Joe" will have to suffice.

Ginger is friendly with a nurse who works in a hospital that is situated between Waltham and Grimsby. He says that although she is smitten with his Gary Cooper looks she dislikes his night time activities because they keep her awake.

'We always know when there's a raid on,' she's told him, 'it's the only time one can get a seat in the pub.'

She is not the only person to complain. A chap who lives near the airfield reckons that the noise from our "Merlins" stops his chickens laying their eggs, and a local farmer reckons we upset his cows to such an extent they won't give milk.

Harking back to his nurse Ginger tells me she is fond of dancing, and wants to pay a visit to the *"Gaiety"* in Grimsby. He is not keen though, for he knows that what R.A.F. drill corporals and sergeants the length and breadth of the land have always claimed is true - he has two left feet! And there is another reason for his reluctance. A visit to the dance hall for the two of them would set him back a couple of bob, which is mighty off putting for a tight wad like our Harold. Scouse says he should take her to the dance held at a local church hall where there's a 6d reduction in admission price for men in uniform, and a free lock-up for cycles.

Tiny, a navigator acquaintance of mine, is built like a tank. Six feet three inches tall, with massive chest and huge thighs, he is Charles Atlas personified. Heralding from Wales, his life has been all singing and rugby. He hails from some unpronounceable place not far from Tonypandy, and claims that he was a good enough heavyweight to be engaged as a sparring partner for Tommy Farr.

Having donned a pair of boxing gloves I was coming off worst in an encounter with a punch bag when Tiny appeared. 'You should take it up seriously when the war is over,' he observed, with a lilt in his voice and a twinkle in his eye.

'Pull the other one,' I panted.

'Seriously though, boyo, there's a dearth of male ballet dancers, don't you know. Now stop prancing about like a pox doctor's clerk and come here.' As he spoke he adopted a defensive stance, with fists, elbows and arms protecting his body and chin. 'Now, hit me. Try to knock me out.'

Knock him out indeed! I couldn't land a blow anywhere on his body, never mind his chin. Each punch I threw was picked off by his huge forearms, and periodically something flattened my nose which soon began dribbling a liquid as red as the gloves he was hitting me with.

Instructions poured from his smiling mouth. 'Keep your guard up.' 'Lead with your left.' 'Stop dropping your right.'

A timely appearance saved both my pride and my bacon. It was Ginger who, after ensuring we were out of punching range, told Tiny to pick on someone his own size!

I hear that when Tiny was due to fly on an "op" some time ago the raid was scrubbed at the last moment. Having swallowed his "wakey-wakey" pill sometime earlier he had then spent a sleepless night all by himself playing solitaire. Pardon me while I snort with laughter through my damaged proboscis.

09 TARGET FOR TONIGHT: - COLOGNE.

Wednesday/Thursday. 16th/17th June, 1943. A mostly Lancaster raid of 212 aircraft, 14 of which were lost including one from 100 Squadron - Sgt. Boughton and crew in ED 553. Sgt. L.H. Wright, piloting EE140, crash landed on his return to Waltham, having been badly shot up by a Ju 88. Ginger, always a mine of information, says that another Lanc., EE 140, is damaged beyond repair, and Boughton's mid-upper was about forty years of age, which surprised me because I had no idea that anyone remotely approaching that age could fly on "ops".

Another aircraft that nearly failed to return that night was our ED 749. With the North sea many thousands of feet below our aircraft began to spiral out of control, and confused voices over the inter-com indicated that we had "iced up". Skipper it seemed was fighting a losing battle with the elements, confirmation of which came moments later when he gave the order to prepare to abandon aircraft.

With the Lancaster twisting and turning in an alarming manner I was filled with horror at the prospect of a watery grave but as I struggled to open the turret doors the order was rescinded, and ere long the aircraft had resumed straight and level flight.

All of a dither I wondered where we were in the night sky. Nev our "Nav" also appeared to be somewhat confused but when a "fix" established that we were miles off track, with no hope of reaching the target on time, the decision was taken to abort the operation. A while later, breathing huge sighs of relief, we crossed the Suffolk coast north of Southwold and headed for base.

'Bloody gremlins!' a gaunt and tired Ginger moaned as we waited for the crew bus to collect us at dispersal. 'Some chaps will have it that it's hail and other adverse weather that wears off the gunge that is smeared on the leading edge of an aircraft's wings, but they're wrong, it's gremlins. And not just any old gremlins, they are the greedy sort who enjoy the taste of de-icing paste.'

Gremlins or not I knew that I had stared death in the face an hour or so ago, and the memory of it would stay with me for the rest of my days.

It seems we were not the only crew to have had a "shaky do" due to ice. F/Sgt. Pickles returned early in W.4999 having had most everything 'freeze-up', and when Squadron Leader Davies, flying ED 815, was twice attacked from the starboard quarter by an unseen aircraft his gunners had been unable to reply because the firing pins of their Brownings were frozen.

Returning from a "daylight" on Wilhelmshaven and Cuxhaven our American cousins claim to have shot down over one hundred Nazi fighters! A ludicrous and extravagant claim that reminds me of a rather vulgar ditty we enjoy chanting.

        'The Yanks are flying Fortresses at forty thousand feet,
        'The Yanks are flying Fortresses at forty thousand feet,
        'With twelve point-fives and a teeny weeny bomb!'

        'We are flying Lancasters at zero zero feet,
        'We are flying Lancasters at zero zero feet,
        'With no point-fives, but a f.....g great bomb!'

June 18th, 1943. In the mess yesterday Tom said he wished he was stationed at nearby Binbrook. When I asked why all he could say was, 'Rabbits'. I shook my head and came to the conclusion that our recent dicing with death over the North Sea had affected his brain but he continued with, 'I like them, I always had one when I was a lad, and there's a rabbit club at Binbrook.'

A while later, when I arose from my seat to play at darts with Scouse, Tom was still enthusing over, "Old 'English", "Dutch", "Silver Fox", "Flemish" and something that sounded like "Beverages" or "Beverens".

Poor Ginger. Left alone with Tom the look on his face implied that he also wished that our bomb aimer was indeed at Binbrook, or anywhere else for that matter if it would put an end to the long haired mammal monologue.

June 20th, 1943. It is rumoured that Bomber Command is about to issue a new tactical policy. Up to the present we have always made frequent changes of course and height in order to avoid being caught and shot down by fighters or flak, but from now on - in order to obtain the utmost accuracy from our bombing - aircraft are to fly straight along the route to and from and also over the target, except of course when singled out for engagement when existing manoeuvres should be used.

Protection will be obtained by crews adhering scrupulously to the ordered route, with continuous intensive search by air-gunners in order to avoid surprise attack by enemy fighters. If an aircraft is attacked by a fighter then the immediate use of the rules governing air combat are to be used, the diving turn and the corkscrew being the most effective. Gunners will vigorously engage the enemy with fire, co-operating with the pilot to obtain the correct timing of manoeuvres. An aircraft's action when coned in searchlights is to fly as quickly as possible by the shortest route out of the lit area, making another approach to the target if the bombs have not been released.

By straying from the ordered route crews risk their own lives, and jeopardise the remainder of the force because they reduce the concentration of aircraft in the stream. Flying an erratic course over the target may result in a collision with an aircraft endeavouring to obtain good bombing results by flying straight. With the introduction of this new tactical policy Command is obviously determined to ensure that the bombing offensive will be carried forward with ever increasing success by skilled and determined crews.

'So you are not to nod off in future, Ginger,' I laughed, 'you must be wide awake at all times if you wish to avoid a surprise attack by an enemy fighter. Non-stop searching from now on, my lad.'

'I always search,' growled our mid upper, 'particularly on the bombing run with its wretched straight and level. God, how I detest those few seconds. They seem like eternity and from now we'll be expected to do it all the way to the target and back. Ruddy suicide if you ask me. Why those characters at Bomber Command H.Q, the ones with scrambled egg on their caps, think that frequent changes in course and height don't contribute to our safety I've no idea. They should get off their fat backsides and do a few ops before making such loony decisions!'

10 TARGET FOR TONIGHT: - KREFELD.

Monday/Tuesday. 21st/22nd June. 1943. Total number of bombers on raid: -705, of which 262 were Lancasters. Number of aircraft lost: - 44, of which 9 were Lancasters. From the 22 aircraft put up by the Squadron one failed to return - ED 556. P/O Thurlow, and crew. Cloudless conditions prevailed en route, and marking of the target by Pathfinders was spot on. Visibility was excellent. I witnessed two combats and although night fighters were much in evidence we ourselves were not attacked. Flying as usual in ED 749 we dropped our "cookie", 500 pounders and incendiaries on the red target indicators from 20,500 feet, at 01.36. As we left the target fires were taking hold on the ground, and there was considerable activity in the night sky with flak damaging our aircraft. The port rudder fin and tail plane received hits, but fortunately for me the rear turret remained intact.

Ginger, when things had quietened down, not realising that he had left his inter-com switched on entertained us by first humming *"Solitude"* and then croaking the opening lines of *"Deep in the Heart of Texas"*.

'To blazes with the night sky over Texas, mid-upper!' Skipper admonished. 'It's the night sky over Germany you should be concentrating on.'

A click in my ear signified that Ginger had received and understood the message, for from that moment on silence reigned supreme, except for the synchronised roar of our four Merlins.

Visits to Germany have meant that we have not been able to visit the *"Tivoli"* in Grimsby. As a result we have missed something billed as *"The Big Revue Sensation"*. *"These Dames Make News!' Four Chelsea Models and Six Picked peaches! Oh Boy! What Views! These Dames Make News!"*

According to one of the ground crew we were fortunate to have missed the show for the "models" had lived up to their billing by being imitations of the "real thing", and the peaches had been plucked a long, long time ago!

23rd June, 1943. 70,000 people have lost their homes in Krefeld. Intelligence reports state that the updraught of a firestorm caused winds of hurricane velocity to uproot trees before carrying burning debris which fed other fires. The level of devastation and number of civilian casualties has caused Dr Josef Goebbels to rant and rave. Referring to the bombing he declared - 'The war has come to us in its most terrible aspect but the day will come when we shall meet terror with terror.'

He admits that what the populations of bombed areas have had to endure has been unbearable, and confirms that in the past month over 10,000 tons of bombs have fallen on the Ruhr.

The people of nearby Louth hope to be able to raise more than £120,000 during their *"Wings For Victory"* week. It is estimated that the money will pay for twenty four Spitfires.

11 TARGET FOR TONIGHT: - WUPPERTAL.

Thursday/Friday, 24th/25th June. 1943. Total number of bombers on raid: - 630, of which 251 were Lancasters. Total number of aircraft lost: - 34, which included 8 Lancasters. The 17 aircraft dispatched from Waltham all returned safely to base. The marking was accurate and the bombing concentrated.

Over the target, as Tom requested, 'bomb doors open,' I caught sight of what appeared to a parachute floating down into the hideous inferno below. What would happen to the poor devil dangling from it I wondered, recalling tales I'd heard of the vengeance exacted on aircrew by the citizens of Ruhr towns. Determined not to end up in the living hell that was Wuppertal I crouched over my guns and searched the multi-coloured night sky, then held my breath as flying straight and level we added our lethal load to the bubbling cauldron below.

25th June, 1943. Information from a neutral source suggests that there is growing discontent in the Ruhr, where grave problems are being created by our bombing. Grave problems, indeed! Very apt, I'm sure. Our local paper claims *"The Other Half of Wuppertal Got Its Share Last Night"*. I can certainly vouch for that!

For our entertainment an air-gunner consumed a razor blade this morning. He chewed hard on the three-hole tit bit, shaped it into a ball on his tongue, displayed it for all to see then swallowed the delicacy in one gulp. Needless to say, he's completely round the bend. Another little trick of his is to enter a Nissen hut - not his own - throw live ammo into the red hot coke stove then depart in a hurry!

Just in case we have to ditch, come down in the drink that is, an air-sea rescue launch is on permanent standby at Grimsby docks. This is nice to know because I'm a lousy swimmer, Tom can't swim a stroke and Scouse is frightened of water. Maybe other persons besides the natives of Lincolnshire should be called "Yellow Bellies".

The Russians want more action, like a second front for instance. "Butch" Harris disagrees. He insists that Bomber Command will win the war all by itself.

12 TARGET FOR TONIGHT: - GELSENKIRCHEN.

Friday/Saturday, 25th/26th June, 1943. Total number of bombers on the raid: - 473, of which 214 were Lancasters. Number of aircraft lost: - 30, of which 13 were Lancasters. Sixteen aircraft of 100 squadron took off from Waltham, one failed to return - ED 988. F/Sgt. Naile and crew. ED 749 was airborne for 4hrs 5mins.

28th June, 1943. It would appear that the raid on the coal and steel district of Gelsenkirchen was not a success. The marking by P.F.F. "Oboe" Mosquitoes was poor resulting in bombs being scattered over a wide area. Dusseldorf, and a town called Solingen, suffered far heavier damage than the intended target.

Today a different type of exercise saw us co-operating for two hours with our local anti-aircraft batteries. I wonder if they shot us down?

Before long I shall be displaying a ribbon on my chest for the King has instituted a 1939-43 Star for all members of the services who have fought in the war, except that is for the victors in North Africa who will get a gong of their own.

Intelligence from Germany suggests that more than 1,000 fighter planes and 30,000 anti-aircraft guns will soon be protecting the cities of north-western Germany.

Bloody Hell!

2nd July, 1943. Seven days leave. Many hours of sleep, glorious sleep, followed by breakfast in bed. I was never pampered like this in peace time A glance at the *"News Chronicle"* reveals that the war is carrying on quite well without me, and after consuming a tasteless banger I read that Lord Woolton, who is in charge of the country's food, longs for the time when there will be real meat in his sausage!

Mum has a treat in store for me tonight. Lentil soup, followed by battered spam or something similar. Tomorrow potato cakes will be on the menu, and Welsh rarebit. We shall be eating in the kitchen because the dining room is not a dining room any longer. It was, before I joined the R.A.F, but since then father has purchased one of his so called "real bargains" - a huge display-cabinet-cum-book-case. This mahogany monster, together with the piano and air raid shelter, has left no room for other furnishings. The shelter is a *"Morrison"*. Well over six feet in length and about five feet wide it affords adequate protection from any stray bombs the Luftwaffe might drop. However, as father says, with a twinkle in his eye - 'If your mother puts on any more weight she won't be able to get in the thing!'

A group of children, neighbours of my Aunt Lizzie, put on a "back-garden" show yesterday.

I discovered them near the end of their performance and found that the material used was mostly from *"ITMA"*. One lad, with a very red nose, had the juvenile audience in fits with Jack Train's "I don't mind if I do," and a little girl with her hair in curlers was roundly applauded for Mrs Mopp's "Can I do you now, sir" and "T.T.F.N.". A boy, looking remarkably like an illustration in Richmal Crompton's *"William"*, made a mess of something called *"Last Saturday's Football Match"*, and when a young lady assured us rather flatly that there would be, 'bluebirds over the white cliffs of Dover,' I departed - but not before I had put sixpence in the pudding basin labelled *"Wings for Victory"*.

6th July, 1943. Tomorrow I return by train to Grimsby. I have done my best not to "line shoot" or appear "big-headed" but with relatives and friends asking countless questions it has not been easy. One thing's for sure, I have not vouchsafed any of the careless talk that costs lives. To please my mum and dad I have been with them to a service at Hill Top chapel, to please myself I went to a dance at the Castle Hotel, and to please no one in particular I visited my former place of work. Chapel was boring, tedious, out of touch with reality. The dance was a waste of time for not one heart-throb from my past was tripping the light fantastic. At work, none of my former pen-pushing colleagues were double-entry book-keeping because they had all been called up for the duration of the present emergency. I went alone to the "*Roxy*" cinema in Hanley and averted my gaze when the usherette's flashing torch momentarily illumined the back row of the rear circle, but only because the double seats reminded me of a certain young lady's charming attributes. Yesterday I carried my father's clubs around Wolstanton golf course, and listened again to the tale of his recent "hole in one".

Shall I be glad to get back to the squadron? I have asked myself that question more than once these past few days but it remains unanswered. Here at home the war seems a million miles away. Life is dull, enlivened only by Whist Drives and Spelling Bees. The exploits of near neighbour Mrs Clark continue to provide some excitement, this time a black-out offence has cost her the mandatory fifteen shillings. Life is safer here of course for the Luftwaffe rarely pays a visit, and even then it is only to jettison a bomb or two intended for Manchester or Liverpool. If I had a choice, then being on leave would probably triumph but only because the mess cooks at Waltham can't hold a candle to Mum!

What I am not looking forward to is the "good-byes", for I know what will be uppermost in my parents' mind and my own. For all our sakes I shall do my best to appear cheerful. Keep a stiff upper lip and all that jazz. Knowing that the whole family will troop down to the railway station to see me off fills me with dismay. I shall become more and more self-conscious and all of a dither as I pray for the 11.45 to arrive on time, something I feel it has failed to do in years of faithful service for its long suffering passengers.

7th July, 1943. Today my worst fears were realised for even Parson Potts and his wife joined the throng gathered at the railway station. Father pressed my hand and bit his bottom lip, Mum pecked at my cheek, sis wept crocodile tears and my brand new nephew sicked up. With a sigh of relief from me, and a wheeze from its ancient self, "Billy" eventually puffed out of Longport, leaving me to search through corridors filled mostly with service men and women in a fruitless quest for a seat.

At Stoke station a civilian climbed aboard. Looking distinctly out of place in a sea of khaki and blue he was carrying a large case and clutching a newspaper. Sitting down on the former he spread out the latter which enabled me to read the upside down headlines of its front page. Tut, tut! In my absence Bomber Command had raided Cologne without my help, and apparently with some success.

Cologne! Agh!

Suddenly the war was back with a vengeance, and hours later when I entered the mess at Waltham I knew that I too was back with a vengeance, when a familiar voice proclaimed – 'Confucius 'e say, "Sergeant who make love to Waafy on roof, 'im 'ave one on 'ouse."'

Three cheers for the chaps who man the Skegness life boat, for they have rescued yet more aircrew from the North Sea.

The Author, 26 June 1943, 100 Squadron R.A.F.

13 TARGET FOR TONIGHT: - COLOGNE.

Thursday/Friday. 8th/9th July, 1943. An all-Lancaster attack aided by six P.F.F. Mosquitoes - 282 aircraft in all from which 7 were lost. ED 749, damaged by flak en route, pressed on regardless! I had earlier felt quite apprehensive when I discovered that Cologne was the target, haunted as I was by the memory of the "icing-up" of June the17th.

Bombs, it seems, have exploded at nearby Binbrook! From what I hear a Lancaster was being prepared for a raid when an entire load fell from its bomb bay. There was no mention of any casualties but two other aircraft are thought to have been destroyed.

Winston C. has received the Freedom of the City of London. Speaking in the bomb damaged Guildhall he forecast that before autumn leaves begin to fall there will be heavy fighting in the Mediterranean and elsewhere.

According to a BBC broadcast German "U-boats" are being defeated, their sinking of our shipping being only one quarter of the April figure.

R.A.F. Transport Command, tired no doubt of us bomber boys getting all the accolades, has created a "first". One of its aircraft has towed a glider across the Atlantic, a distance of some 3,500 miles in 28 hours!

'Hey Tommy, why do you call that bomb-aimer mate of yours "*Harpic*"?'
'Oh come on Ginger, you must know why.'
'No, I don't.

'Gawd, where have you been all your service life? I thought everyone knew that oldie. It's because, like *"Harpic"*, the lav cleaner, he's clean round the bend. He's done his best to get out of going on "ops" twice of late, and most of his spare time is spent hanging around sick bay.'

'Sounds like he's suffering from L.M.F.'

'Oh no!' I sympathize, 'I hope not. You know what might happen. He could be paraded in front of the whole squadron and stripped of his brevet and stripes.'

'That's happened to a flight engineer I trained with,' Scouse confides. 'He's been kicked out of the R.A.F. I think he's been sent to work in a coal mine.'

'That's a bit much.'

'It might have been worse, he could have been transferred to the army as a latrine cleaner. The powers that be reckon that lack of moral fibre, or cowardice if you prefer, would spread like wildfire if it was not stamped on. That's why it can be a court-martial job, with the offending bod being whisked away from his squadron as soon as possible.'

Ginger shook his head. 'A latrine cleaner, eh? I'm sure he wouldn't have minded as long as there was enough *"Harpic"* to keep him from going clean round the bend!'

When alcohol is mentioned, Tom reckons we should frequent the "Barrel", claiming that it's a proper pub, not like the *"Ship Hotel"*. He likes spittoons, or cuspidors as Skipper calls them, and mysterious sounding places like tap rooms, snugs and four-ale bars. Ginger prefers the inn at Barnolds... somewhere or other, and Scouse favours the *"King's Head"*, because the publican there 'knows how to look after his ale.'

Personally I couldn't care less for beer tastes foul to me no matter where it is dispensed. I doubt very much if some of the other chaps are all that keen either, methinks they only drink the stuff in order to work up enough Dutch courage to ask "female members of the opposite sex" for a dance at the *"Gaiety"*.

Ah, the "*Gaiety*" dance hall. Now that's preferable to any pub, in my opinion. I like to arrive at the hall during the Saturday night interval because when that's finished, at 21.20 precisely, Bob Walker's twelve-piece band gives out with Count Basie's "*9.20 Special*". The tune becomes a very lively quick step under Bob's baton, and I thoroughly enjoy doing my one, two, three, together, as I avoid planting my size nines on my partner's toes.

Members of the National Fire Service invited a few of us to one of their parties recently. Most of the so called "games" played were real shockers. One of the least objectionable started with the gullible participant being shown a row of crazily angled chairs. He was then blindfolded and told that a prize awaited him if he successfully "negotiated the course".

As soon as the blindfold was affixed, the chairs were removed and holding on to someone's hand the unsuspecting one performed all manner of contortions as he attempted to avoid non-existent furniture.

Cries of 'Careful,' 'Move a bit the left,' 'Lift your right leg,' 'Slow down a bit,' etcetera, brought howls of laughter from the onlookers but eventually success was achieved. To shouts of, 'Well Done!' and, 'Bravo!' the "winner" was then instructed to reach down and feel for his prize.

When he did so, and his hand made contact with a liquid, his blindfold was promptly whipped off, and he found himself feeling into a chamber pot full of well-done sausages and lemonade.

The disgust and cry of dismay that issued from the "victim" when the blindfold was removed had to be both heard and seen to be believed!

Bob Walker's dance band – "9.20 Special".

The Ship Hotel, Grimsby,
where, for the author, the mild was anything but!

14 TARGET FOR TONIGHT: - GELSENKIRCHEN.

Friday/Saturday. 9th/10th July, 1943. Total number of bombers on the raid: - 418, of which 218 were Lancasters. Total number of aircraft lost: - 12, of which 5 were Lancasters. "Oboe" marking was used by P.F.F. We bombed the release point flare from 22,000 feet at 01.14 hours but ten-tenths cloud meant that we were unable to ascertain whether the town's oil refineries had suffered any significant damage.

Gremlins were out in force tonight. Over the North Sea I developed cramp, first in my right foot and then in my left. As we approached the enemy coast my backside itched like crazy and the electrically heated suit began to malfunction. With the temperature outside registering thirty below I was fiendishly cold on my "port" side but piping hot on my "starboard" side, and from time to time tiny electric shocks affected the whole of my body. Returning to base I attempted to use the pee tube but that too was frozen, and the end result was extremely unpleasant.

After interrogation we wandered slowly towards our mess. Above us in the night sky an aircraft's engines droned.

'It doesn't sound like one of ours,' I observed.

'It isn't,' said Tom, 'it's a Junkerschmitt.'

'A what?'

'A Junkerschmitt. Surely you know that all unidentified German planes are Junkerschmitts!'

11th July, 1943. It seems the Gelsenkirchen "op" was a bit of a flop due to equipment failure in some of the P.F.F. Mossies. An intelligence report states that most of our bombs fell to the south and east on Bochum and Wattenscheid.

As long as they fell somewhere in the Ruhr does it really matter?

There is good news from a variety of war zones. The Serbs under Mihailovitch have inflicted heavy casualties on two Axis columns, the Japs have lost six ships in the Kula Gulf, and a great allied force has landed in Sicily which means that the invasion of Europe has begun. Uncle Joe will be pleased!

Sex goddess Rita Hayworth occupies pride of pin-up place in our hut.

'I would gladly use her faeces for tooth paste,' says Tom, turning over onto his belly to admire her.

'You really are disgusting, Jackson,' remonstrates a bomb-aimer pal of his who has called in for a chat.

Tom ignores the rebuke, blows a kiss in smiling Rita's direction and bursts into song. 'You were never lovelier darling, than you are...'

It takes three pairs of hands and two pillows to silence him.

'I find this hard to believe,' Ginger remarked, scratching various parts of his body.

'Do you now, and no doubt we are going to hear what it is that you find so hard to believe. What's that you're reading?'

'"The Lincolnshire Standard".'

'Phew! And there I thought it was some kind of third rate rag like the "*Times*" or "*The Manchester Guardian*".'

'Well it says here that when a local authority health official visited a council house in Skegness he saw a boy's hair move on his head it was so alive with fleas, and his neck and chest were covered in bites. The kitchen was filthy, remains of many meals lay on the table and clothes on the line had been washed but were still black. What bit of furniture there was in the living room was covered in dust and filth, and the bed and dressing table were equally deplorable. The whole place reeked, the beds were alive with bugs, and when he got home he discovered twenty-two of the blighters on his own underclothes.

'Where's Woodhall Spa?' asked Scouse, peering over Ginger's shoulder.

'Not far. I think 619 fly from there. Why d'you ask?'

'There's an advertisement here for something called "*Kinema in the Woods*". "*The Ghost Goes West*" is showing there. Robert Donat's in it.'

'Not good old Robert Donat, we called him "doughnut" at school.'

'He's a jolly good actor. How long would it take to cycle there?'

'Ages on your clapped-out steed. Are you thinking of going?'

'Maybe. And "*Hellzapoppin*'" is coming shortly. I've seen it but I wouldn't mind seeing it again. Ole Olsen and Chic Johnson are in it, and Mischa Auer and Martha Raye.'

'Ole what and Chic who?'

'Olsen and Johnson. By the way you know what they say about girls with big mouths, well Martha's got the widest in Hollywood. She's great, you should hear her belt out, "Watch the birdie, take a candid camera shot".'

The Author in 1943 - shame about the negative scratch.

15 TARGET FOR TONIGHT: - TURIN.

Monday/Tuesday, 12th/13th July. 1943. An all-Lancaster attack of 295 aircraft. Two aircraft from 100 Squadron - EE 183 and ED 561, captained by F/Sgt. A. G. Sadler and F/Sgt. W. R. Caldwell respectively, failed to return.

Our longest operational flight to date: 1970 miles with ED 749 airborne for eleven hours. At briefing I felt it would be an easy "op", a "piece of cake", for I knew that the Italians were a useless shower. And so it proved to be. After leaving our shores in the vicinity of Beachy Head there followed a long stooge over France. From Grenoble the scenery altered dramatically with majestic Mont Blanc basking in brilliant moonlight surrounded by other snow-capped peaks. St. Elmo's fire, with its flame like electrical discharge dancing about the aircraft's tail unit, proved to be far more frightening than Turin's wayward searchlights and ineffective anti-aircraft fire. We dropped our "cookie" and incendiaries from 18,000 feet at 02.02 hours, and figured our four thousand pounder burst west of the river. After setting course for home I gazed in awe at the Haute-Alpes, and when they disappeared a not completely blacked out part of France passed beneath me. Before long Bordeaux was to port and then, following a wonderful sunrise, landfall was made over the Cornish coast. We had been instructed to land in Cornwall if necessary but Scouse's skill saw us reaching Grimsby with gas to spare. After so many hours seated in a cramped turret Waltham airfield was for me a most welcome sight but following touch down I found standing erect almost impossible, so much so that the rest of the crew promptly christened me Quasimodo. Skipper on the other hand was quite sprightly, he having had an "easy ride" with most of the "driving" done by P/O Burbeck who had flown with us as second pilot.

Talk about tit for tat. While we 100 Squadron types were raiding Turin our host town of Grimsby got clobbered by the Luftwaffe!

14th July, 1943. According to to-day's newspapers the main weight of our bombs fell to the north of the centre of Turin. 800 people are reported dead with many more injured. A report just in states that Wing Commander Nettleton V.C. and his 44 [Rhodesia] Squadron crew failed to return from Turin. His Lancaster was one of thirteen that failed to make it back from what I'd called an "easy op".

17th July, 1943. Yesterday someone in authority decided that the Squadron would benefit from a spot of formation flying, a decision which saw us airborne with wings too close for comfort over Sleaford, Northampton and Huntingdon, before returning to Waltham.

The flight proved to be my last in Lancaster ED 749 for today our crew split up, with Skipper, Godfrey and Scouse leaving to join a Pathfinder squadron based in Cambridgeshire, and Sparks bidding us all farewell - he having completed his second tour of operations. So Tommy Jackson, Ginger Whitmore and I have become "spare bods" with uncertain futures.

21st July, 1943. The various newspapers strewn about the mess are naturally full of war news. A violent battle in the Kursk salient has resulted in the Germans suffering grievous tank losses, and the invasion of Sicily is proceeding steadily with the 8th Army pushing towards Catania.

16 TARGET FOR TONIGHT: - HAMBURG.

Operation "Gomorrah". Saturday/Sunday, 24th/25th July, 1943. Total number of bombers on the raid: - 791 of which 347 were Lancasters. 12 aircraft lost, of which 4 were Lancasters.

Fred, my friend from the Potteries, flies with the Aussie, Andy Gersekowski, and when one of the chaps in their crew went sick I was asked to take his place in ED732. HW "L". At briefing we were warned to keep our eyes peeled because there were several night fighter airfields close to the city, heavy flak batteries just about everywhere and a huge number of searchlights. For the first time something called "Window" was to be used, and it was hoped that the dropping in sufficient quantities of these strips of black paper, with aluminium foil stuck to one side, would play havoc with the German defensive system. The news was greeted with derision by the assembled crews, and dismissed as yet another daft idea dreamt up by some crazy boffin.

Lancaster HW "L" lifted off at 22.15 hours, and part way over the North Sea the dropping of "Window" commenced at the rate of one bundle per minute. After crossing the enemy coast close to the German/Danish border Andy turned south to avoid Kiel and Lubeck, which were themselves to get small diversionary raids. Avoiding Bremen's searchlights we proceeded to the target where Fred Peake dropped our bombs at 01.05 hours from 21,000 feet. The fires beneath me seemed to build up extremely quickly, and there was a considerable amount of smoke. We recrossed the coast between Bremerhaven and Cuxhaven, then flew to the south of Heligoland, shortly after which a halt was called to the "Window" dropping. Andy then stuck the aircraft's nose down and brought us safely back to base.

26th July, 1943. Adolf has no illusions about Benito. He has threatened to bomb Italian cities should the Duce surrender. Musso, however, after a reign of twenty-one years, no longer has the stomach for a fight so he's handed in his resignation to King Victor Emmanuel.

Meanwhile, the Germans in Sicily are digging in but the digging is being done by their former allies, not themselves. As further punishment the Italians are emptying latrines and performing other menial tasks.

Oswald is a tortoise. He hails from Boston, Lincs, not to be confused with Boston, Mass. According to the local paper Oswald has recently laid two eggs!

17 TARGET FOR TONIGHT: - HAMBURG.

Operation "Gomorrah". Tuesday/Wednesday, 27th/28th, July, 1943. Total number of bombers on the raid: - 787, of which 353 were Lancasters. 17 aircraft lost, of which 11 were Lancasters. One 100 squadron aircraft failed to return - EE 169. HW "O", W/O Gafford and crew.

Being well acquainted with Fred and Andy meant that flying with them on the first Hamburg raid had been fine, but I did not find the "spare bod" role to my liking when I flew on this raid with W/O Wright. I felt like an interloper, a stranger in a strange crew, a person they were being forced to take with them because one of their number had fallen sick. I had never had any dealings with the warrant officer or any of his crew, in fact the only thing familiar about them was their faces which I'd seen from time to time in the mess. Another reason for my lack of enthusiasm was that I was having to fly in a crew position new to me, that of "mid-upper", but I consoled myself with the thought that it would be another "op" done on the way to the elusive thirty.

The route to the target was similar to the earlier raid, the main difference being that we flew directly over Lubeck before turning towards Hamburg. At briefing the reading of a congratulatory message from Harris regarding our efforts on the 24th/25th was greeted with derisory cheers. Later, as I waited at dispersal to climb aboard Lancaster "J2", I suddenly felt quite bereft - missing as I did the warmth of Tom's toothy smile and the strength of Ginger's craggy features.

Over the target yellow T.I.s and the greens of the "backers up" dropped into an absolute inferno, the like of which I had never seen before. I was aghast, surely no living creature could survive such a hell on earth. Smoke from the sea of fire reached to our height. Exploding flak shells added to the grim spectacle. Searchlights waved aimlessly, fighting a losing battle as Hamburg gradually became one great mass of flames. An hour after leaving the target area I could still see a red glow from the fires.

30th July, 1943. Goodbye Waltham. Farewell 100 Squadron. As for its motto death had not got me, and there had been precious little glory. Cheerio Grimsby with its fish tower. Au revoir "*Gaiety*", home of bruised female toes. Good bye to the "*Ship*". With a lump in my throat I went out to dispersal to shake hands with the ground crew, then patted the fuselage of Lancaster ED 749 for bringing me back safe and sound on so many "operational" occasions.

Hail Lindholme. Conversion Unit number 1656, with its memory of crashing there in a Halifax on the 10th of April last, when I'd been a very inexperienced airman. Three and one half months have flown by, quite literally, and now I'm an old sweat with seventeen operations written in red ink in my log book. Tom and Ginger are here with me and, together with our kit, we have brought with us a host of corny gags, dirty jokes and silly sayings.

   Chorus [Self & Ginger] 'Sister Anna, you'll carry the banner.'
   Tom [falsetto] 'But I carried it last week.'
   Chorus .... 'And you'll carry it again this week.'
   Tom [falsetto] 'But I'm in the family way.'
   Chorus .... 'You're in every buggers way.'

Saturday, 31st July, 1943. This morning Tom, Ginger and I became acquainted with S/L George Alan Roden D.F.C., our new skipper. Stockily built, fierce looking with bristling ginger moustache, he's not a "Duration of the Present Emergency" bod like ourselves but a regular, an aviator who was in the R.A.F. long before Pontius was a pilot. When we met up with him he had in tow a flight sergeant-navigator by the name of Weller who had more "ops" to his credit than the rest of us put together, and Steve, a Flight engineer, with a similar number in his log book to myself. A rather diffident inexperienced wireless-op called George then presented himself and lo and behold we were a crew. Needless to say George will be Sparks to one and all, and F/Sgt. Weller, though I am quite sure it will cheese him off, will be "Sam".

Tuesday, 3rd August, 1943. Flying a "cross-country" in Lancaster ED 585, S/L Roden and crew got airborne as a unit for the first time today. Taking off from Lindholme after an early breakfast we made for Carlisle, then the Mull of Galloway, Bardsey Island and Thame before heading back to base. Later at 22.30 hours we flew with a F/L Noden who explained to S/L Roden the intricacies of taking off and landing a Lancaster in the dark.

Come fly with Noden and Roden! I thought. Aerial Artistes! Exciting take-offs! Hair raising landings blamed on kangaroo petrol!

Noden, however, soon departed and Roden took over. Much to my dismay we then practiced "circuits and bumps" for five hours.

Hitler refuses to visit Hamburg! I'm not surprised, he would be lynched if the locals got their hands on him. A press release states that the city had a greater tonnage of bombs dropped on it in the recent raids than London had during the whole of the attacks of 1940-41. Seven square miles of the city are completely devastated. Mass evacuation has been organised and more than 130,000 homeless people have been sent to eastern Germany. An eye witness reports that a tunnel under the River Elbe has been completely demolished, shipbuilding yards have received terrific damage and several U-boats lie destroyed in the slips.

News from Sicily. The Allies are on the verge of capturing Catania, and the Egadi islands to the west have surrendered.

'The what islands?' asked Ginger. 'Never 'eard of 'em.'

Wednesday, 4th August, 1943. Managed forty winks after breakfast but by mid-afternoon Roden had us in a mark one Lancaster, Q 4883, indulging in a spot of fighter affiliation with a Spitfire.

'Achtung Spitfeuer,' I warned over the inter-com when our adversary appeared, then promptly wished I hadn't - for Skipper spent the next few minutes tearing me off a strip for being facetious. I doubt if my gunnery skills improved during the exercise but I certainly learned one thing - clever dick non-essential remarks over the inter-com were "strictly verboten".

Roden had other rules too. Smoking was strictly taboo. No one was to leave his position in the aircraft without permission, and Ginger and I were to be forever vigilant - particularly so when returning from an "op" in case there were intruders in the circuit.

A warrant officer, based here at Lindholme, has just returned from seven days leave spent in his home town of Nottingham. Chatting to some of us he criticised the food we had just eaten, then went on to moan about how most people in civvy street were eating like lords and hardly knew there was a war going on.

'I took my nephew to a circus and zoo at Wollaton Park on Monday,' he declared. 'There was a huge crowd there having the time of their lives. I'm not over fond of such things but I must say the trapeze artistes were pretty daring, and there was a bloody great lion which the ring-master claimed was not only the biggest but the most highly trained in captivity.' Before long the W.O.'s audience had dwindled quite perceptibly, and when Sam signified he had heard enough we made good our escape.

'My mother took me to a circus once to see the world's biggest pig.'

'Really Ginger, you do surprise me, I had no idea Hitler had been to England.'

'This one was called Billy, not Adolf. It was the size of an ox, weighed at least half a ton and regularly ate more than that well known glutton Tommy Jackson. Two cases of rotten apples, double figures in cabbages, several pounds of potato peel and a box of chocolates being its standard fare. After swilling down a bucket of milk it walked a tightrope carrying six little kiddies on his back. There were fleas there too, up to their tricks. They climbed ladders, did handstands, and performed somersaults. One of them was quite worn out with her exertions, so much so she refused to have sex with her husband!'

'Eh? How could you possibly know that?' I asked, suitably mystified

'She complained of a headache.'

'Um, why don't you remuster to a turkey and get stuffed.'

12 SQUADRON
"Leads the Field"

No. 1 Group
R.A.F. BOMBER COMMAND

Wickenby, Lincolnshire, England

CREW ROSTER: - OPERATIONS 18 - 29.
AUGUST TO NOVEMBER, 1943

R.A.F. S/L G. A. Roden	Pilot (Captain)
R.A.F. Sgt. S. P. George	Flight Engineer
R.A.F. F/Sgt. B. Weller	Navigator (Ops: 18 - 28)
R.A.F. Sgt. L. C. J. Street	Navigator (Op: 29)
R.A.F. Sgt. T. R. Jackson	Bomb Aimer
R.A.F. Sgt. G. H. Brittle	Wireless Operator
R.A.F. Sgt. H. W. Whitmore	Mid-Upper Gunner
R.A.F. Sgt. A. H. Alcock	Rear Gunner

5th August, 1943. Joined 12 Squadron, based at Wickenby. Called "Shiny Twelve" it has a "Fox" emblem and a "Leads the Field" motto.

6th August, 1943. Flew on a 'bullseye' in Lancaster DV177, "K2", taking off at 23.15. Carried out infrared bombing of Westminster Bridge before proceeding to the Isle of Wight, then back to London and base. The exercise took four hours.

8th August, 1943. Made the short flight to Waltham in Lancaster "G2". Had lunch in the mess there then off to the coast for bombing and gunnery practice.

18 TARGET FOR TONIGHT: - NUREMBURG.

Tuesday/Wednesday, 10th/11th August, 1943. Total number of bombers on raid: - 653, of which 318 were Lancasters. Number of aircraft lost: - 16, of which 6 were Lancasters. Two weeks since my last "op", and I felt quite apprehensive about returning to "dice with death". I was truly scared and hoped it didn't show. Take off was at 22.00 hours in Lancaster LM 321 "H2". Bomb load: One 4,000 lb. "cookie" and a great load of incendiaries, the I.O. having remarked at briefing - 'Nuremburg's buildings are medieval, they should burn well.' Fuel: 1,850 gallons. Routed out over Beachy Head and Le Treport we found the target partly obscured by cloud. Pathfinder green ground markers and scattered fires were visible and there was considerable searchlight activity. Airborne: 7 hours 30 minutes.

The clouds were still glowing red on our return when I observed tracer to port. Crouched over my four machine guns I searched anxiously with eyes sticking out like a dog's b's, but nothing else untoward happened in the night sky and the tracer ceased as suddenly as it had begun. Pondering over its possible significance, I began to feel rather light headed. Voices over the inter-com seemed unusually distant, and I discovered what felt like ice in my oxygen tube. Feeling ever more peculiar, I informed Skipper who promptly instructed Sparks to make his way to the rear turret using an oxygen bottle for his own survival, and carrying a spare flying helmet for me.

After what seemed an eternity a bang on the turret indicated that Sparks had arrived, and after the two of us had managed to open the doors he handed me the replacement headgear. My initial sense of relief was short-lived, however, for when I donned the helmet I found that there was no oxygen tube attached. I immediately panicked, knowing that I could not survive for long without oxygen at the height we were flying, so I grabbed hold of the supply tube and thrust it into my mouth. The rest of the flight was sheer pantomime, with the frozen metal refusing to part company with my lips, and Sparks's face was a picture when he returned to find out why the idiot in the rear turret remained incommunicado.

Back at base a medical orderly came out to the aircraft and after the two of us had performed a variety of contortions, both in and out of the rear turret, the offending tube was removed from my lips. Later, mumbling through bruised and bleeding lips, I left no one in any doubt as to what I thought of the clueless git who had handed me a helmet minus its oxygen tube. Poor George! And him on his first operation!

11th August, 1943. Low cloud and rain brought an early "stand-down" today. There was no peace for the wicked, however, and I got thoroughly soaked taking part in dinghy drill with the rest of the crew.

The bombs dropped on Nuremburg appear to have flattened a number of industrial buildings and part of the old town. Several of the squadron's aircraft had, however, failed to get to the target. Unserviceable rear turrets resulted in two of them aborting; another developed an oil leak over base, and W.4380 bounced on take-off after the wheels had been "selected up". Acting on instructions from the control tower the aircraft flew out to the coast, dropped its bomb load into the North Sea and returned to base to successfully belly flop. The crew survived, and no one was hurt physically but I could not but wonder what the crew had suffered mentally.

14th August, 1943. After spending a quiet Saturday evening in the mess with Ginger I retired early to bed only to have Tom, back late from a visit to the White Hart pub, disturb my slumbers by announcing in stentorian tones that as Double Summer Time would end during the night everyone in the hut should arise and adjust his watch. 'You could arrive over the target one hour early if you don't,' he hiccupped, wagging a finger, 'or would it be one hour late? D'you know somethin', I don't know which way to turn the bloody finger!'

'Never mind its finger, just pull your own out, Jacko, and get into bed,' growled Ginger, pulling his blankets over his head.

I said nothing, merely reflected that some say "Good old Tom", while others speak the truth!

If Double Summer Time is ending, though, I feel sure Ginger will be pleased, for he was complaining only yesterday that when he went out with his nurse it never got dark enough to snog.

But will he?

Suddenly I am as confused as Tom, for in my soporific state I am unable to figure out if it will get dark earlier or stay light longer!

19 TARGET FOR TONIGHT: - MILAN.

Sunday/Monday, 15th/16th August, 1943. 199 Lancasters took part, 21 of which were from 12 squadron. Take-off - 20.00 hours in LM 321, "H2", the same aircraft we had flown on the Nuremberg operation. Bomb load: 4,000 lb. "cookie" and incendiaries. Fuel: 2,050 gallons. Airborne: 8 hours 40 minutes. Route: Selsey Bill, thence to the northern end of Lake Bourget and the target. There was no cloud en route. The alps looked magnificent. The sky was clear over the city which was marked by green target indicators. We dropped our bombs from 19,000 feet. Wayward searchlights groped for us and the flak was inaccurate.

With take-off delayed we had been standing around at dispersal when Tommy Jackson unwittingly "dropped me in it". He had first tried to catch Ginger out with a silly gag which involved the use of an extremely crude word but Ginger wasn't taken in, and later neither was I.

Tom was convinced, however, that our gullible wireless op would fall for it, and after waiting impatiently for Sparks to finish a conversation with a ground crew wireless technician he greeted him with a crafty smile. 'Hi Georgie, I've got a tale for you but there's one thing you must remember, there are four stages. Four stages. OK? It's about a Waaf on a train who is bursting for a pee.'

George, taken aback on being informed of the content of the "tale", pulled his face but Tom was not to be put off.

'Now in the first stage our Waaf can't have her pee because the train is non-corridor, so she crosses her legs and says to herself, "Be patient c..t, be patient".'

That the "c" word both surprised and disgusted Sparks was obvious but Tom pressed on regardless. 'The second stage of the story, and let me impress upon you that it is the second stage, sees our poor little Waaf getting desperate. So much so that when the train finally pulls into a station she hurtles out only to find that the door to the ladies is locked. So back she comes to the compartment, sits down, crosses her legs and repeats to herself, "Be patient c..t, be patient".'

Sparks, obviously embarrassed by the repetition of the four letter word, stared down at the floor.

Tom meanwhile, with a malevolent smile on his face, prepared to deliver his coup de grace. Slowly and deliberately he said, 'Now, in the fourth stage...'

'Don't fall for it, Sparks,' I pleaded under my breath. 'Don't say "but what about the third stage", because if you do Tommy will shout in triumph, "Be patient c..t, be patient".'

Sparks duly obliged by not falling for it, instead he turned on his heel and said with considerable disdain, 'You must think I was born yesterday, Jacko.'

The crestfallen look on Tom's face had the rest of us chortling, and when the sound of our laughter reached Skipper's ears he sauntered over and asked me what had caused such merriment.

'A joke, just a joke, sir,' I said, through lips still sore from the oxygen incident.

'And a good one too, I'd say, judging from the noise you all made.' With that Skipper turned as if to leave but after consulting his watch he paused and said, 'We still have a few minutes to spare, so how about telling me the joke.'

'Oh, it's not really very funny, sir.'

'I'll be the judge of that. It was sufficiently funny for your guffaws to be heard all over the airfield. Come on, out with it.'

Please earth, open up. Please God, smite down those rotten buggers, those so called colleagues of mine, who have deserted me and are climbing aboard the Lancaster. Base-born cowards, who have no wish to become involved in the proceedings, especially that miserable so-and-so Sergeant Thomas R Jackson!

'It's Jackson's joke, er tale, sir. He tells it much better than I do.'

'Oh, do get on with it, sergeant.'

'But it has a very crude word in it, sir.'

'Crude word!' scowled Skipper, eyes flashing, moustache twitching. 'Crude word! I wasn't born yesterday? Ye gods, I was in Baghdad before you were in your dad's bags. Get on with it, and that's an order!'

Get on with it! How could I with that word involved? What if he fell for it and asked, "But what about the third stage?" I couldn't tell a Squadron Leader, a regular with a D.F.C., that not only had he to be patient but also that he was a "c..t". Oh dear, oh dear, oh dear, woe is me!

'Well!' the mighty one roared.

'It's in four parts, sir, the joke is'. I stuttered. 'Jackson calls them stages and he says it's very important that one remembers that there are four of them. In the first stage we have a young lady who is most anxious to pass water but she can't because there isn't a corridor.'

'Eh?'

'Oh, I forgot to mention. She's in a railway carriage, sir.'

'My God, Alcock, I hope you're better at shooting down the Hun than you are at telling jokes. Now let me see, have I got this right? There's a female on a train who wants to urinate but she can't because the carriage she's in is non-corridor.'

'That's correct sir, but I've forgotten to tell you that she's not a female she's a Waaf.'

'You do surprise me, I thought all Waaf were female. Is it important to the tale?'

'Not really, sir. Come to think of it she could be any sort of young lady.'

'Oh dear,' says Skipper wearily. Then, with an air of resignation he asks, 'So what does this female or whatever she is, do about it?'

'She just sits there, digs her finger nails into the palms of her hands, licks her lips, crosses her legs, grits her teeth, and tells herself to be patient using the crude word I mentioned.'

'Crude word, what crude word?' Roden's question is followed by a further inspection of his watch. At a nearby dispersal a Merlin engine bursts into life. 'Um, time to get cracking, your tale will have to wait. Crude word indeed. Don't forget, I shall want to hear this joke of yours when we get back, crude word and all. Come on chaps, let's go. Huh! Aboard already are they, my but they are keen tonight.'

16th August, 1943. With Wickenby covered by heavy cloud the squadron was 'stood-down' today from operations. In a letter from home father tells me that an uncle of mine is thinking of keeping pigs. Wandering round declaring, 'Take care of the pig and the pig will take care of you,' he appears to have taken leave of his senses. Father also mentions my cousin Douglas who is, 'somewhere in Africa,' surrounded by horrible great spiders and four inch long beetles. More to the point the Army authorities will not grant him compassionate leave, even though his mother is close to death. Bolshie Mrs Clark has been stroppy again, she's been fined a further fifteen shillings for allowing yet another unscreened light to pierce the blackout. My mother cried a lot sitting twice through "*Mrs Miniver*". She certainly gets value for money from her threepenny matinees, does Mum. Chapel is mentioned of course, with a local preacher in a sermon of not far short of an hour's duration warning the congregation of Christ's coming. 'Be ye ready!' he'd thundered.

This longer than usual letter tells of a visit to a concert by my parents where the comedian had them in stitches. Dad, thinking perhaps that I need cheering up, has penned a few examples of the comic's wit. For instance -

Barber: 'Do you want a haircut?'

Customer: 'Well, I really came in to have them all cut.'

'Quack doctors in Switzerland are amassing fortunes from the nervous disorders of the Swiss people - there's gold in them there ills.'

'Emily is taking violin lessons.'

'How come, she hasn't the slightest ear for music?'

'I know, but she has beautiful elbows.'

I would never have believed it but there is someone out there whose jokes are cornier than Tommy Jackson's.

17th August, 1943. Photographs taken by the P.R.U. show that parts of Milan were severely damaged in the early hours of Monday morning. Many factories were destroyed and LM 321's photograph shows that our bombs were bang on target.

20 TARGET FOR TONIGHT: - PEENEMUNDE.

Operation "Hydra". Tuesday/Wednesday, 17th/18th August, 1943. 12 Squadron put up 25 aircraft for this attack, beating Binbrook's total by one. Number of bombers on raid: - 596, of which 324 were Lancasters. Number of aircraft lost: - 40, of which 23 were Lancasters.

At briefing the target was described as a Radio Location Research Plant situated on a small peninsula south of the island of Rugen, where research was being carried out by the Germans on a radar controlled night fighter system. There were to be three aiming points and our group was to bomb the second of these. It was stressed that as the target was of vital importance to the enemy it was to be completely destroyed, and if we failed in our attempt to do so we would have to keep going back until we had succeeded. To fool the Germans into thinking that their capital was the intended target eight Mosquitoes were to do a spoof attack on Berlin. A "Master Bomber" or "Master of Ceremonies" would verbally control the bombing by "shifting" the markers. Take off 21.40, in Lancaster ED 424, "E"2. Down at 03.55. Bomb load: 11,000 lbs.: 1 x 4,000 lb., 6 x 1,000 lb. and 2 x 500 lb. Fuel: 1750 gallons. Bombed at 00.34 hours from 8,000 ft. 196 deg. mag. 160 mph. Visibility good, no cloud. Ground opposition in the target area which was alive with bomb bursts. A smoke screen was becoming active as we left. One 12 Squadron aircraft lost: S/L Slade and crew flying in DV 168, PH "F". The Squadron Leader had been in charge of "A" flight.

The diversionary attack by the Mosquitoes drew the night fighters from the bomber stream and the first two waves to attack the target benefitted from this ploy. The third wave, however, was savagely mauled by the frustrated fighters.

19th August, 1943. Seating ourselves in a pressure chamber of sorts the M.O. explained, for the benefit of the dim wits amongst us, that air becomes thinner the higher you go. He then talked about deficiency of oxygen and decrease of atmospheric pressure. Wearing our flying helmets with the oxygen supply switched off we reacted to commands given outside the chamber, from where we were also observed. Inside the chamber, with his oxygen at "on", a medical orderly waited to come to our rescue. After first writing down my name, rank and number I carefully obeyed several other instructions, anxious to prove that I could reach dizzy heights without oxygen. I glanced about and saw that Ginger's writing had become somewhat spidery, while to my left Sparks appeared to have dozed off. *Piece of cake this. I'll make 20,000 feet, no trouble at all... Strange, I don't remember switching my oxygen on. Is that scrawl on the paper in front of me really my handwriting?*

Sitting back I breathe in deeply, and when the medic adjusts George's oxygen supply I realise that he must have done the same for me. Before long the seven of us are chatting merrily away, boasting of how long we had survived without the odourless gas so essential to our existence.

Tom reckons English is a daft language because in the magazine he is reading it claims that if a chap who is putting up for Parliament takes a certain stand when he runs, he will have a walk-over.

21 TARGET FOR TONIGHT: - LEVERKUSEN.

Sunday/Monday, 22nd/23rd August, 1943. Total number of bombers on the raid: - 462, of which 257 were Lancasters including 25 from 12 Squadron. Number of aircraft lost: 5, of which 3 were Lancasters. Take off 21.20 in Lancaster DV 200, "F2". Airborne - 4 hours 50 minutes. Bomb load 10,840 lbs.: 1 x 4,000 lb. "cookie", 3 x 1,000 lb. and incendiaries. Fuel: 1,400 gallons. Clear weather over base, Mablethorpe and the enemy coast, but 10/10ths cloud over the target with tops to 20,000 feet. The aiming point was the I.G. Farben factory but with the T.I.s not visible we bombed on E.T.A. The flak was in barrage form but the many searchlights were ineffective due to the cloud.

The "op" was lacking in incident but when I eventually hit the sack at around 04.00 sleep eluded me. I tossed and turned, straightened my bed clothes half a dozen times, sipped water and punched my pillow but all to no avail. By 7 a.m., however, I was sleeping fitfully, and in one of many crazy dreams Skipper chased me along the never ending corridor of what appeared to be a railway carriage. When I eventually surfaced I was surprised to find that it was nearly lunch time, that we were once again on the battle order, and judging from the amount of fuel Steve says "F2" has greedily consumed we are in for a long trip.

A newspaper in the mess claims that several Ruhr towns were bombed last night, which really means our bombing was scattered. The same paper reveals that Winston S Churchill had a narrow escape from being killed by a bomb while dining at number 10, Downing Street, during the London blitz in November 1940. The powers that be certainly kept that quiet at the time.

Tom is into slang in a big way, and I am forced to listen to words and phrases that would baffle anyone not wearing Air Force blue.

"Bang on" means correct; "bind" is a duty that is tedious; "to boob" is to blunder; "chocks away", means it is time to get started; "Crump Dump" describes the Ruhr; "dim" is stupid; "drink" is the sea and "duff gen" is false information.

None of this slang originated with Tom of course, he is merely slave to its usage. German tracer and cannon shells are "flaming onions"; to "flap" is to panic and "Gone for a Burton" means that an aircrew chap is missing, presumed dead, or known to be dead.

He recently came up with something I had not heard before when he called a Waaf, who had spurned his advances, a "huffy", and he baffled me with "kipper kites" which turned out to be Coastal Command aircraft protecting convoys. "Ladybirds" are W.A.A.F. officers, and when I fire my machine guns I apparently "loose off" a few rounds. His latest picturesque figure of speech refers to the recently issued 1939-43 star, which he calls his "N.A.F.F.I. gong".

George says the Waaf parachute packing mommas call me, 'Pilgrim.' The reason being that whenever I go into their section I try to make progress with one of them.

22 TARGET FOR TONIGHT: - BERLIN.

Monday/Tuesday 23rd/24th August, 1943. Total number of bombers on raid: - 727, of which 335 were Lancasters. Total number of aircraft lost: - 56, of which 17 were Lancasters. As Steve our flight engineer forecast the amount of octane fed into PH "F2" had indeed meant that we were in for a long stooge. I had hoped it would be Italy again, but no such luck; it was the dreaded "Big City". I had known that Berlin was bound to be the target eventually, no matter how much I willed it not to be. My worst fears were confirmed when it resulted in the heaviest loss suffered thus far by Bomber Command - with one 12 Squadron aircraft amongst the fifty-six that failed to return, F/O N. Ashburner and crew in DV 158.

A light shower from a cloudy sky accompanied us to the briefing room. There the sight of a ribbon stretching to Berlin on the wall map brought forth a gasp of dismay from the assembled aircrews, together with a sinking feeling in the stomach for myself. Take off was 20.39 in Lancaster DV 200, PH "F2" and the trip would last seven hours. The weather was clear as our "kite" transported 10,080 lbs. of bombs and 1,700 gallons of fuel over Holland, before progressing south of Bremen and north of Hannover. Avoiding Brunswick, we passed south east of Berlin, then cut back to bomb red and green target indicators.

No sooner had we bombed than we were coned, and though Skipper "got weaving" in the truest sense of the phrase the searchlights refused to be shaken off. Despite the steep dives and climbing turns which threatened every rivet in the aircraft my turret remained bathed in a whiteness of incredible brilliance, which rendered me both blind and useless. Sweating profusely I tried desperately to shield my eyes, and waited for the hail of cannon fire I felt sure would come. Twisting and turning Fox Two fought for her life, and when another dive rid us of the searchlights I experienced the blackest black I had ever known. For one blessed moment I felt secure, cocooned in inky darkness, but suddenly danger loomed in the shape of a Ju88 night fighter. Knowing that the enemy's guns could soon be raking "F2" from stem to stern I opened fire with my four Brownings, giving Skipper the necessary evasive action as I did so. The incident lasted only a few seconds but it was long enough for me to register hits, and when the aircraft disappeared from view an engine appeared to be on fire.

Large conflagrations were now much in evidence on the ground and smoke had risen to our height. Within me, as we returned to base, I felt a grim satisfaction. Roden's reprobates had raided the "Big City", had successfully escaped from its searchlights and possibly downed an enemy fighter. Even more important we had started what Bomber Harris had so often threatened, we had helped light a fire in the belly of the enemy that would eventually burn his black heart out.

25th August, 1943. Having flown over Denmark on the return from Berlin I was today intrigued to find a magazine article in the mess which told of the current state of affairs in that country. The inhabitants are certainly "doing their bit". They have adopted a policy of "cold shouldering" the German troops, are committing acts of sabotage and organising strikes. The article also tells of the serious clashes that have resulted in the death of many brave Danes since Copenhagen was occupied.

'Wake up, Cocky.'
'I wasn't asleep, you long streak of you-know-what.'
'Oh, so you can read with your eyes closed, can you? D'you fancy going into GY tonight?'
'Can't, I'm strapped for cash. And talking about being penniless, you know that blonde job in the parachute section, the one who is always complaining of being broke?'
'You mean the wench Tom mentally undresses whenever he sees her?'
'I thought he did that with all of them. Anyway, she was carrying on in her usual manner when Lefty from Pete's crew walked in. He listened for a while then gave her an old fashioned look and said, "Oh, quit moaning girl, don't you know you're sitting on a gold mine?"'
'Gosh, Al, that's an oldie, the last time I heard it Tom claimed he was the one who had asked her the question!'

The newspapers are full of the Berlin raid. They claim it was the heaviest yet on the German capital with 1,700 tons of bombs dropped in an attack which lasted fifty minutes. Smoke had risen to a height of over twenty thousand feet from fires visible two hundred miles away.

"Recce" photographs show that considerable damage was inflicted on the industrial districts of Charlottenburg and Wilmersdorf, and the Siemen's works was well and truly clobbered. Other areas suffered too but it is not known to what extent because of the great pall of smoke covering the city.

I hear that my former squadron, number 100, suffered severely with four Lancasters failing to return. I hope trusty old ED 749 wasn't one of them.

27th/28th August, 1943. Nuremberg was the target last night but Roden and crew were not on the raid from which 33 aircraft failed to return. One 12 squadron aircraft was lost - W/O L. W. Aspden and crew, flying in Lancaster DV 187, PH "A".

The newspapers reports of the raid differ considerably. One claims that most bombs fell in open countryside, another that the Zoo was hit and a couple more reckon that city was wiped out. Our bombing may not be spot on at times but one thing's for sure, we are a damn sight more accurate than the denizens of Fleet Street.

Tom has been wittering on about his soccer skills, and his bragging has resulted in George boasting about a silver cup he won as a lad at a swimming gala. This joint showing off brought forth a denunciation from Ginger of all forms of physical exercise, unless it involved the opposite sex.

'That happened to me on one occasion,' I said.
'What d'you mean?'
'Physical exercise with the opposite sex.'
'How come?'

'Well, once upon a time, a young and innocent airman attended an Air Force sports day where a flight lieutenant invited him to take part in the various activities, one of which was a three-legged race. At first the youth was reluctant to do so but when he clapped his peepers on the absolutely gorgeous Waaf the officer had chosen to partner him, his enthusiasm knew no bounds. Sitting on the grass next to the auburn-haired beauty our hero found fastening the rope that was to make the two of them three legged posed a dual problem. Firstly her tantalizing close proximity, and secondly her perfume which drove me, I mean him, wild with passion.'

'Lordy, lordy, what have we done to deserve this?' asked Tom, rolling his eyes and whistling through the gap in his teeth.

'Be patient Tommy, be patient. Eventually he, er, I, succeeded in my quest but not before I had been forced to literally manhandle my partner's shapely leg and trim ankle. Trying to stand up then proved to be as difficult as it was enjoyable, so much so that when several airmen and airwomen came to our assistance I found myself wishing they would leave us alone. After a few practice steps we were in perfect synchronisation and when the officer called, 'Ready, steady, go,' we went off at a gallop and were soon way ahead of the opposition. Glancing to my left I realised that I was already half in love with the blue-shirted honey who, with come-to-bed eyes, luscious lips and heaving bosom, was panting by my side. A few more steps and we would reach a climax and breast the tape together.'

I paused, glanced at my listeners, and discovered to my surprise that they were agog with disinterest.

'And what happened next?' asked George, with complete lack of enthusiasm.

'The stupid rope untied itself didn't it, and although we were the first past the finishing line we were disqualified. You should have seen and heard my running mate! With eyes flashing she gave me a right verbal lashing, calling me every name under the sun for not tying the rope securely. She told me to get stuffed, get lost, get knotted and drop dead.'

'Now there's a thing,' sighed Ginger. 'I feel quite disappointed. I thought fairy tales always finished up with the ugly airman and the beautiful Waaf getting married and living happily ever after.'

23 TARGET FOR TONIGHT: - MUNCHEN GLADBACH/RHEYDT.

Monday/Tuesday, 30th/31st, August, 1943. Number of bombers on raid: - 660, of which 297 were Lancasters with 23 of them from Wickenby. Total number of aircraft lost: - 25, of which 7 were Lancasters. One 12 squadron aircraft failed to return - Lancaster III, ED 972, PH "R". F/L A. Booth D.F.C., and crew. Flying with F/L Booth was Wing Commander J. G. Towle, our new Commanding Officer. Taking off at midnight we were routed out via Sheringham and Knokke. Over the target there was thin cloud with tops to about 5,000 feet. Bomb load:11,840 lbs.: 1 x 4,000 lb., 4 x 1,000 lb. and incendiaries. The bombing of the twin towns was very concentrated. We were airborne for 4 hours 20 minutes in Lancaster DV 200, "F2", the same aircraft we had taken to Berlin seven nights earlier.

Something happened tonight that has left me with a feeling of guilt. I feel pretty sure I dozed off! Relaxed, warm and comfortable as we sped homewards, I was relishing the prospect of bacon and eggs plus lashings of tea when suddenly the rhythm of our four Merlins ceased to dance in my ears. I sat bolt upright, filled with dismay. Had I nodded off? I must have done. Had Skipper tried to contact me over the inter-com? How could I find out without making him suspicious? Should I call him up on some pretext or other? Maybe not, I would probably sound full of guilt and give myself away. How long had I been asleep, if asleep I had been? Only a matter of seconds surely, but what if an enemy fighter had chosen that moment to attack.

Suddenly I was no longer warm and comfortable, I was sweating, wretched and dismayed. My duty was to defend the aircraft, to protect to the best of my ability the lives of my fellow crew members as well as my own. Whatever would the chaps think if they knew I had nodded off? I knew what Skipper's reaction would be. He would have me tied to the tail wheel and flogged, or maybe he would make me finish the four-stage tale of the young lady who was dying to spend a penny. But this was no laughing matter and I resolved there and then that in future I would take a "wakey-wakey" tablet, a drug I'd mistakenly thought I could do without.

2nd September, 1943. Over half of Munchen Gladbach was destroyed on Tuesday night and our Squadron also suffered. We had lost F/L Booth, F/S Patterson had aborted because of a u/s starboard outer, W/O Green's "B" had been severely damaged by a fighter, and F/O Snell failed to take off after colliding with a bomb trolley as he taxied from dispersal. Leaving all this excitement behind me I set course for Stoke-on-Trent, a.k.a. "Smoke-on-Stench", for seven days leave.

3rd September, 1943. Friday. Today, on this the fourth anniversary of the outbreak of war, the King has requested that it be observed as a national day of prayer. Being on leave I attended a special church service with mum and dad, then later met a certain party from Cross Heath. Sitting in the shade of what was most certainly not an old apple tree, on a seat thoughtfully provided by the local council for the use of tired old codgers or randy young lovers, we kissed and cuddled. With the petting growing ever heavier the desire to lose my virginity mounted within and without of me. The young lady's fear of what "going all the way" might result in acted as a brake, however, and as the sun went down so did most everything else.

Mum was "waiting up" when I hobbled into the kitchen. She showered me with questions but got only non-committal grunts in reply. Had I managed to catch the late bus home? Did I want a cup of cocoa? Had I been to the pictures, if not what had I been doing?

Not quite everything I thought, shifting uncomfortably in my chair. My mind wandered as I sipped the cocoa, just as my hand had done earlier. Something stirred, and it wasn't just the spoon.

7th September, 1943. Returning from leave, George, our wireless op, took the opportunity to visit Lincoln cathedral, where he was given an unofficial guided tour by an obliging "yellow belly".

'There was an awful lot to see,' Sparks enthused. 'Got a crick in my neck from peering upwards but it was the misericords I enjoyed most.'

'The what?' I asked, revealing my complete ignorance of all things ecclesiastical.

'Misericords. Lots of old churches have them. Lift up a seat and there they are.'

'What's so special about them?'

'The carvings.'

'Angels and things?'

'Well, some are religious, like the *Ascension*, the *Resurrection* and the *Adoration of the Magi*, but mostly they depict everyday goings on. A woman using bellows on a fire, a man with sacks of grain, and pigs eating acorns that have fallen from a tree. Some are really cute, like the mermaid with a comb and a swan with a queen's head. There are smaller carvings too. A dragon with its prey, and a monkey riding a queer looking creature which my guide said was a griffin. The one I liked best though was a fox in a pulpit preaching to geese. Next time you go to Lincoln you should give the "*Saracens Head*" a miss and visit the Cathedral, I'm sure you would enjoy the experience.'

'Um! I learn something new every day, as Jerry Colonna would say.'

'Jerry who?' George sounded mystified.

'Don't tell me you've never heard of Jerry Colonna. You know all about mystery chords or whatever but know nothing of Jerry, he of the weirdly pitched voice, straggly 'tache and poppy eyes. You obviously haven't seen *"Star Spangled Rhythm"* with its host of stars. People like Bing, Bob, Betty Hutton, Paulette Goddard and Alan Ladd. My, but your education's been severely neglected. Next time you go to Lincoln give the cathedral a miss and go to a cinema, I'm sure you would enjoy the experience.'

'You know what you can do!' said my colleague, waxing bold with a "reverse victory salute."

12th September, 1943. Formation flying laid on but it was a case of "duty not carried out", to use official phraseology. And there were no "ops" either because the squadron's navigators were learning how to use *"H2S"*.

I received a letter from my sister to-day. Judging from the content it would appear that I have dropped an almighty clanger! Back home, it seems my name is mud! Returning from leave I had written two letters, one to "my lady of the lovers seat", the other to an aunt. Using passionate words I had informed the young lady of my love for her and of what we might get up to on my next leave. In the other I had sympathised with aunt regarding a recent operation which had resulted in the removal of certain internal organs.

And the clanger?

I put the letters in the wrong envelopes. My declaration of sexual intent has horrified aunt, and my lady friend will forever wonder which of her reproductory organs have been removed without her knowledge!

14th September, 1943. Two hours thirty minutes of flying in formation followed by a lecture. I managed to avoid one of Skipper's "physical jerks" sessions but as a result was forced to endure a Tom and Ginger trivial tirade. As usual our bomb aimer did the "falsetto" bits.

'Marry me, or I'll throw you off the bridge.'
'But I can't swim.'
'You won't have to, it's a railway bridge.'

And:
'Submit to my feelthy advances.'
'No, no, I'm only thirteen.'
'I'm not superstitious.'

And:
'To the woods, wench.'
'But my mother won't like it.'
'Your mother isn't getting it.'

'Did you hear about the tart who stayed cool, calm and collected?'

'Only birds and fools fly and even birds stop at night, except for the ogo-pogo bird which flies around in ever decreasing concentric circles until it disappears up its own arsehole.'

'There we were. Toss all on the clock, all engines gone, upside down and still climbing!'

Tom, hair pulled down over his left eye, fakes a moustache by placing the index finger of his left hand across his upper lip. Saluting Nazi style he rants, 'I vant peace, a piece of Austria, a piece of Czechoslovakia, a piece of Poland, a piece of Denmark and a piece of Norway.'

Ginger, arm also raised in salute, inverts his palm, waggles his middle finger and shouts, 'I'll tittle 'er.'

'Tell me airwoman, are you religious?'

'I know about psalms, sir.'

'And what do you know about psalms?'

'They are sacred songs in which the 'p' is silent as in swimming or bath.'

As we enter the mess Tom removes a pretend cigar from his mouth. 'We are going on to the end. We have fought over France. We have fought over seas and oceans. We have fought, with absolutely no confidence and growing diarrhoea, in the air, and never in the field of human conflict has anyone ever before had to eat the pig swill this place calls food.' Reverting to his own voice he asks, 'I wonder what's on the menu, bet you anything you like it's bubble and squeak again.'

Tom's opinion of our food is on a par with mine regarding his and Ginger's humour. When I eventually get to see and hear the newly formed station concert party, the "Ad Astras", I hope their repertoire will be an improvement on what I have just had to suffer.

17th September, 1943. To Skellingthorpe and return. Skipper implied that the visit was official R.A.F. business but I reckon he wanted to chew the fat with an old buddy of his. Not that I minded one bit for the trip afforded excellent views of Lincoln Cathedral. How kind are the powers that be, letting me sightsee at their expense!

20th September, 1943. Fighter affiliation. Today a Beaufighter, using a cine camera gun, attacked me with all the vigour of a night fighter over Berlin. I replied with equal enthusiasm. I wonder if we shot each other down? The thought had me remembering some of the chaps who had gone missing since my last "op". W/O Green and crew on a Big City raid, F/O Leader Williams and crew on a Mannheim trip, and two members of F/Sgt. Hutchinson's crew who had gone down with their Lancaster when it sank off Spurn Head. Bound for Munich the aircraft had suffered engine failure twenty minutes after taking off. As Sam says - 'You don't have to be crazy to fly on "ops" but it sure helps.'

22nd/23rd September, 1943. A fine day which improved dramatically when I found that our crew was not one of those detailed to bomb Hannover. And what a hive of activity Wickenby became with twenty-one aircraft being prepared for the raid, and the completion of several buildings which included a new Flight Office, Station HQ, Main Stores and Sick Quarters.

24 TARGET FOR TONIGHT: - MANNHEIM-LUDWIGSHAFEN.

Thursday/Friday, 23rd/24th September, 1943. Number of bombers on raid: - 628, of which 312 were Lancasters, including 19 of 12 Squadron. Number of aircraft lost: - 32, of which 18 were Lancasters, two of them from our squadron: - W 4991, PH "Q", F/L Harper, and crew, and DV 225 PH "H", F/O Guthrie, and crew. Take off was at 18.50, and we were routed out over Clacton. Bomb load: 10,080 lbs. 1 x 4,000 lb., 2 x 1,000 lb. and incendiaries. Heavy flak greeted us on our approach to the target which was well ablaze when we arrived, and Skipper wasn't fooling when he said over the inter-com that the natives seemed hostile. White flares were dropped from above us to help enemy night fighters, but, though I observed combats, our aircraft PH "G2" was not attacked. Return to base was via Selsey Bill and Reading.

A Halifax bomber based at Lissett, which had been on the Mannheim raid, crashed near to our airfield. Two of the crew were injured. They were taken to Lincoln Military Hospital where their injuries were said to be non-life-threatening.

26th September, 1943. Reports confirm that we caused considerable damage to the I.G Farben factory at Ludwigshafen, and many thousands of people in Mannheim have lost their homes.

Ginger is teaching me the words of *"T'was on the good ship Venus"* - or maybe trying to teach me would be more accurate. I have no difficulty remembering the first two lines but from then on I get confused.

'T'was on the good ship Venus,
You really should have seen us.'
'Go on, you could remember the next line yesterday.'

'I know but I've been asleep since then. Now er, let me see, er...

    'Astride a rampant...'
'No! No! Our figurehead was a whore...'
'Oh yes...
    'in bed, beside a rampant penis.'
'Astride, you twit, not beside.'
    'Our figurehead was a whore in bed,
    'Astride a rampant penis.'
'That's it. Now what comes next?'
'The penis? D'you think Skipper would let us paint a Venus on the side of a Lanc, with penises instead of bomb symbols showing the number of operations done by the aircraft.'
'I doubt it. Carry on.'
'Is it the cabin boy or the captain's daughter who comes next?'
'Oh Al, you're bloody hopeless.'
'I remember the last bit about the junk getting sunk in a sea of...'
'Yes, yes, but then you would, wouldn't you.'
    'The best was at the China station,
    'We really caused a great sensation.'
'Oh, belt up! Don't ever try to learn 'Eskimo Nell', I'm told it has more than forty verses.'

28th September, 1943. A Lancaster, returning from a raid on Hannover, crashed here early this morning, and a 101 Squadron aircraft based at Ludford Magna was shot down by an intruder. The crew of eight were killed.

2nd October, 1943. I was in the flight office this morning when a brand new crew captained by a sergeant named Butterfield came in for one of Skipper's pep talks. They looked very young, bits of kids hardly out of school. When he'd finished, Pop, I mean Skipper, dismissed them in his usual abrupt manner, and as they filed out of the door I felt quite old - all 21 years 6 months of me.

25 TARGET FOR TONIGHT: - MUNICH.

Saturday/Sunday 2nd/3rd October, 1943. An all-Lancaster attack of 294 bombers which included 21 from 12 Squadron. 8 aircraft lost, one of which was from Wickenby - DV 222, PH "G2", the kite we had taken to Mannheim a week or so ago. Take off: 18.30 hours in JA 864, PH "D2". Airborne 8 hours 25 minutes. Bomb load: 7,672 lbs. 1 x 4,000 lb. and incendiaries. Fuel: 1,926 gallons. Routed out over Orfordness, returned via Beachy Head. Cloudy over France and most of Germany. P.F.F. marked the target with Red and Green indicators. Considerable flak at 20,000 feet, and a host of searchlights.

Two aircraft aborted because of u/s rear turrets, and PH "H2" suffered flak damage. Three of our aircraft coned by British searchlights on their return over London saved themselves by firing off the colours of the day!

Skipper's' know how' of all things relevant to bombing and operational flying must have impressed Group, because he has been asked to write a special report for H.Q concerning the Munich raid.

Later, when I discovered that Roden and crew were operating for a second, successive night, I greeted the news with my usual apprehension - which increased when I heard that it was Butterfield's aircraft that had failed to return from Munich.

26 TARGET FOR TONIGHT: - KASSEL.

Sunday/Monday, 3rd/4th October, 1943. Total number of bombers on raid: - 547, of which 204 were Lancasters, which included 17 from 12 squadron. Number of aircraft lost: - 24, of which 4 were Lancasters. Took off in JA 864, PH "D2", at 18.25. Bomb load: 9,464lbs. 1x 4,000 lb., 1 x 2,000 lb. and 866 x 4 lb. incendiaries. Fuel: 1,600 gallons.

Having waved farewell to a murky looking Mablethorpe on the Lincolnshire coast we encountered considerable cloud over the North Sea, avoided flak from Texel and negotiated Holland safely. South of Bremen some pretty deadly stuff came up at us and this continued as we flew south east towards Hannover. By the time we reached the target we were at 22,000 ft. As we commenced our bombing run a huge explosion lit up the night sky to the north-east. Flak continued to be troublesome as we returned between Bonn and Koblenz but things quietened down over Belgium. Base was reached via the south coast of England.

One of the least enjoyable things about "ops" occurs when we return to base to find other Lancasters awaiting their turn to land. Stacked up five hundred feet or so apart we follow instructions given to us by a Waaf in Flying Control. After what seems an eternity we eventually get permission to pancake. Such occasions are fraught with danger, with friendly aircraft too close for comfort and unfriendly intruders waiting to pounce.

5th October, 1943. P.R.U. photographs show that major damage was inflicted on Kassel's many factories. The huge explosion I saw was due to an ammunition dump taking a direct hit.

6th October, 1943. My former navigator, the cultured and charming Flying Officer S. C. P. Godfrey D.F.C., with whom I flew on 15 ops with 100 squadron, failed to return from a recent raid on Frankfurt. A member of 156 Squadron, he was not, on that occasion, flying with my former skipper, F/L Anset, but with S/L Cook D.F.C. D.F.M. This war of attrition we are waging with night fighter crews and anti-aircraft gunners in the skies over Germany is a bloody rotten business, and if hostilities continue for much longer then the cream of Britain's youth will not be around to help face the problems peace will bring. They will instead be filling the cemeteries of Holland, France, and Germany, or lying at the bottom of the North Sea.

'This is foul-tasting muck,' complains Tom, pushing aside a cup of tea.

'Now, now, Thomas, you mustn't complain,' I reprimand, tongue in cheek. 'Think of those unfortunate people in civvy street who are forced to drink tea made from blackberry leaves, and coffee ground from dried acorns. Poor souls, their only meat is liver and lights. Their marmalade is made from carrots, and they're forced to eat the tasteless utility loaf which isn't white but an unappetising shade of grey.'

'Yeah, my heart bleeds, though I doubt if many go hungry. Take Ginger's family for instance. His dad's a butcher so they won't go short, and as for that ruddy Uncle Bert of mine his lot want for nothing. My blood boils when I go home on leave and find my mum doing her best to live on her rations, while Uncle gets eggs and other dairy produce from a Mrs Bentley who has a small holding.'

'And what's your uncle got that makes this woman offer him such favours?'

'A large holding, I guess.' A smile wrinkles Tom's features. 'We Jacksons are well endowed you know.'

7th October, 1943. There's a flight sergeant in the mess who plays "Boogie-Woogie". He's *"Speckled Red"*, *"Cow Cow"*, Jimmy Yancey, Albert Ammons and Meade Lux Lewis all rolled into one. My, but what a left hand he's got! *"Honky Tonk Train Blues"*, *"South Side Stuff"*, *"The Fives"*, *"The Dirty Dozen"*, *"Cow Cow Blues"*. His eight to the bar repertoire is endless, and when a pal of his joins forces with him, their four handed piano attack really does have the joint jumping. Man alive, let's dig that jive.

George was in the Air Training Corps prior to being called-up and on one occasion he attended a lecture given by a pilot who, after being shot down over the Ruhr, evaded capture and eventually made his way back to this country. According to our wireless-op the lecturer possessed a first rate sense of humour, and the A.T.C lads were in fits of laughter when he made light of jumping out of his stricken bomber. Landing safely he had got rid of his parachute, turned his battledress blouse inside out to hide his true identity, and blackened his face with still hot embers. Using schoolboy German to good effect he'd shaken his fist and cursed the "terror fliegers" up there in the night sky, all the while doing his best to prolong the life of the fires the locals were attempting to extinguish.

27 TARGET FOR TONIGHT: - STUTTGART.

Thursday/Friday, 7th/8th October, 1943. An all-Lancaster attack of 343 aircraft which included 19 from 12 Squadron. Only five aircraft were lost, which was probably due to a diversionary raid on Munich designed to keep enemy fighters away from the main force. Take off, 20.15 in Lancaster "J2", JA 922. Airborne 7 hours 10 minutes. Bomb load: 8,120 lbs.: 1 x 4,000 lb. 1 x 1,000 lb. 780 x 4 lb. incendiaries. Yellow indicators backed by reds and greens marked the target, with white flares at ten second intervals.

No cloud until 50 miles from the target, then 10/10ths thin layer cloud to 8,000 feet. After leaving Stuttgart, I discovered a shadowy shape lurking low down to port. Was it an enemy fighter or dirt on the Perspex? The uncertainty had me on tenterhooks. From time to time the mystery object seemed to slide slowly from port to starboard before rising sharply to disappear from view. Was it a spot before my eyes, or a figment of my imagination? It did not resemble a night fighter but nevertheless its presence really began to niggle me.

'Come on you swine,' I challenged under my breath, before warning Ginger over the inter-com of my suspicions.

We were over the sea before my tormentor eventually disappeared. Never before had I felt so agitated. Was I becoming flak, or fighter, happy? Going round the bend? Maybe the fact that I was coming to the end of my first tour of operations was getting to me!

Returning from dispersal an incident occurred that resulted in me temporarily forgetting my own "spot" of trouble. Lancaster "R", safely back from Stuttgart, was due to land when its port outer engine burst into flames. The aircraft promptly left the circuit and disappeared. At de-briefing the I.O. told us that "R" had come to rest in a field a few miles from base, and that the crew had escaped unhurt.

8th October, 1943. I have had a jolly good look at the Perspex of "J2"'s rear turret but the inspection revealed nothing, so whatever it was that I saw or didn't see last night will remain a mystery. There was no blemish, speck, scratch or particle of dirt visible, and I was forced to agree with Ginger when he said I had been imagining things. He also hinted that I should pull my finger out and stop flapping.

According to the BBC we really "pranged" the target last night. The P.M. in a recent speech said that one of our objects was to de-house the German population, and we have certainly done that to the inhabitants of Stuttgart.

After lunch I sat on my bed and sowed a bright shining crown above the three stripes on my battledress blouse, having been promoted to flight sergeant. When Sergeants Thomas Jackson, Harold Whitmore and George Brittle enter this Nissen hut of ours I shall most certainly "pull rank" and issue a few orders. And I know for sure what their reaction will be!

The target for Friday/Saturday, 8th/9th October, 1943, was Hannover but S/L Roden and crew were not on the battle order, having already "operated" three times in less than a week.

The night turned out to be a stinker for the squadron for both W/O Joy and Sgt. Collins failed to return to Wickenby, and a 12 squadron Lancaster, EE 202, on loan to 460 squadron at Binbrook, was also lost. Gloom and doom prevailed, and the fog did little to help.

'This bloody Station's a right bloody cuss,
'No bloody pubs and no bloody bus

Hitler has told Goering he doesn't want his Luftwaffe intruder aircraft to shoot us down over our bases on our return to this country, he wants us to be destroyed over Germany so that the wreckage of the aircraft can be seen by the populace.

Tom's home-town sweetheart has fallen for a big mouth from God's own country. Like all Yanks he had more to offer a girl than any of us Brits of similar rank, and the whole affair has soured our bomb-aimer.

Huh! If only he was in the U.S.A.A.F. serving with "The Mighty Eighth"! He would be over-there, over-paid, over-fed, over-sexed, and all the other "overs" including a uniform covered all-over in medal ribbons. One for being a Yank, one for being abroad, one for being in England, one for cutting himself while shaving, a couple of dozen for flying a few "missions" over Germany, one for jitterbugging, one for non-stop gum-chewing, one for having to associate with Limeys and many, many more for similar "deeds of daring do".

No longer would there be just "coffee and cake money" in his pockets, instead they would be stuffed with tenspots and greenbacks. With a "blonde job" on each arm no way would he be a punk hoofer. Aloft in a B17 "Flying Fortress" he would be aboard the mightiest bomber ever built, safe and sound in his flak vest. He would always hit the target, the incredible Norden bombsight would see to that. A bomb in a barrel from 20,000 feet? Easy, every time without fail. Jeez, what accuracy, what eyesight!

28 TARGET FOR TONIGHT: - LEIPZIG.

Wednesday/Thursday, 20th/21st October, 1943. An all-Lancaster attack of 358 aircraft from which 16 were lost. Take off: - 17.40 in Lancaster "J2", JA 922. Airborne: - 7 hours. "The weather conditions were appalling" - Bomber Command's words, not mine. 10/10ths cloud, electrical storms and severe icing. With the red and green target indicators hardly visible, our bombs finished up scattered all over the place. Even the welcome home smile, which I received from the Waaf driver of the crew bus that took us from dispersal to interrogation, failed to lift my spirits.

26th October, 1943.
'How's Jane?'
'Fine! Her skirt's gone missing!'
'Oh, half naked, eh? Through no fault of her own, I suppose?'
'Is it ever?'
'And Fritz?'
'The faithful hound is leading a dog's life, which in his case is most enjoyable because he's watching his mistress take a bath.'
'Lucky beast. Bags the Mirror when you've finished reading it.'
'Sorry, you'll have to join the queue.'

Sergeant Leslie Charles John Street has replaced "Sam" Weller in our crew, and because his first two initials are L C then that's what he will be called – Elsie! A quiet, undemonstrative sort of chap, he is at 34 much older than the rest of us. I was surprised therefore when he hurried into the mess holding his nose, pulling his face and generally carrying on.

'Is it that unpleasant in here?' I asked.

'No. I've just managed to escape from Jumbo. I was standing minding my own business in the lav when he bounded in, pointed his Percy at the porcelain and broke wind with a shock wave greater than any block buster. It wasn't the noise that offended me, though, because I expect that sort of thing from him, it was the effluvia! I told him he was a filthy sod but all he did was laugh and give an encore. 'Better an empty house than a bad tenant,' he shouted, as I beat a hasty retreat.

27th, October, 1943. I received a letter from home today. It seems that Mrs Proctor's son has been turned down for flying duties, he having in some strange way perforated an ear drum. He is terribly disappointed of course, he did so want to fly.

Yeah, I'm sure he did. He must be really upset because it means he will be forced to carry on working in a munitions factory, where he will only earn three times as much as I do. Which is right and proper of course with him being so near to something that might go off with a bang! Heaven forbid, it might perforate the other drum!

Cigarette smoke frames Lana Turner. Sweater-clad, she smiles colourfully down at a half-dressed Ginger who gives her a wink as, stretched out on his bed, he puffs on a "*Piccadilly*" fag and darns a sweaty sock.

Until last week the photograph adorned a staircase leading to the upper circle of a Lincoln cinema. How the "sweater girl" has finished up over old craggy face's "pit" I can't imagine.

29 TARGET FOR TONIGHT: - DUSSELDORF.

Wednesday/Thursday, November 3rd/4th, 1943. Total number of bombers on raid: - 589, of which 344 were Lancasters, twenty one being 12 squadron aircraft. 18 aircraft lost, of which 11 were Lancasters. Two 12 squadron aircraft failed to return - DV 218 PH "G2" and JB 536 PH "F". We were airborne for 3hrs 55 minutes having taken off at 17.30 in ED 424, PH "E2". Bomb load: 11,760 lbs. 1 x 4,000 lb. 2 x 1,000 lb. and incendiaries. Fuel: 1,500 gallons. 10/10ths cloud en route over the North Sea with tops in excess of 15,000 ft. The cloud thinned as we approached the target, leaving ground haze only. Heavy flak between 16,000 and 18,000 ft, and night fighter activity above.

Homeward bound, my mind dwelled on the blazing inferno I had just witnessed, and I allowed myself a cynical smile when I remembered our government's claim that only military objectives were being attacked! The Germans call our 4,000 lb. cookies *"Bezirk Bomben"* - "District Bombs", because one of them can make a whole block of buildings disappear

This operation saw us bidding farewell to Steve on the completion of his first tour. A sergeant with the rather impressive name of Henri Antonius Van Hal will be our flight engineer from now on.

4th November, 1943. This afternoon we flew Lancaster JB 559 on an acceptance test which lasted one hour forty minutes.

5th November, 1943. 'Oh, I do like to be beside the seaside,' Ginger warbles, as a 15 cwt truck takes us to a distant dispersal where JA 922, "J2", is waiting to whisk us away for a spot of air to sea firing in the Mablethorpe area. 'Oh, I do like to be beside the seaside, I do like to be beside the sea.'

I wait for the usual caustic comment from Skipper. When it fails to materialize I am forced to assume that our pilot is mellowing in his dotage.

626 SQUADRON
"To Strive and Not to Yield"

No. 1 Group
R.A.F. BOMBER COMMAND

Wickenby, Lincolnshire, England

CREW ROSTER: - OPERATION 30.
18th/19th NOVEMBER, 1943

R.A.F. S/L G. A. Roden	Pilot (Captain)
R.A.F. Sgt. H. A. Van Hal	Flight Engineer
R.A.F. Sgt. L. C. J. Street	Navigator
R.A.F. Sgt. T. R. Jackson	Bomb Aimer
R.A.F. Sgt. G. H. Brittle	Wireless Operator
R.A.F. Sgt. H. W. Whitmore	Mid-Upper Gunner
R.A.F. F/Sgt. A. H. Alcock	Rear Gunner

7th, November, 1943. We, the crews of 12 Squadron's "C" flight, have become part of a newly formed squadron numbered 626. The coding is UM, and rumour hath it that before long Skipper will be promoted to take charge. I rather fancy having a Wing Commander for a skipper, the rank sounds far more impressive than that of Squadron Bleeder.

15th November, 1943. This is the life. Today, after a late breakfast, we took off at 11.30 in Lancaster "F2" for Sherburn in Elmet, where we were introduced to a high-ranking pal of Skipper's. What he thought of us I can't imagine. I was unshaven. Ginger needed a haircut. Tom was wearing his good luck scarf of Waaf scanties, and George couldn't stop burping.
'Excuse my friend, he's a pig,' Tom whispered, over lunch.
'Tell him to get his head out of the trough then.'

When the meal was over we flew to Castle Donnington, where our Lancaster attracted even more attention than it had at Sherburn.
'Sherburn in where?' Ginger asked, recording the flight in his log book.
'Emlet.' I said, affixing a new nib to the pen I was using.
'Elmet.' Tom corrected.
'Are you sure?'
'Sure I'm sure. I was the map reader, after all.'

Occasional visits to Lincoln's Brayford's pool have helped improve my rowing technique, and an inspection of the cathedral in George's company has seen me craning my neck to spot the Lincoln Imp. I have inspected thirteenth century glass, marvelled at the magnificent Nave, and sat in the Choir Stalls where my friend was determined to show me the misericords. On a recent visit to the city I did my best with the oars, and was so exhausted that when the time came to climb Steep Hill I felt like going down on my knees – not because I was "out of puff" but to thank the Lord for the hand rail placed there to assist me.

I am becoming a dab hand at shooting clays these days, and when not engaged in that sporting activity I thrash Ginger at snooker but get soundly beaten by Tom at darts. George invariably wins our shove-halfpenny contests, Henri shows me no mercy at chess and Les is teaching me the principles of photography. From time to time we get the cards out for a pontoon session, and most of the 'winnings' seem to end up in Tom's pocket.

30 TARGET FOR TONIGHT: - BERLIN.

Thursday/Friday. 18th/19th November, 1943. 440 Lancasters, 23 of which were put up by 12 and 626 squadrons. 9 Lancasters failed to return. We took off at 17.03 and were airborne for 8 hours 10 minutes. Bomb load: 8,320 lbs. 1 x 4,000 lb. "cookie", 56 x 30 lb. and 660 x 4 lb. incendiaries. At briefing eyebrows were raised when it was announced that to counter the German night fighter tactics the bombing period would last for only sixteen minutes instead of the usual forty-five or so, a dramatic shortening which meant that about twenty-seven Lancs would be attacking each minute of the raid. I glanced at Ginger and the look on his face confirmed that his thoughts were my own, that there would be collisions galore! The met forecast was for clear weather but there was eight to ten-tenths cloud from the Dutch coast.

Our aircraft, UM "C2", arrived over the city at 21.00 hours. Hundreds of searchlights greeted us but they were ineffective due to the thick cloud into which our red T.I.s, backed up by greens, quickly disappeared. There was little fighter activity but the flak barrage more than made up for its absence. So intense was it, a line-shooter could have been forgiven for claiming that it was thick enough to land on.

As crews were collected at the various dispersal points and taken to interrogation the conversation in our transport became quite animated.

A gunner complained that he had never before been bedevilled by so much ice, how he had spent most of the trip scraping the stuff off his controls. There was also talk of a mighty explosion on the deck.

'The bloody sky was alive with bursting shells,' claimed a flight-engineer. 'I reckon we'll find shrapnel has turned our Lanc. into a colander when we inspect it in daylight.'

'Must have been forty below,' sighed a gunner who, after lighting up a cigarette, coughed and spluttered to such an extent that it gave the lie to the much advertised claim that a "*Craven A*" was good for his throat.

20th November. 1943. Our visit to the "Big City" has made the headlines. BIGGEST BLITZ. BERLIN HIT BY HUNDREDS OF COOKIES. Waves of Britain's biggest bombers streaming out towards Europe brought about a complete radio black out. Berlin, Deutschlandsender, Bremen, Leipzig, Hamburg and Cologne were all off the air. The main weight of the attack is reported to have fallen on the southern part of the capital. The subway had direct hits in several places and railway sidings were smashed.

According to one newspaper our all-Lancaster force had battled through ice and cloud to reach the hidden target, where we had dropped our bombs on T.I.'s which cascaded through the clouds. A series of violent explosions were visible through the clouds even when the bomb flashes were hidden.

The "news" to which the newspapers are not privy is that 12 squadron's "N" aborted with a u/s rudder, both starboard engines of "E" cut eighty minutes from the target and all the electrical equipment failed on "S". 626 fared little better with "H2" making an emergency landing away from base due to extensive flak damage, and "K" having to feather a starboard engine. As the man said - 'Don't try to live forever, you will not succeed.'

21st November, 1943. Tired of reading the newspapers I switched on the radio in the mess. Through the loudspeaker came the well-known voice of Mr. C. H. Middleton, well known that is to me and millions of gardeners - not that I was ever a gardener but my father is.

'Good afternoon,' C. H. boomed, before revealing to his green-fingered listeners the technique of successful carrot growing. My father - an avid listener when it comes to anything to do with gardening - will be listening I'm quite sure, for he never misses Middleton's *"In Your Garden"*. Digging, weeding, planting, growing, hoeing, raking, hedge clipping, border trimming, grass cutting and pruning is a sort of religion for my parent, second only in importance to Methodism.

Before I joined the R.A.F. dad was never very happy if I mocked "chapel", but he always chuckled when I imitated the slow, deliberate voice of God number two - Mr Middleton. 'Good afternoon. Is your rhubarb backward, then bend it forward.'

I find "listening in" on Sundays very heavy going. Lots of classical music. Nothing by German composers of course, that wouldn't be patriotic! Serious talks, news and church services. Occasionally the Forces programme manages to lift the gloom with *"Jay Wilbur's Orchestra"*, *"Johnny Canuck's Revue"* and *"ITMA"*.

Ginger is looking forward to his next leave. 'I shall go up to town,' he says. 'I want to see the Agatha Christie play *"Ten Little Niggers"* at the *"St. James"*, and *"Revudeville"* at the *"Windmill"*, the theatre that boasts about never closing throughout the blitz.'

22nd/23rd, November, 1943. Berlin was again the target for tonight but S/L Roden and crew were not on the battle order.

The newspapers called this Berlin's heaviest pounding of the war, with over 2,300 tons of bombs dropped on the burning capital. 'We have had horrible hours,' the *"Aftonbladet"*'s Berlin correspondent reported. 'Berlin burned throughout the night. Industrial areas still burning from the raid last Thursday night were smashed again.'

One of the eleven Lancasters lost on this "Big City" trip was from 156 squadron. Captained by S/L D. C. Anset, D.F.C. - with whom I had done 15 operations at Waltham with 100 Squadron - JB 304, GT "Z", had lifted off at 16.55 on the 22nd from Warboys but failed to return.

So Godfrey, Anset and Scouse Walker who was flying with him, have all failed to return. Maybe there's some truth in the assertion that the Grim Reaper will get you in the end!

Germany is preparing for a fifth winter of war by mobilising all possible man power for military service, in some instances using men as old as fifty on the battlefronts. Every German man who can carry a weapon must now perform military service.

In northern Italy men in the classes 1924 and 1925 have been called up for service with the Germans. They will be used in the Coastguard and anti-aircraft defences.

German flak gunners have a new weapon at their disposal. Experts say it is the most effective and dangerous that has so far been used against us. It is a rocket driven shell!

LEAVE: - TAKEN AFTER FIRST TOUR OF BOMBING OPERATIONS

Seven days leave for me but a lousy period for Wickenby's two squadrons. Number 12 was the first to suffer when a Lancaster was lost on a Berlin raid, F/O C.E. Jones and crew in JB 537 PH "N". On 26th/27th November, with the "Big City" once again the target, 12 lost a further two aircraft, with PH "O" crashing on its return to Wickenby and PH "D" belly flopping on the approach to Binbrook. 626 suffered its first losses, F/Sgt. K. N. Windus, and crew, in DV 295 UM "M2" which crashed in Norfolk and F/Sgt. Kindt and crew in DV 388, UM "S2". Returning from Berlin that night, LM 362 UM "A2" crashed at nearby Lissington, and on the 29th of November another 626 Lancaster came to grief on a "cross-country" training exercise.

30th November, 1943. There has been a great public outcry because Sir Oswald Mosley, who founded and then led the British Union of Fascists in the early 1930's, has been released from detention on health grounds. Students of Bristol University have hung his effigy on a lamp post outside the Students' Union building, and miners in Yorkshire have protested vigorously. According to my father my brother-in-law has proclaimed, 'That so and so, he should be brought to trial not set free.' The Home Secretary, Herbert Morrison, is to tell Parliament why he has released Mosley from detention.

Photographs released to the newspapers show what we did to Hamburg in July, and what we did seems to have resulted in the complete devastation of a once important city. Half a chimney leans at a crazy angle, a gutted church stands forlorn, a factory is a mere skeleton of bricks, and a street stretches out into the far distance with not one building standing. Everywhere there are mountains of rubble.

As my leave neared its end, early morning shivers and occasional sneezes turned into a real stinker of a head cold.

Mum, acting like a mother hen, clucked and fussed.

Dad contacted our doctor who took one look at me and promptly wrote out a chit, informing R.A.F. Wickenby that the overstaying of my leave was "legit".

I sweated and protested but Mum was adamant, caring nought about what that Harris person might think, say or do. I was going nowhere until I had recovered.

Three days later, with thick head and sore nose, I returned to Wickenby to find that S/L Roden and crew had taken off in Lancaster JA 864 "D2" on the 2nd of December for Berlin but had failed to return.

When the news was first conveyed to me I could not take it in. *Skipper and the rest of the chaps missing? Impossible! No way!* Surely my informants were mistaken.

But they were not, and when I was assured yet again that nothing had been heard from my crew since take off, I accepted the inevitable and tears began to flow - to the utter consternation of the members of a new crew who had already been allocated the beds recently occupied by George, Les, Tom, Ginger and Van.

Anger replaced shock and after I had roundly cursed the Almighty nightmares took over, which resulted in my being moved to an empty Nissen hut.

Before long I had become an embarrassment to 626 Squadron. Surplus to requirements I was sent away on yet more leave, unloved, unwanted and with no mention of the "gong" that Skipper had hinted at.

On the train journey home familiar faces appeared behind my closed eyes. Tom, weighed down by a scarf made of silk stockings and knickers, grimaced to reveal the gap in his teeth. Ginger, gaunt and weary, waved a boney hand. George, glancing up from the pages of a book, looked bewildered. Skipper, moustache bristling, eyed me fiercely, and, when his face dissolved, those of Anset, Walker and Godfrey took its place.

One face did not appear, however, that of the sergeant who had taken my place, and it failed to do so because I had never met him.

An hour's wait at Derby did nothing to improve my state of mind, and more memories held sway. I remembered W/O Lawrence, F/L Goldsmith and F/O Taylor who, with their respective crews, had also failed to return from Berlin. Wickenby had, in fact, suffered an unsustainable loss rate that night.

When Tutbury became Marchington and Uttoxeter gave way to Blythe Bridge, I began to wonder what might have been if I had not caught the cold that still lingered in my head.

Would I now be listed as 'missing'?

Dead possibly, or maybe a prisoner of war?

Would my parents have received the dreaded telegram?

On the other hand could I have done something that might have resulted in JA 864 D2 returning safely to base? Like informing Skipper for instance of the nearness of heavy flak or searchlights at some point en route to the target, a warning that would have had him altering course by the merest fraction.

If I had been with my crew and not lying sweating in bed would I, benefitting from the experience of flying for seven months on "ops", have seen the night fighter in time to warn Skipper of its presence, if indeed it was a fighter's cannon shells that had resulted in "D" Dog's failure to return to Wickenby?

By the time the train clanked out of Etruria I was beginning to wonder why I had been spared and whether the misfortune that had overtaken my six comrades and my replacement could in some way be attributed to me.

CREW ROSTER: - TARGET FOR TONIGHT: - BERLIN.

Lancaster JA 864, "D2", on the 2nd/3rd December, 1943.

R.A.F. S/L G. A. Roden KIA	Pilot (Captain)
R.A.F. Sgt. H. A. Van Hal KIA	Flight Engineer
R.A.F. Sgt. L. C. J. Street KIA	Navigator
R.A.F. Sgt. T. R. Jackson KIA	Bomb Aimer
R.A.F. Sgt. G. H. Brittle KIA	Wireless Operator
R.A.F. Sgt. H. W. Whitmore KIA	Mid-Upper Gunner
R.A.F. Sgt. A G. Luke KIA	Rear Gunner

(KIA: - Killed in Action)

HEY, DON'T YOU REMEMBER?
You called me Al

PART THREE

"Genned Up"

Chapter 10

New Boots for Old

(Early Spring 1944)

The icy wind of winter blows unkindly from the sea and grains of sand whip smarting into my face. I grind my teeth grittily, convinced that January is not the best month of the year to be posted as an Instructor to this seemingly inhospitable Isle of Man. An airman, his face bluer than his uniform, who has assisted me thus far with my kit, comes to a sudden non-military like halt. He extends a finger through tattered mittens and points to a Nissen hut standing in secluded isolation near to grass waving dunes.

'That's yours, flight sergeant,' he shouts. 'That's your hut.'

I thank him for his help but doubt if my words reach his balaclava covered ears. He beats his arms, freed at last, against his great-coated sides, and returns to the main camp.

I open the door to the hut and find that the grim unfriendly look of the exterior is echoed by the interior. There are three beds spaced well apart, three lockers, half a dozen unclean curtain-less windows, and the ubiquitous coke-burning stove. Neatly folded blankets lie on two of the beds but the third is already made up.

I dump my kit on one of the beds, stamp my frozen feet, and am wondering what sort of chaps my hut mates will turn out to be when the door swings open to admit a flight sergeant and a chilling blast of wind. Slamming the door shut he removes a large scarf from round his neck and blinks in my direction.

'Hi! So this is the bracing sea and mountain air, not to mention the gorgeous Manx scenery I've heard so much about!'

'It's the Isle of Man alright but I have yet to see a cat without a tail.'

'I'm Ted,' he laughs, introducing himself. 'Is this one free?'

'I guess so. I've only just arrived myself so I'm no wiser than you.'

We busy ourselves with bed making and the unpacking of kit, then head for the sergeants' mess. I haven't eaten since leaving Fleetwood in the early hours of this morning so I'm feeling quite peckish, and though the bubble and squeak I'm offered for late lunch looks stodgy it's welcome nevertheless. I can't say the same for the unidentifiable afters though, for the inedible mass looks like a sticky mix of bread and butter pudding and roly-poly.

'What's this place called?' asks Ted, pushing his half eaten afters to one side.

'Andreas.'

'Oh yes, of course, Andreas. D'you know what sort of kites we'll be flying?'

'Avro Ansons.'

'Limping Annies! Gosh, I trained on those. The undercarriage has to be wound up by hand you know. Many a sore knuckle I've had in the past but it won't be my hands that'll be suffering this time round.' And the malevolent laugh that accompanies the threat makes me feel rather sorry for Ted's future pupils.

'Why do you call them "Limping Annies"? I've never heard that expression before.'

'Because of their uneven engine note. Have you just finished your first tour?'

'Yes, I was on Lancs.'

'The heavy mob, eh? I was on Bostons. We used to hear some hair-raising things about Bomber Harris. What a ruthless old so and so he was, and that sort of thing.'

'I don't know about ruthless but if he ever heard our moans he'd have been in no doubt as to what we thought of his choice of targets.'

'All the big cities, eh?'

'Yes. I arrived at my squadron in time for the Ruhr bashes, then Hamburg and when I finished it was Berlin.'

My new found colleague and I while away the evening playing shove-halfpenny and darts, but when yawns begin to take the place of conversation we elect to have an early night.

'Gosh but I'm cold,' sighs Ted, climbing into bed. 'I must get some more blankets from stores tomorrow, this really is brass-monkey weather.'

I agree and point to the other bed. 'I wonder when our room-mate will honour us with his presence.'

'I don't know and I don't much care.' And with that terse comment Ted switches off the lights.

The fingers on my watch glow a pale green as they point luminously to one o'clock. I lie, miserable in my bed, listening to strange noises emanating from the region of the unknown one's bed space. Muffled curses accompany growls and grunts, and when these are followed by the sound of running water I wonder if the hut is about to be engulfed by the Irish Sea. I make no attempt to find out but bury my head instead under coarse blankets, and remember nothing more until my time-piece indicates that it will soon be three-fifteen. I lie quite still and listen to yet more weird noises and foul language. I also have Ted's snores to contend with. My head remains firmly under the blankets for I can now hear something being dragged across the floor.

Ye gods! Is the unknown one a mass murderer? Am I about to become his next victim?

A shiver runs through my sparse frame and I know that my hair would be standing on end if it were not trapped beneath a pillow. Gradually, as the noises subside, I stop holding my breath and drift into a welcome sleep.

My luminous watch has lost its luminosity for it is eight-thirty and time for breakfast. In the mess, the station warrant officer pauses by my side to enquire how Ted and I are 'settling in'.

'Fine, thank you sir, but I didn't get much sleep.'

'Same here,' agrees my hut-mate. 'Talk about things that go bump in the night! I don't know what that chap who shares our hut was up to but he woke me up on at least three occasions.'

'Oh, that's Smithy. Sergeant Smith.' laughs the S.W.O. 'You mustn't take any notice of him. Being a regular you'll find he's not over fond of what he calls the "bits of kids" who've invaded his mess. He won't take kindly to you two that's for sure, you being flight sergeants and him still a sergeant after twenty years' service.'

'What does he do?' asks Ted, crunching on a piece of toast.

'Apart from guzzling beer, you mean? He's in charge of the stores. He's a real loner and very fond of company, just so long as it's his own. You'll find him propping up the bar most nights, and at lunch times as well for that matter. Never speaks to anyone apart from the barman and then it's only to order another pint. I don't know if you've heard the expression "he's got hollow legs", which is used to describe someone who can sink a pint or two, well I reckon whoever created it had Sergeant Smith in mind!'

Ted and I have spent most of today getting acclimatised to life at Andreas. On visiting sick bay for the customary "free from infection" check the M.O. informed us that Andreas held a proud record, that of having had more Waaf discharged from the service due to pregnancy than anywhere else in Training Command. He'd added, with a smile of resignation on his face, that no doubt Ted and I would keep up the good work, and if that was our intention we might like to know that a tomb in the village churchyard had a shape so bed like and a scroll so pillow like, that it was immensely popular with both airmen and airwomen alike.

Tomorrow will see us airborne in the "Limping Annies", so Ted and I have retired early to bed in the hope of getting a good night's sleep. Stretching out contentedly under the additional blankets I've acquired I remember nothing more until I'm shaken rudely awake by someone who smells like a brewery. In the pale light of the moon I see that my assailant is a sergeant, and from the way he's behaving I assume it is Smithy.

'Are you the bugger who piddled in my gum boots last night?' slurps the drunken one.

From the direction of Ted's bed I hear a faint snigger, which gradually swells to a roar of laughter as the accusation intensifies.

'Well? Was it you what did it, or was it that laughin' hyena over there?'

With that final accusation the drunken one lurches towards his bed, protesting all the while about, 'Kids, bits of bloody kids.'

Darkness reigns but not quite supreme for a shaft of moonlight picks out Sergeant Smith's bed. I lie silent, wide awake, unable to sleep. Suddenly he sits upright, snorts himself awake and feels tentatively for the floor with his right foot. I raise my head and watch a pantomime unfold. Smithy's left leg has joined his right and he's crouching on all fours, searching for something under his bed. He's muttering all the while and his language is so foul it's a wonder the moonlight doesn't turn blue. Then, with a snort of triumph, he drags out a gum boot, and this is followed by the sound of running water as he empties his bladder. More curses follow but after several failed attempts he manages to prop the makeshift gazunder against the wall of the hut. Returning unsteadily to his bed he collapses on a pile of blankets. Within seconds he snores himself into oblivion.

This morning I've done a couple of flights in one of the Ansons and am now trying to implant a little aircraft recognition into the minds of would be air-gunners. I hold aloft a model of an Fw190, and am pointing out its characteristics when the door opens to admit an excited looking Ted.

'I've come to say cheerio, Al!' he shouts, waving a travel warrant.

'Cheerio!' I stare at him in astonishment. 'Cheerio! You've only just arrived!'

'True, very true, but you know the R.A.F. Give 'em half a chance and they'll cock anything up! It seems that I shouldn't have been sent here in the first place, I'm supposed to be in Northern Ireland. So it's pretty much a case of hail and farewell old chap, for I'll soon be off to catch that funny little train into Douglas.'

'But you can't go!' My protest is so violent I almost bring down a Bristol Blenheim that dangles from the ceiling. 'Have a heart. You can't leave me alone in that Nissen hut with Smithy.'

'Sorry about that old bean but don't blame me, blame the Air Ministry. Anyway, you should look on the bright side, Sergeant Smith can't keep on peeing in his wellies.'

'Why not?'

'Because he'll rot 'em if he does, and then he'll have nothing to pee in.'

'Huh! That's what you think, but you're wrong. He most certainly will have something, he's not the sergeant in charge of stores for nothing!'

The "Capetown Castle".

Chapter 11

See Naples and...

(Late Spring 1944)

Reclining on one of the many decks of the *"Capetown Castle"*, a Union-Castle Mail Steamship vessel of some twenty seven thousand tons, I idle away time by watching two shapely and agile Waaf indulge in a game of deck tennis. They are all smiles and nubility these girls, and when one of them bends to retrieve the quoit her facial features remind me of a Waaf who had departed on the same day as myself from R.A.F. Andreas.

That young lady's two official duties had been to issue parachutes to trainee aircrew, and to record take-off and landing times of the Anson aircraft. In her spare time her unofficial duty had been to accommodate as many airmen as possible on the bed like tomb in the village churchyard, an exercise that had resulted in her becoming with child. The unfortunate lass had absolutely no idea who had fathered her future offspring, but as she'd walked awkwardly ahead of me, lugging a suitcase through the main gate, there was no doubting the pregnancy which had resulted in her discharge.

I thought at the time what a rotten shame it was and the feeling has lingered. By now she will have given birth to an unwanted baby and be back in the bosom of her family, a family whom, according to a caustic comment she'd once made in my hearing, she'd joined the W.A.A.F. to escape.

A quoit lands at my feet.

'Sorry. Could I trouble you?' one the charmers requests with a smile.

I toss the rubber ring to her and reflect that though her features are similar to those of the Andreas Waaf her shape is very different.

Ah well! Life, as I have often realised of late, can be surprisingly cruel.

Tearing my eyes away from the sporting beauties, I find that there's not much else to see but the sea, apart from the other vessels that make up our convoy. I'm not bothered though because on the "*Castle*" we are not short of things to do, and there's plenty of space in which to do them because the ship is nowhere near full. The reason for this, as the "know-alls" had been quick to point out when we'd set sail from Liverpool, was that if there was any trouble with U-boats ours would be the ship that picked up survivors.

This is the life! Eat, drink, sleep and sunbathe, for tomorrow we may... I'm on a Mediterranean cruise that is all the more enjoyable because it is free, with the government picking up the bill. To add to the enjoyment a jazz group performs daily. It is part of a regimental band that's on board, and when it isn't playing the rest of us are - at "housey-housey".

A boxing tournament has been arranged. So, having learned a few tricks from a navigator pal of old who had been a sparring partner for the heavyweight champion Tommy Farr, I've put my name down to fight in the ten to ten and a half stone class, but only after a close inspection of the opposition has revealed they are a seemingly clueless lot. I select a pair of boxing gloves and note with some satisfaction that there are a number of Waaf and Wrens amongst the spectators. Huh! I'll show them a thing or two!

To polite applause, my opponent and I enter the ring. We touch gloves and I'm perturbed when I see that he's a lithe, good-looking chap, with the cross of Lorraine emblazoned on his vest. Strange, I hadn't noticed him before; in fact, I was not even aware that there were any "Free French" bods on board.

'Ladies and Gentlemen,' announces the master of ceremonies. 'This is a welterweight contest of three, three minute rounds. He then introduces me as representing the R.A.F, and for France, Henri somebody or other, who hails from Nancy.'

Representing the R.A.F indeed! What a load of codswallop, I'd only entered for a lark. Nancy, eh? Let's hope he fights like one.

Clang!

The noise from a hand-bell has hardly faded before a left fist sinks into my solar plexus, and a right connects with my chin. I had danced out of my corner in sprightly fashion to meet my adversary but already I'm flat-footed and back pedalling.

I throw a left. It misses by a mile and a glove the size of a house flattens my nose. I'm bleeding, my eyes are full of tears. I can hardly see my opponent. I go into a clinch, hang on for dear life and ignore the order to break.

The referee pulls us apart. I search in vain but am unable to find the Frenchie.

Ouch! That hurt. I think it was a right jab.

Oops! That hurt even more. I'm sure this chap has secreted rocks in his gloves.

Clang!

I collapse on my stool and advice fills my ears. 'Keep your guard up'. 'Watch his left.'

Clang!

Round two sees me attacking with fists flailing. I fail to connect; in fact I have yet to lay a glove on my opponent. It's different for him though, he's got my distance and his two handed hitting has me reeling. *Please ring the bell, please.* He's an all action fighter this chap, he's also Free French, free with both his fists and verbal taunts.

Clang!

'Look out for his left,' I'm advised.

How can I when I can't see him, let alone his fists?'

Clang!

It's the third and last round. Heaven be praised!

Ahhh! Surely he should be disqualified, that punch was way below my belt!

Ouch, that wasn't, it was on my chin.

Get into a clinch, you fool! Impossible, I'd have to find him first.

What the heck am I doing on the floor? Stand up you clot, don't you realise that the honour of the Royal Air Force is at stake! Get on your feet.

I'm up and holding on.

Clang!

The bell has sounded for the last time but it's the ref who has to disentangle himself from my desperate embrace, not my suave smiling opponent who, dancing round the ring, is acknowledging the roar of the crowd.

I slink towards my corner, bloodied and bowed, eyes downcast in order to avoid the looks of contempt that I know will be showing in the eyes of those Waaf and Wrens I'd been so keen to impress. After some kind person has removed my boxing gloves I retire from the ring vowing, through bruised and blood-stained lips, to forever detest the French and to never again indulge in a bout of fisticuffs.

This morning I've been shaken rudely awake and put ashore with some twenty other R.A.F. aircrew at Oran. But the authorities have made a mistake, dropped a clanger in fact, for we should have remained on board and not left the ship until it reached Algiers.

With the Capetown Castle a mere speck on the horizon some other mode of transport has to be found, and an ancient lorry is commandeered to take us to the rail depot. There, we are loaded into wagons, which, according to labels written in French, are meant to hold eight horses.

The uncomfortable journey of some forty-eight hours is made almost bearable by dramatic views of distant mountains, and enlivened by the occasional appearance of wild dogs that become targets when free reign is given to the Smith and Wesson "thirty-eights" issued to us in Blighty. The immediate foreground becomes full of spurting sand and contorting hounds. Alas, no hits are registered! Which is a pity, because "*Canus Africanis*" might have made a pleasant change from our diet of bully beef and hardtack.

After Algiers has shimmered and finally disappeared like an ethereal white mirage in the early morning light, a rather disreputable vessel called the "*Banfora*" sails grudgingly, with a marked list to port, towards Naples. On board my disgruntled colleagues and I are missing the good food, undisturbed sleep and spacious comfort of the "*Capetown Castle*", for on this tub the grub is disgusting and the comfort non-existent. Any attempt to fall asleep in the low ceilinged hold full of perspiring bodies swinging to and fro in hammocks is doomed to failure, which is mainly due to the foul stink left behind by the previous cargo - a herd of goats. To add to our misery we R.A.F. bods have been detailed to man the ship's Oerlikon twenty millimetre automatic antiaircraft cannon, in shifts of four hours on, four hours off.

Some of the chaps do manage forty winks but for me sleep is out of the question because my hammock hangs next to a cabin occupied by a member of the ship's crew. He's a half-naked mountain of a man, a lascar with black stumps for teeth and a completely bald pate. Thirsting continually for two things, booze and trouble, the man never sleeps, and because of him neither do I.

Tired and cheesed off I'm finding it well-nigh impossible to keep my eyes open. Searching the sky for hostile aircraft I doze fitfully and my mind wanders when I gaze beyond the blue horizon in the direction of North Africa, where my stay in Algiers had been so tantalisingly brief I'd found no time to search for Hedy Lamarr - which means I'll never know if Charles Boyer really did invite that sexy lady to go with him to the Casbah.

I yawn, then give vent to my feelings by spitting at a gull that has used me as a target.

Four hours on, four hours off! I scratch, stretch, and sigh with relief for my stint will soon be over. 'Please, god of sleep, Morpheus, or whatever your name is, please let the slant eyed horror be on duty and not in his cabin for the next four hours.'

'Wakey, wakey,' shouts my relief, tapping me on the shoulder. 'Time for you to get some proper shut-eye.'

'Fat chance,' I grumble.

'Things should be OK down there from now on,' laughs my informant, a flight sergeant navigator.

'How come? Has Ulysses rid us of the monster?'

'No. Some of the chaps were so fed up they complained to the Chief Mate and he's given our friend a right rollicking.'

I slip and slide down several flights of metal stairway in joyful anticipation of an undisturbed sleep.

The hold is indeed peaceful, in spite of the din from the propeller shaft, and I undress as quickly as I can, fearful of making a sound. Clambering with some difficulty into my hammock I swing gently to the ship's motion and am soon asleep.

I awake with a start. My hammock is swaying violently, propelled by two huge fists. Banana-sized fingers clenched tightly together sink into my ribs, assault my buttocks and lambaste my head. I'm frightened stiff and the misery is further compounded when my evil looking neighbour swigs from a bottle before spraying foul smelling liquid all over me.

'If I catch the yellow bellied bastard who ratted on me, I'll kill 'im.'

My hammock swings crazily. A mouth full of ugly, black, broken teeth looms so close I feel that I am about to be eaten alive.

Thump! Thump! Thump!

'If I catch the yellow bellied bastard who ratted on me, I'll kill 'im.'

Thump! Thump! Thump!

'If I catch the yellow bellied bastard who ratted on me, I'll...'

Mercifully the threats and blows come to a stop but only because some of his fellow crew members have overpowered the fiend, and dragged him away.

'Don't look back,' a voice warns as aching all over and black and blue to boot, I make my way slowly down the gangplank to disembark.

I ignore the advice, glance over my shoulder, and promptly wish I hadn't for leaning over the ship's rail is the lascar. The look in his eyes defies description. I shudder and press on.

'Told you not to look back,' says my friend the navigator. 'He was giving you the jettatura.'

'The what?' I query, clambering over the capsized wrecks of ships that provide a walk way to the quay.

'The jettatura, the evil eye! I hope you've got your coral horn or a piece of bone with you, because if you haven't you're as good as dead!'

A sergeant who shares my room here at Portici transit camp is complaining again. Nothing ever satisfies him. The food is bloody awful, the heat is unbearable, and he's convinced that the authorities have forgotten his very existence. The more he chunters the more he gets up my shirt for, with my posting imminent, I'm forced to stay put, something which prevents me from seeing the "sights" which abound in the area. My "colleague", on the other hand, has all the time in the world but he does nothing but moan. How I wish I could exchange places with him. I wouldn't spurn, as he does, the opportunity to visit Naples, or turn down the chance to see more of the aftermath of Vesuvius's recent eruption.

He has been on one "outing" though, to Pompeii or "Pompey" as he calls it, and he only went there because someone had told him about the brothel. Every conceivable position of "you know what" is painted on its walls he'd informed me on his return, before going on to complain about the hefty tip the guide had expected.

As for Vesuvius, huh, he won't go within a mile of it because he's had it on good authority that it will erupt again before long. He also says he won't be visiting a place up the road, Torre de Greco, del Greco, or something like that, because it's been covered over in lava more times than he's had hot dinners.

This Sunday morning, as I lie half naked on my bed, I hear from somewhere in the distance the lilting melody of "*I Cover the Waterfront*". The "seventy eight" shellac record from which it emanates is obviously well worn and badly scratched, but even though it is being played non-stop I find the melancholy tune infinitely more agreeable to the belly aching of my roommate.

Suddenly the complaining stops and the sergeant informs me that it's time for his little friends to have some grub.

'Here we go again,' I think, and smile to myself when a fly is swatted with a rolled up copy of a well-thumbed *"Illustrated"*.

With the deed done the magazine is tossed to the floor and, as it unfolds, I see that Poland's bald-headed premier, who adorns the cover, has suddenly acquired a blood stained nose. I roll over and watch as the fly is placed some two inches away from a crack situated in a corner of the room, where the wall meets the floor.

'There, that's a nice fat one for you,' says the fly killer, returning to his bed where he props himself up on one elbow and waits.

I too watch and wait. Within seconds two ants appear. They also watch and wait, before slowly advancing to inspect their free meal. Suddenly one of them makes a lightning thrust, and when this produces no response from the fly the second ant joins in. Eventually, having satisfied themselves that no resistance is forthcoming, the two return to their hidey hole.

Suddenly ants, dozens of them, are forsaking the safety of their hole in the wall. More close inspections of the fly are undertaken after which some of the braver chaps, or maybe they are fearless girl ants, crawl underneath the dead creature. One of their number, probably a boss-ant, then makes for home and the funeral cortege follows with ants carrying, pushing and shoving with all of their might. Slowly the two inches to the wall is traversed and then, after its wings have been removed to facilitate ease of entrance, the fly disappears into the hole together with the ants.

'Wait for it!' The command is followed by a shout of triumph from the sergeant when an ant re-appears. 'I knew it, there's always one of them comes out for a quick peek, just to make sure a rival ant tribe isn't about to attack.'

Having been informed that my posting has been put back twenty-four hours I have gladly accepted the offer of a lift into nearby Naples, and boy does it stink! If I should die here and now it will be from asphyxiation brought on by the incredible number of foul smells assaulting my nostrils, not because of any "jettatura".

Mouth tight shut, I take in the sights but am obliged to keep to the main streets of the city for the side alleys are "Out of Bounds" to allied servicemen. This, I feel, is a great pity because they appear to be crammed with medieval buildings and ancient churches, whose elegant facades cry out for closer inspection. Everywhere, street traders vend their wares. Urchins of tender years offer me tyres swiped from a jeep, together with items that have fallen off the back of an army lorry. They also, but only rarely, offer legitimate "souvenirs de Napoli". Performing monkeys dance atop hurdy-gurdies, and the mechanical music competes with tenor voices singing Neapolitan bel canto to the accompaniment of mandolins. "*O Sole Mio*" and "*Santa Lucia*" bring joy to my ears.

Postings are what Portici is all about, and as I prepare to depart the issue of a topee helmet would appear to confirm the rumour that I'm destined for Egypt.

So, farewell Napoli. I've seen you and I haven't died!

Stumbling and cursing, for my body still aches from the attention paid to it by the "Free Frenchman" on board the "*Capetown Castle*", and more recently the lascar, I drag my heavy case and lumpy kit-bag over the upturned bottoms of boats, and laugh when I remember the "jettatura" warning. What a load of duff gen that had been.

I shake my head at silly superstition and slowly climb the gangplank of the ship that is to transport me to the land of the pharaohs. It's a tatty looking vessel that would certainly benefit from a coat of paint.

I pause to rest my weary bones and see, to my surprise, my erstwhile friend the navigator gazing down at me.

'Taking a chance aren't you,' he shouts, pointing with his finger at the name painted on the side of the ship. The combination of sun and sea water has taken its toll over the years but as I peer more closely the letters become clearer, and my stomach ties itself into knots. Ye gods, is it the "*Banfora*"?

Chapter 12

Shoe Shine Boy

(Early Summer 1944)

Cairo! Where East meets West. I'm billeted in a flat in the Heliopolis suburb of this sprawling city awaiting a transfer to the Bitter Lakes area where I'm to join the South African Air Force - or to be more exact I've become temporarily attached to that outfit. I have recently become acquainted with a certain Mike Platt, who, like me, is a flight sergeant. Mike completed his first tour of "ops" on Stirlings, and he's got the hard neck to compare them favourably with that most magnificent of all four-engined heavies - the Lancaster. Huh!

Cairo! Where presumably West meets East. Like all conscientious tourists the two of us have visited the Pyramids at Giza and stood in awe in front of the Sphinx, where Mike offered to teach me a "feelthy" poem about the inscrutable smile that adorns the face of that lion with the human head. He's a veritable cornucopia of naughty jokes and uncensored songs is my new found friend, his favourite ditty being one that is most uncomplimentary to the King and Queen of Egypt.

Poor Farouk! He's requested to hang his genitalia on a hook, and as for Farida - well, I'll draw seven veils over what servicemen are apparently yearning to do to her!

The Cairo natives everywhere offer worthless trinkets. Third-hand wristwatches, "jewelled" rings which Woolworths wouldn't sell and wallets in imitation leather. There are saucy postcards too, and judging from the almost obliterated naughty bits they date from the Great War of '14 - '18.

A sight of the wallets is guaranteed to get Mike's hackles rising for within five minutes of disembarking at Port Said an Arab had sold him just such an item, only to pinch it back again moments later. Happily we are not being pestered at this precise moment for being Englishmen, and therefore mad dogs, we have come out in the midday sun and are suffering the consequences.

I puff and pant as the heat becomes more and more unbearable, and scold myself for not taking the siesta recommended by knowledgeable airmen who have been stationed out here for yonks. My khaki shirt is fast turning black with sweat, and to add to my discomfort squadrons of flies alight continually on the exposed parts of my body.

'I wouldn't be surprised to find that swatting and flicking is a national sport in this country,' laughs Mike, fighting off a winged insect.

Quite without warning, a small boy confronts us. Agile in his white robe he moves backwards, clutching the tools of his shoe cleaning trade to his chest. He flashes a cheeky white toothed smile in my direction. 'Hey Johnny, you want shoe-shine? Me very good, best shoe-shine boy in Cairo.'

'Scram! Clear off!' I say, with a lethargic wave of my hand.

The boy ignores me, and as I admire his sinuous body movements I suggest to Mike that we could well be gazing upon a ritual thousands of years old. A shoe-shine performance the like of which King Tut himself might well have witnessed.

'Yeah,' scoffs my companion. 'What puzzles me is where the devil he gets his energy from.'

The boy gyrates a while longer. Then, slowing to a stop, he asks again if we want our shoes shined.

'No, scram, push off,' I say.

'You want my sister? She fourteen, very sexy.'

'I'm getting tired of this cheeky little so and so. What d'you suggest we do about him?' asks Mike.

'Give him a bloody good clout.' The advice comes from an army sergeant who happens to be passing. 'It's the only language these little buggers understand. In future you should wear the brothel creepers you'll no doubt have been issued with, they don't need blacking.'

We have no need to act on his advice, however, because his arrival has resulted in the boy scurrying into one of the many dark, forbidding alleys which abound in the area. I peer apprehensively, and am not surprised to see that they are marked "Out of Bounds" to servicemen.

'Our dancing friend showed a healthy respect for the army,' grins Mike, 'far more than he shows for us.'

'Yeah, perhaps the little so-and-so wouldn't have pestered us if our knees were brown. Phew, but it's hot. What do you fancy doing tonight?'

'I don't mind. Just as long as I'm nice and cool doing it.'

'How about going to the Eden, the casino we visited last week?'

'No thanks. I object to buying coloured water at extortionate prices for wenches who are supposed to provide us with female companionship. All they do is simper and if you try to hold their hand they shy away. It wouldn't be so bad if they could speak English.'

'Yeah, but what girls they are! Real beauties, sort of half French, half Arab.'

'You make 'em sound like they're bred for the race track.' Mike laughs, flicking at a fly that has made a six-point landing on his Adam's apple. 'Why don't we try and find the joint Taffy mentioned, the one that sounded like something out of a Hollywood gangster flick? You remember him telling us about it, don't you? They slide open a grille and give you the once over before opening the door to let you in.'

'Um, I do recall him saying something about some such place. Didn't he say you have to be a member?'

'Yeah, but surely we could get someone to sign us in. I don't want to leave Cairo until I've seen the sacred donkey do its tricks.'

'You want shoe-shine, Johnny?'

Bloody hell, the infidel is back!

'You want my sister? She very good. Knows her stuff.'

Mike, with a display of energy that makes a mockery of the heat, grabs hold of our tormentor. He shakes him violently, cuffs him about the head, and orders him to clear off.

The boy breaks free and retrieves the utensils of his trade which are scattered on the pavement. Shouting what I assume to be obscenities he moves away to the seclusion of one of the blacked out alleys, from where he gesticulates in our direction.

A sense of unease that I had felt earlier returns. I search for some support, should the situation turn ugly, but there is none. Increasing our pace we cover a couple of hundred yards in double quick time.

'Phew! I think we can slow down.' Mike pants, glancing over his shoulder. 'I don't think we are being followed.'

I am only too happy to oblige for the exertion has left me breathless, and the few hairs of an embryo moustache adorning my upper lip feel quite damp. My feet are excessively hot, and my knees are turning fiery red not the required brown.

'This area looks vaguely familiar,' says my friend, screening his eyes from the sun. 'If my memory isn't playing tricks I think we're near to the Tipperary club. D'you you fancy a cool drink?'

'You want shoe-shine, Johnny?'

The undernourished urchin, clad in a robe that is no longer white, performs an arabesque in front of us. He has once again put his knowledge of Cairo's back alleys to good use.

'Right my lad, you've asked for this.' But when Mike lashes out the little pest sways out of harm's way. Using one of his brushes as a sling he aims a jet of black fluid at my friend.

'You bloody little heathen, I'll kill you!' screams Mike, as liquid blacking flows down from his forehead to his nose, mouth and chin, from whence it drips down to blacken his khaki tunic and shorts before finishing up on the toe cap of one of his shoes.

'I'll kill you! I'll bloody well kill you, you 'orrible little sod. Just wait until I get my hands on you, I'll kill you!'

But the "'orrible little sod" has no wish to die. Within seconds he has disappeared and there is no bloody little heathen for Mike to get his hands on, let alone kill.

Chapter 13

A Bitter Tale

(Mid-Summer 1944)

With the completion of a low level "cross-country" and bombing exercise our flying for the day is over and I am trying to relax on burning hot sand under a relentless Egyptian sun.

Doing my best to ensure that I tan evenly I roll over onto my stomach in time to see an airman shuffling by. Little more than a skeleton in khaki-drill he's a pathetic figure, a mere shadow of the chap I first became acquainted with in Cairo two months ago.

'Poor blighter,' I sympathise, as he makes for the canvas construction that is our latrine.

'That's Walters isn't it, what's wrong with him?' asks Dusty, with whom I share a tent here at Kabrit, a satellite of 70 O.T.U., Shandur.

'Dysentery, I reckon. Gyppo gut, non-stop diarrhoea. That's his second visit to the karzy since we've been lying here.'

'I'm glad I'm not in his brothel creepers. I wouldn't fancy having to make continuous visits to that foul stinking place.'

Dusty's comment is only too true for our latrine is both foul and stinking.

Basic would best describe the place with its rough wooden plank suspended over a yawning trench. There's always a revolting smell, and privacy is non-existent for the plank is invariably full of airmen seated side by side jostling for position. On arrival at the camp I'd avoided the place for several days, but in the end an insistent clamour from my bowels had triumphed over a queasy stomach. To make matters worse flies gather there in their hundreds. They lay siege to parts private, which always places me on the horns of a dilemma. Do I lift one of the hands that are my only means of support in order to brush away the little horrors, thereby increasing my chance of falling into the miasmal muck below, or do I hang onto the plank with both hands and endure excruciating torment as my scrotum is used for circuits and bumps?

My decision never varies and I've yet to end up in the mire!

'Filthy bloody things,' I moan, as one of the "terror fliegers" lands on my invitingly large nose.

'It's a vicious circle,' says Dusty, who is apparently on the same wavelength as myself. 'The 'orrible creatures enjoy themselves in our bog before flying off to the mess where they settle on the food. Little wonder so many of the chaps complain of bellyache.'

An odour, almost as unpleasant as that from our own latrine, wafts over us.

'They're at it again,' I complain. "They" being the locals who perform menial tasks about the camp. White-robed characters who gather together daily at this hour to relieve themselves upwind.

'Come on then,' cries Dusty, rising to his feet. 'We can escape from it by swimming out to the raft.'

I pull a face but he refuses to be put off.

'Stop fussing,' he says. 'It's a piece of cake. Just remember what I've taught you and you'll be fine.'

My stomach churns as he speaks. Little does my swimming instructor know how much misery his words instil in me. I've always wanted to be able to swim but fear grips my heart the moment I come into contact with water, and it makes no difference whether it's the public swimming baths back home or this Bitter Lake in Egypt.

'Come on,' Dusty insists. 'It's less than one hundred yards, and you know you won't sink because of the amount of salt in the water.'

'Oh won't I, just watch me.' But my words fail to reach his ears for he is already "crawling" with great vigour towards the raft.

I'm debating whether sun bathing in a foul atmosphere is preferable to attempting to swim in a lake full of salt when a shout of encouragement from Dusty helps make up my mind. I make for the water's edge, wade out up to my waste but put off any further action by pausing to watch a ship sail majestically through the sands of the desert. Well that's how it appears to me for the water of the lake is not visible from my vantage point. All I can see is sand and ship.

Dusty has reached the raft. He beckons and when the smell from the Arab encampment increases I thrust myself forward and attempt to breast stroke. Alas, despite the vast quantities of salt, I sink. With arms and legs thrashing wildly my feet search for the bed of the lake, and when they finally make contact I stand up and search for my goal. Oh heck, the raft looks further away than it did before.

Full of determination I fill my lungs with air, and immediately wish I hadn't for the stink sickens me. Oh boy! Am I between the devil and this deep blue lake!

Come on, you wet weekend, put into practice what Dusty's taught you. Push both hands forward and together from the chest. There, that's easy enough. Now bend both knees, draw up your feet, and swim. Yuk, why did I open my big mouth?

I spit out a quantity of very bitter water, wipe my eyes with the back of my hands, and remember more enjoyable breast strokes. Another determined attempt to swim fails because of a complete lack of synchronisation between my mind and body. Despite Dusty's earlier reassurance that I am in a salt water solution so concentrated that I cannot sink, I do so! With an effort bordering on the superhuman I perform a variety of strokes that bear little resemblance to swimming, yet they move me forward a little. But this is not my lucky day for when some miserable wretch of an airman collides with me my head submerges. Fighting for breath I surface, turn over onto my back, and float. Oh, blessed relief!

Please dear gods, help me. Please Neptune, or any other deity with water connections, command the current to carry me out to the raft.

I bob up and down and just as my confidence begins to grow, I sink. For absolutely no reason at all, I sink. My eyes, ears, nose and throat are filled once again with salt water.

'Help! Help! I'm drowning!'

Any moment now my past life will flash before my eyes. I'll be coming up for the third time and that'll be curtains. An arm encircles my waist.

'Oh thank god you came, Dusty.' I cry, for it is his arm that supports me. 'I was drowning!'

'Drowning my eye! I doubt even a pillock like you could drown in six inches of water. Why were you swimming - if that's the right word to describe your crab-like antics - parallel to the shore?'

Without more ado he propels me out to the raft where I cling thankfully to its sides. I breathe in great gulps of reasonably fresh air and reflect on how wonderful it is to be alive. With my head and shoulders above the surface of the water I feel safe because the rest of my body is in contact with the raft.

An airman, tired of sun bathing, dives gracefully into the water. I admire his swallow like performance and occupy the space he's vacated.

Oh boy, this is the life! I close my eyes, stretch out languorously and try my best to dismiss the nagging thought of how I'll get back to the shore.

Come on sun, do your stuff! It does, and my body starts to sting and smart. I sit up and discover to my horror that my arms, chest, stomach, thighs and tops of legs are covered with a multitude of cuts. Blood oozes from these angry looking wounds, and as the sun burns and the salt dries I writhe in misery.

'Hey!' I shout. 'Look what's happened.'

The other chaps sit up and inspect me. 'Did you float under the raft?' one of them asks.

'Yes,' I cry, thrashing about in agony as sun and salt act together in cruel unison.

'Huh, it's true what they say, there is one born every minute! This raft's been here since the year dot and the underside is covered with razor sharp barnacles. Come on chaps, we'd better get this head-case to the M.O.'

Without further ado, a posse of swimmers come to my aid and I'm conveyed funeral style over the lake to sick bay, where a medical orderly dabs at the affected parts with a lotion that looks suspiciously like gentian violet.

'Good grief,' laughs Dusty, sticking his head through the tent flap. 'You look like an ancient Briton covered all over in woad.'

'Is that better than being covered all over with sweet violets?' I quip, piling on the self-pity. 'When you bring grapes on your next visit will you make sure they are black and seedless. And no flowers please, by request. Oh yes, one other thing, I prefer toffees to chocolates.'

'All you'll get from me is a swift kick up the arse and a swimming manual. When is the M.O. throwing you out?'

'Never, I hope. I doubt I'll ever fly again.'

'Hate to disillusion you, my friend, but we have an exercise at six tomorrow morning. So you'd better pull your finger out!'

Sergeant Walters, skeletal in his khaki-drill, returns from yet another visit to the latrine. He pushes past Dusty and climbs awkwardly on to his bed.

'Nice try,' he says, giving me a sickly smile, 'but if they won't send me back home in my state, you don't stand an earthly!'

"Knobbly Knees" Egypt 1944 (Author far right).

Chapter 14

Dario

(Late Summer 1944)

Summer has turned into early autumn and my Egyptian tent has changed to something similar in Italy. This transformation has been achieved by flying for thirteen hours forty minutes in a Dakota aircraft from Cairo West to Pescara, with stops en route at Malta, Rome and Bari. The outlook therefore is no longer desert sand and Suez Canal but a newly constructed airstrip and the Adriatic Sea.

Dusty is here with me and we will be flying as members of the same crew with the South African Air Force. Coincidentally, my squadron number has not changed. Twelve months ago I was flying with number 12 Squadron R.A.F. Bomber Command. Now, it's the same number but of the S.A.A.F. and Desert Air Force, with its Springbock astride a winged bomb and Primus in Acien (First into battle) emblem. Before long, if the weather remains favourable, I will be starting my second tour of operations over German occupied territory. This time, however, the targets will be in Italy, and they will be clearly visible for I shall be flying by the light of day.

Within hours of our arrival at Pescara an Italian lad offered his services as a sort of "batboy", an offer we gladly accepted. Since then he has relieved Dusty and I of all domestic chores. He makes our beds with extreme care, always making sure that lizards have not secreted themselves between the sheets, and fetches and carries with alacrity.

With our approval he has organised his close relations into a support group. His mother is our laundress, his aunts are bearers of fruit in baskets and vino in bottles, his sister fills us with desire and the lad himself supplies us with eggs, cheese and a hard but pleasant tasting bread. Consequently the overall quality of our food has improved, and we are no longer reliant on standard mess fare. This close contact with an Italian family has also improved our knowledge of their language, with uova, pane, formaggio, pasta chutta, late, frutta and vino replacing eggs, bread, cheese, macaroni, milk, fruit and wine.

The services performed are not gratis but the cost is negligible for Dario, that's the name of our "little treasure", is over the moon when presented with worn out khaki shirts, shorts and socks, and his luminous brown eyes glow with gratitude when we reward him with the occasional tin of cigarettes. He acts as if the latter were the crown jewels, not the foul tasting evil smelling *"Springbok"* and *"Cape to Cairo"* brands that are gifted to us by the S.A.A.F. authorities. The delight he shows makes me realise that cigarettes are extremely hard to come by in Italy.

'Anyone for Chieti?' a S.A.A.F. wireless-op shouts, sticking his head round the flap of our tent.

'Chi, what?' I ask.

'Chieti.'

'Sure.' says Dusty, answering for the both of us for he knows that I am as keen as he is to see the "sights".

We clamber aboard a truck and head for the town which we are assured is one of the most attractive in the Abruzzo region of Italy. Determined to miss nothing of the scenery, I grasp the side of our transport for support and peer over the top of its cab.

On reaching the outskirts of Pescara my attention is drawn to a number of Italian civilians seated on a bench outside a low roofed building. To my surprise there is a South African sergeant amongst them. The airman's compatriots, my fellow travellers, do their best to attract his attention but he affects not to see them.

'What's he sitting there for?' I ask.

'He's awaiting his turn.'

'His turn for what?'

'A knock off. It's a brothel, and it seems to me like he'll have to wait a long time for his bit of grumble and grunt. There are nine Eyeties in front of him in the queue and there's only one woman employed there.'

'Really! How do you know?'

'Ah, that would be telling.'

The chap who had invited us to visit Chieti is flabbergasted. 'Bloody hell,' he cries. 'Ten blokes! The poor woman won't know whether she's been punched, bored or counter-sunk by the time that lot have finished with her!'

'And she'll make the princely sum of two hundred lire, for the going rate is twenty lire a go,' says our informant.

'Two hundred lire! That's roughly the equivalent of an English quid,' gasps Dusty. 'For...'

I do not hear the rest of his comment because our coloured driver has put his foot down. He's driving as if there is no tomorrow and I'm forced to hang on for dear life as the bends in the road become more and more acute.

Then, to my surprise, I'm not looking at delightful scenery, but at the disc of a wheel revolving at speed only inches from my face. I cling grimly to the side of the truck with one hand but when the vehicle squeals to a stop I find myself lying in a heap at the side of the road.

Several of the chaps come to my aid and after inspecting my limp arm they decide to abandon the sightseeing and elect to return to camp. I thank them for their consideration, apologise for ruining the excursion, and survey my wrist which feels very tender in the area where I fractured it a couple of years ago.

We return to Pescara and, when a herd of goats slows our progress, the sound of laughter and raised voices has me glancing over the side of the truck. The South African, who had earlier been awaiting his turn outside the brothel, is standing by the side of the road. Looking thoroughly cheesed off he does his best to ignore the questions fired at him.

'What's the matter, hadn't you got twenty lire?'

'Didn't she fancy you?'

'Had your contraccettivo got a hole in it?'

'She just bloody packed up, didn't she,' the airman scowls.

'Why was that?' someone asks.

'How should I know?'

'It's not surprising, she's probably heard all about you and didn't want her livelihood ruined.'

'He's a rum so and so, that one,' a S.A.A.F. pilot confides as the truck pulls away. 'Take my advice and stay well clear of him for he's completely round the bend. He detests you English, so don't fly with him if you can help it because if you do he'll speak in Afrikaans, which could prove to be a bit awkward in a tight spot. The Eyeties don't rate him either. The other night he got drunk as usual, and when the owner of the vino establishment eventually refused to serve him he emptied the contents of a thirty-eight into her door. He's lucky he didn't kill someone.'

'He's a hard case alright,' says another of the chaps, 'and never short of a smart arse retort. We were walking into camp yesterday when one of those floozies, you know the ones who hang around the entrance offering themselves for a few lire, asked him in broken English if he wanted something new. "Why?" he asked. 'What have you got? Leprosy?'

Back at camp a medic gives my wrist a cursory inspection. 'You've sprained it,' he says. 'Here, put your arm in this sling, you'll be fine in no time.'

I return to my tent and find that Dario has just arrived with our clean laundry.

'That was quick,' I say, with a smile.

He returns the smile and is about to leave when from my Jan Smuts "glory-bag", a free gift from the "Union", I produce some barley sugar.

'Grazie, molte grazie.' The lad's smile broadens as I present the sticky mess to him.

'Prego,' I reply, with that studied air of nonchalance only an expert linguist, someone like myself who has managed to learn ten words of the Italian language, can command.

Chapter 15

A Second Tour of Operations.

(Autumn 1944)

The medic's diagnosis that followed the aborted Chieti excursion was spot on for my wrist was indeed "fine" within a matter of days, a return to full fitness which coincided with the squadron embarking on a non-stop spell of bombing in support of the Eighth Army.

Gun emplacements on the "*Gothic Line*" were our initial targets, and I soon realised that I was "dicing with death" again when one of our aircraft was destroyed by enemy flak at the end of August.

After the capture of Fano, which was quickly followed by that of Pesaro, the announcer on the Eighth Army's "fighting man's radio" reported that our aerial bombardment had killed hundreds of Germans.

The enemy was, however, determined to hold on to Rimini and day after day, occasionally twice in one day, we bombed areas to both the south and west of the town. On the 4th of September heavy flak greeted our arrival, and, though holed by shrapnel, we successfully bombed our target - an enemy strongpoint. On the 9th of September tragedy struck, but this time on the ground, with seven men losing their lives when a Marauder blew up while a bomb was being fused.

Taking off at 08.00 on the 10th of September our Marauder "R" was damaged over the target, as were four other aircraft, even though the flak was only moderate in my estimation. Later that same day we took off at 15.40 in "Z", flying in number three position in the usual box of four aircraft but this time we returned unscathed.

Doing our best to avoid the republic of San Marino - perched on the edge of Monte Titano, some fourteen miles from the Adriatic - we continued to bomb the Rimini area: twice on September the 11th, once on the 12th, twice on the 13th, and on the 14th we dropped anti-personnel bombs on enemy troops one thousand yards ahead of our own troops.

Ten-tenths cloud over the target resulted in us being recalled to base on the 15th but we hit our targets on the 16th, 17th and 18th. The Eighth Army captured Rimini on the 21st of September, which saw us turning our attention to the Ravenna area where our bombs overshot the target – a road bridge, to which we returned the following day with more success. On the 26th of September, flying in Marauder "S", the target was San Angelo, a hamlet full of enemy troops, vehicles, and other equipment.

This "operation" proved to be our last from Pescara airfield which had become a quagmire due to incessant heavy rain. All flying ceased, and I spent my time attending lectures or on leave in Rome.

Two promotions now came my way. First, on the 9th October, 1944, to Warrant Officer, and then - following an interview with the exceedingly high-ranking "boss" of Desert Air Force at Caserta, where I lied in my teeth about being fond of dogs, for he had a Labrador sitting at his feet - I became, on the 9th of December, 1944, a commissioned officer in King-George-the-Sixth's Royal Air Force.

R.A.F. Officers Cap Badge.

Chapter 16

That Thin Blue Band

(Early Winter 1944)

Immaculate in my new uniform I come smartly to attention. After inspecting myself in a full length mirror I adjust the angle of my cap, check that my buttons are fastened, and perform half an about turn to satisfy myself that my trousers are not hanging at half-mast. I straighten an already straight tie, and make sure my shoes are shining like cherry blossom. This repeated checking of my person is not for narcissistic reasons. I am merely delaying the moment when, for the first time in my life, I shall present myself to the outside world as a gentleman. For that is what I have become, an officer and therefore, by definition, a gentleman!

I come to attention in front of the mirror knowing that the King has reposed a special trust and confidence in my loyalty, courage and good conduct, and that from henceforth I am to carefully and diligently discharge my duty. I am also to discipline in their duties inferior officers and airmen, and what is also apparent is that if I delay my entry into the officers mess here at Desert Air Force headquarters any longer I shall arrive too late for lunch. I execute one more careful check of my person, pluck up courage, and set forth.

Within seconds a hazard presents itself in the shape of an airman. How I wish the earth would open up and swallow me. It doesn't, so I prepare to accept his salute, his acknowledgement that I hold the King's commission.

Well I'll be blowed, he's ignoring me! This distinctly inferior person has turned his head and looked the other way!

I cannot allow this to happen, he must be disciplined, must be taught a lesson! But what sort of a lesson? And as I deliberate the culprit disappears from view, leaving me with a half raised right arm and egg on my face.

Normally an easy fitting size fifteen, my collar now holds my neck in a vice like grip. An uncontrollable twitch affects my right eye, and both of my knees have turned to jelly. Ahead of me, laughing and joking, a group of officers are approaching the mess. I mingle with them and enter a dining hall that is a sea of blue, the blue of uniforms, cigarette smoke and language. I make for the first available seat and immediately feel that I have become the centre of attention. I'm convinced that hundreds of pairs of eyes, critical and questioning, are focussing on me and on me alone!

'Soup, sir?' A waiter dances attendance.

'Yes, p, p, please.' Surely that's not my voice?

'Minestrone sir, or would you prefer tomato?'

Tomato! He's only suggested that because he thinks it will match the colour of my face.

'M, m, minestrone, please.' That's definitely not my voice, it can't be, I don't stutter!

'Very well, sir.'

Both of my eyes are twitching now. Nearly all the officers in here are aircrew, men with excellent vision. They are watching and waiting, anticipating my first clanger.

I'm licking my lips with a dehydrated tongue when to my dismay the seat opposite is occupied by a three ringed person, a Wing Commander no less! My desert-air-force of a mouth craves water and Winco seated opposite to me or not, I must quench the thirst. I reach for my tumbler, accidentally strike the rim a ringing blow, and watch with considerable trepidation as the glass rolls towards the superior one. To my relief it stops short, and my gaffe appears to have gone unnoticed. In fact the gentleman opposite is more interested in the menu than in my clumsy-clottedness. I retrieve the glass and attempt to fill it from an extremely large jug full of water. Though half blinded by smoke from countless cigarettes I manage to pour out a quantity of the lifesaving fluid.

An officer, on my immediate right, reaches out for a basket that contains bread rolls, and I'm replacing the water jug when his outstretched hand brushes against mine. Water spills out onto the table cloth and the linen darkens in front of the mighty one who now is most certainly aware of my presence. His handlebar moustache twitches and he withers me with a piercing glance.

'Your minestrone, sir.' The waiter deposits a bowl of steaming soup in front of me. Did he really have to emphasise the "sir"?

I spread a table napkin over my knees but they are knocking with such violence it falls to the floor. To steady myself I grip the edge of the table with my left hand before reaching down to retrieve the fallen object. En route my right hand makes contact with the haft of a table knife which promptly joins the napkin. With body bent double, and my head at table top level, I glance upwards as I grope.

The Wing Commander returns my gaze. His eyes have in them a look of utter disbelief. He is clearly unable to comprehend the lunatic antics of the bleary eyed idiot crouched before him. A pilot officer who is fast replacing P.O. Prune as the biggest clot in the R.A.F.!

A wine waiter fills the Winco's glass with vino rosso. He first sniffs then sips appreciatively at the wine.

I pick up my spoon and partake of the minestrone. After several successful transfers of soup from bowl to mouth I feel confident enough to take the one remaining bread roll from the basket. An officer to my rear chooses that moment to rise from his seat. The back of his chair comes into contact with mine and the jolt thrusts me forward, causing the roll of bread - which is firmly grasped in my hand - to torpedo the three ringed one's wine glass amidships. Vino spills out over the already wet table cloth, and when the glass topples it spills its blood-red contents into the lap of the bewildered one!

'I don't believe it! I just don't bloody well believe it!' The Wing Commander cries, jumping to his feet. Picking up his table napkin he dabs furiously at the large wet patch spreading over an embarrassing place on his trousers.

But I believe it, and I am also on my feet. Without more ado I race from the mess and do not stop until I reach the sanctuary of my billet. Numerous airmen have paid their respects but not one of them has had his salute returned, which is all to the good because I'm still clutching a bread roll in my right hand.

Xmas Dinner Menu, Officers Mess,
12 S.A.A.F. Squadron, Jesi, Italy.

Chapter 17

Papal Blessing

(Late 1944)

'You wouldn't know there was a war going on,' observes Dusty, referring to the Christmas menu that lists the various delicacies prepared for our dinner.

'There won't be for much longer.' Smithy, our wireless operator forecasts as he partakes of his hors d'oeuvres. 'Mark my words, it'll all be over by spring.'

Dusty eyes him scornfully. 'I've marked your words ever since you first joined our crew in Egypt. You claimed then that the war would soon be over so why are we stuck here in this backwater of an Italian village about to enjoy, and I say that with some feeling, this fifth or is it sixth Christmas of the war?'

'Monsano's not such a bad place, it's better than Pescara. You of all people should be pleased to be here, billeted as you are in the house of the beautiful Maria.'

'I still think it's grotty, apart from Miss Bonechi that is!' cries Dusty, turning his attention to Creme de Celeri.

'His beautiful Maria,' I scoff, sipping a creme de menthe, 'he hasn't got a snowball in hell's chance with her.'

'Now, now, Al, you can't blame him for having a crush on her. She is after all the most gorgeous bit of crumpet in the village.'

'Eh, less of the crumpet, let's have some respect for the young lady,' Dusty admonishes, wagging a finger.

Crumpet or not I'm forced to agree with Smithy. No other female in this village - perched atop a hill in central Italy - can hold a candle to the daughter of Senora Bonechi, whose "casa" is home to Dusty and myself.

Home? Well maybe that's stretching it a bit, for the place often resembles a stable more than a house.

'Who hasn't got a snowball in hell's chance with whom?' asks Dave, our skipper, his grin as quizzical as ever.

'Dusty, with the gorgeous Maria,' I say. Believe me no one will ever get to first base with her, her mother will see to that. I've never come across such a formidable woman. I don't know if you've seen her Dave, she's enormous, yet her husband is just a titch. She's voluble, volatile and vociferous, while he's placid and hen-pecked.'

'Can I have your portion of Christmas pud when we get to it?' Dusty interrupts. 'I doubt you'll have room for it having swallowed so large a dictionary!'

I ignore the sarcasm and continue with my gentle character assassination of our "landlady". 'The most innocent glance directed at her daughter brings forth a warning. It's in Italian of course but the message is clear. I'll say one thing for her though she's extremely hard working, so I suppose it's unfair to liken her place to a stable. She keeps it spotlessly clean, and is as "casa-proud" as my mum's house-proud back home.'

'The place really does become a stable at night, though,' laughs Dusty, 'when all the Bonechi animals get herded into the ground floor. You've never heard such a din! What with birds twittering, and Mussolini bleating.'

'Mussolini?' Dave raises an eyebrow.

'Yeah, the Bonechi's goat. Dusty claims it's animal noises that keep him awake at night but I know better. He can't sleep because the beautiful Maria is lying, innocent and virginal between her white sheets, only feet from him in the next room!'

As I toy with my celery soup Smithy picks up the menu and announces, in execrable French, that we shall shortly be partaking of, 'rotee de pork', sosso pommes and din dunno a la broche.'

'Well, I din-dunno!' cries a surprised Dusty. 'I din-dunno you were a linguist.'

A navigator seated at an adjoining table decides to emulate Smithy, and before long we are all giggling at the sounds and sights of "pommees natural", "chocks flerees a la something or other", and "purtit pees". There are other delights too, like carottees and braces made of celery.

'I've just been talking to the M.O.,' Dave informs me, his face twisting into a boyish grin.

'Oh really Skipper! You've not got, no, you haven't! No, surely not, you haven't caught it! Not after all the warnings they've given us. Who are you blaming it on? The beautiful Lucia of Pescara, or that voluptuous dish in Nino's bar?'

'I thought better of you than that,' he rebukes, but he's still smiling. 'Venereal disease was mentioned believe it or not, and he's quite pleased because there have only been nine new cases this month compared to fourteen in November.'

I look at him in surprise. 'Gosh, I never realised it was that prevalent.'

'You learn something new every day. Would you like to know why the mosquitoes have quietened down?'

'No thanks.'

'Anyone for the theatre tonight?' asks Smithy.

'Why, what's the attraction?'

'An Italian magician who can make things disappear.'

'What's new?' asks a pilot, whose pocket was picked when he recently visited the nearby town of Jesi. 'They don't need a bloody theatre to do that!'

'And there's a R.A.F. concert party called the "*Bully-tins*"!'

'"*Bully-tins*"! That's corny,' quips Dusty. 'How big is the theatre?'

'Seats about one hundred and fifty.'

'That's not bad for a small village.'

'I'd like to go,' says Dave, passing salt and pepper to Dusty.

'Does anyone know just what this is I'm drinking?' I ask, eyeing the contents of my glass somewhat dubiously.

'I've no idea,' laughs Neville, our navigator, 'but if it's anything like the stuff I'm drinking then I suggest we drop it on Jerry!'

His reference to the enemy immediately evokes shouts of, 'Close the hangar doors' and 'Stop talking shop,' criticisms which leave the lieutenant suitably squashed.

An unpronounceable main dish is followed by Christmas pud, and Dusty is dismayed when I manage to make room for it in my stomach despite having eaten a dictionary! Fruits, fromage and biscuits bring the meal to an end and after consuming "café", deliberately mispronounced by Smithy, we make for the lounge where free-issue brandy is being downed in large quantities. Compliments of the season flow as freely as the drink, cheerful tidings that seem somewhat incongruous for tomorrow, Boxing Day, will no doubt see us dropping bombs on the enemy.

Carols, in deliberately distorted form, are being sung with 'God rest ye Jerry Mentalmen' competing with 'While shepherds wash their socks by night', and as things become more boisterous volunteers are called for to take part in an imaginary raid over enemy territory.

'This is where I bow out,' I whisper to Dusty, 'I can't stand these crazy S.A.A.F. antics. I need a breath of fresh air. I've not only eaten too much, I've also had far too much to drink. See you at the theatre.'

I shuffle rather unsteadily across the village square and pause outside the sergeants mess. Remains of the snow that fell a few days ago heralding a white Christmas that never materialised lies dirty against the walls of the three storied building, which prior to the arrival of twelve squadron had been the local school and village office.

A warrant officer, well wrapped up in gloves, scarf and great-coat, is making his exit.

'Jock!' I cry, excusing myself as I stifle a burp. 'I was hoping to run across you.'

'My, my, such manners! I remember cruder noises in the past which never brought forth an apology.'

'But I wasn't an officer and a gentleman then.'

'How very true. Would you like me to salute? I'm surprised you even condescend to speak to me!'

'Now! Now!' I cry, wobbling unsteadily. 'Don't be like that. Will you be going to the concert?'

'I doubt it.'

'Oh, come on, let's go together.'

'No thanks.'

'Let's go an' sing carols outside Mamma's then.'

'She'd soon tell us to clear off, knowing full well that you were only after her daughter. If you want to sing carols then come to the church service with me.'

'What, me, in my state of health!' I hiccup. 'Anyway, you know I'm an atheist, or an agnostic or whatever.'

'Please yourself.' There is an off-hand tone in his voice, and a coolness that has been there ever since we returned from a leave spent together in Rome.

I feel a genuine sense of regret at this turn of events for Jock has been a close acquaintance from the time we first met on a troopship conveying us to Port Said. Several days of that leave in September had been spent viewing the sights of the Eternal City, and the culmination for Jock - he being a staunch Roman Catholic - was a visit to the Vatican. There, to really put the icing on his cake, he had been offered the chance, together with some other members of the armed forces, to have a sort of "audience" with the Pope.

Not being R.C., and having no desire to participate in such goings on I tried to escape, but when the doors closed and officials indicated that we should form up in two lines I was trapped.

What was I to do? Offer up a prayer? If I was then hard cheddar, I didn't know one. Was I supposed to bend a knee or cross myself?   Just what did someone like me do when confronted by the Holy Father? I was utterly confused, and by the time the Vicar of Christ appeared looking like death warmed up I'd become a nervous wreck.

Perched on a sort of sedan chair and born aloft by Swiss Guards his holiness was conveyed between the two lines, pausing only to place his hand on a convenient head.

Were my eyes supposed to be closed while all this was going on? I took a furtive peep at Jock.

Eyes tight shut he was praying, and quite loudly too.

Full of indecision I elected to stare straight ahead and wait for the holy hand to settle on Jock's head but alas it didn't, it came to rest firmly on mine. There were words too, in Latin, but they meant nothing because I had dropped that "dead language", as my father called it, years ago in Form 4a at grammar school. There was no denying it though, I'd been blessed and Jock had not!

To say that my friend's nose was put out of joint by the incident would be a colossal understatement, and though I tried to make light of the affair my facetious remarks served only to make matters worse. And now, as I stand and shiver under a sky teeming with stars, I feel that the gulf between us has got wider.

'I'll be off then.' With that Jock heads for the village church and I weave in the opposite direction towards the theatre. But the encounter has left its mark and I soon tire of the belly laughter that greets every below-the-navel blue joke told by the *"Bully-tins"* red nosed comedian. Excusing myself I steal out into the night and make for the Bonechi casa, where I undress to the accompaniment of cluck-clucks, quack-quacks, bleats, moos and grunts.

I stretch out on my bed but everything spins when I close my eyes.

Curse it! Will I never learn that alcohol and I just aren't compatible? That a *"Green Mamba"* of a Crème de Menthe is certain to lie uneasy in my belly alongside molto Marsala. That a *"Rommel's Prescription"* of a rum is no bed fellow for a *"Red Demon"* cherry brandy. That a *"Sleepers Draught"* of dry sherry does not guarantee a good night's sleep!

A feeling of nausea overcomes me. Opening my eyes I sit up but in doing so make contact with the wall that separates me from Miss Bonechi.

Oh heck! Her mother will be here any minute now accusing me of trying to make contact with her virgo intacta daughter. I lie still, eyes wide open, hardly daring to breathe but nothing happens. The still of the night is broken only by a bleat from Mussolini.

My thoughts meander. I recall how the squadron had moved lock, stock and gun barrel in October to our present airstrip below Monsano, and how the manner of that removal had prompted someone at Wing H.Q. to remark that 12 Squadron no longer requisitioned buildings - it took over whole villages!

I remember a lecture at which the C.O. had berated us for being a slovenly lot! From now on, he'd said, the vino shop would be "off limits" for most of the day. Slackness would not be tolerated, and anyone improperly dressed could expect to be severely dealt with. Failure to salute commissioned officers would be punished accordingly. His final remark had been directed at those of us who enjoyed visiting picturesque Italian towns: - 'See to it that you behave yourselves. You are, after all, ambassadors of your country.'

The spinning slows but confused memories continue to fill my booze-affected brain. Formation flying, tighter ever tighter. A concert by the Desert Air Force band. Seven aside soccer. Seven aside rugger. Gosh, I'm thirsty.

I reach for the glass of water by my bedside and see that Dusty's bed is empty. He'll be sorry tomorrow when, with a thick head, he'll have to dice with death.

Death! How much longer can I go on cheating it? I have already stuck my neck out on fifty six "ops", and no doubt I'll have to continue doing so until the war comes to an end.

I open my lucky locket and return the "watch the birdy" smiles Mum and Dad give me. I'm sure their photographic presence will see me through, like it always has. They won't fail me now, because, as Smithy says, the war can't last much longer.

What sort of Christmas will they have had I wonder? One thing's for sure, they will have been thinking of me as I of them. What must life be like for parents who have a son in the forces I wonder, especially one who has shots fired at him in earnest? Do they daily expect to receive one of those heart stopping telegrams?

Oh stop being so bloody morbid, try to get some shut eye. One of us will have to be wide awake tomorrow, or is it today?

But what's the point? If I do nod off Dusty will be sure to wake me, and he'll take a fiendish delight in doing so.

I toss, turn, and wonder where our next target will be. Udine? Rovigo? Treviso? Oh come on Dusty, come home to Mamma's, I'm tired and need some shut-eye.

Boxing Day! Appropriately named I suppose in the circumstances.

I had hoped that the Christmas period would be sufficiently sacrosanct to warrant a stand down but no such luck. None of the places I forecast was the target though for it was Castelfranco-Veneto that received a belated Christmas present from us, in the shape of 500 and 250 pound bombs. Just to prove me partly right, however, Treviso was the chosen target on the twenty-seventh but we need not have stuck our necks out, for the whole affair was a complete shambles from the moment the lead aircraft developed engine and radio trouble simultaneously. So Treviso's railway sheds and marshalling yards remain intact, and the bombs that were meant to destroy them are keeping the fishes company at the bottom of the Adriatic.

Yesterday our crew was stood down and as a consequence we missed a fairly shaky do, for nine of the twelve aircraft that visited Udine were damaged over the target. A number of aircrew too received minor injuries from the intense accurate flak.

What gluttons Wing H.Q. are for punishment! 12 squadron's punishment that is, for they have chosen Udine again as today's target. I sit with heavy heart hunched up in the top turret of Marauder 'J' Jug, and remember the C.O.'s instructions at briefing. 'Eliminate the marshalling yards, railway tracks and engine sheds, for they are absolutely vital to the enemy's war effort.' Little wonder the Germans had defended the place with such vigour less than twenty-four hours ago!

Twelve Marauders are airborne and most of them show the scars of yesterday's battle. We are flying in two boxes, with six aircraft in each box, and the raid is being led by Major Braithwaite, known to us all as "Tiger". He is piloting "V" Victor and his number four is "S" Sugar, captained by the Belgian, Lieutenant Brichard, with whom Jock is flying.

Earlier, as "S" had taxied out for take-off I was pleased when Jock waved a gloved hand, and I'd returned the compliment with a vigorous up and down movement of the upper turret machine guns.

Brrr! It's chilly up here in the sky some ten thousand feet above the Gulf of Venice.

I shiver and wonder what has happened to the warm underwear we were promised many moons ago. Rotating my turret, I search ahead, for we are fast approaching the target, and I feel relieved when I see no signs of the anticipated flak. Moments later, however, as I admire the excellent close formation flying of "Tiger"'s box, the first tell-tale black puffs appear and the sky darkens.

'Bomb doors open,' Nev requests and Dave obeys his instruction.

The enemy has obviously calculated our height and air-speed with some precision, for the sky is full of bursting shells.

Skipper responds to more terse commands but as our bombs fall away the aircraft is rocked by a terrific explosion, and we are enveloped in a dense cloud of black smoke. A revolting stink, the like of which I have never come across before, fills my nostrils.

'Christ!' Dusty gasps over the inter-com.

More shells explode. Shrapnel strikes the fuselage, and when Dave puts "J" into a steep dive I search frantically for the first box of aircraft but can see nothing.

'There's a Marauder directly beneath us,' Smithy reports from the waist-hatch position as Dave returns our aircraft to straight and level flight.

'Yes, I see it,' Dusty confirms. 'Someone's bailed out, and there goes another 'chute, and another.'

'And a fourth,' yells our wireless operator.

'Coming up to the coast, Skipper.' Neville's voice is admirably calm in view of all the excitement.

'Roger.' Dave sounds equally cool. 'Keep your eyes peeled chaps, there may be fighters about.'

Dusty reports that yet more parachutes have opened and his information is greeted with a spontaneous cheer, for this probably means that all the crew have escaped from the doomed aircraft.

Our delight at the escape of the airmen evaporates when we are informed at de-briefing that three Marauders from the first box have failed to return. Tiger and his crew were the six chaps we saw parachuting to safety, but the fate of Lieutenant Funkey's aircraft and crew is not known.

The news that sickens me, however, is that Brichard's aircraft had exploded, and the general opinion is that no one could possibly have escaped when it had disintegrated into a burning mass of material over the target.

'Oh no, not Jock!' Sick at heart I make immediately for the seclusion of Mamma B's where I find that even she is subdued, for news travels fast on the village grape-vine.

I throw myself onto my bed, and as tears scald my eyes remember that leave in Rome, when a certain hand had touched my head but not Jock's.

Chapter 18

Yet More Operations.

(Early 1945)

Early in the new year 12 Squadron flew across the Adriatic to Zidani Most in Yugoslavia, where bridges and a rail yard were the target. At briefing we were warned that if we had to bail out we should be wary of erstwhile peasants who had become trigger happy partisans. The women too could be "trouble" but no explanation was given as to how or why.

Precipitous gorges and a meandering river made visual identification of the target extremely difficult. Success was achieved in the end however, and the target was well and truly pranged. None of our aircraft were lost, which meant that the partisan ladies failed to get their hands on any aircrew.

The weather now brought an enforced lull but towards the end of January we bombed Castelfranco. The flak there was exceptionally heavy and F/O Dickenson, flying in the number two position in our box of four, force landed at Rimini with over one hundred holes in his aircraft.

February saw the squadron concentrating on marshalling yards. Over Conegliano one air-gunner was killed by shrapnel, and another member of his crew bailed out without being ordered to do so.

A raid on Rovigo provided a chapter of accidents, the leaders of both boxes having total hang-ups. With no Verey light being observed only one of our Marauders dropped its bombs and they missed the target.

Gorizia and Monselice were both attacked with moderate success, and, on the day that our delayed action bombs straddled a bridge at Sacile, welcome news came through that Major Braithwaite and his crew were alive and well - having been taken prisoner after the Udine raid of the 29th of December.

On the 26th of February, for the raid on Arsie in the Dolomites, a new technique was used. A Marauder went ahead with a Spitfire escort to find the correct wind speed which it was to pass to the rest of the squadron. Approaching the target, however, the aircraft developed engine trouble and the resultant bombing was a failure.

Chapter 19

"Nemesis"

(Early Spring 1945)

Medium bomber, Martin Marauder, "N", "*Nemesis*", her twin Pratt and Whitney two thousand horse power radial engines throbbing with power, flies north in an azure Italian sky bound for Conegliano, a town situated some thirty miles to the north of Venice.

Lying snug in the Marauder's bomb-bay is a collection of 500 and 250 pound bombs which it is hoped will cause considerable damage to the target, a rail and road communications centre vital to the enemy's supply lines.

"*Nemesis*" has been airborne for precisely one hour having lifted off from Jesi airstrip near Ancona at ten minutes past ten this fine early spring morning. Dave Dent is captain of the aircraft, Neville Pentz will be dropping the bombs and we three inseparables, Dusty, Smithy and I will be manning the aircraft's defences, listening out on the R/T, and taking photographs of the target.

I rotate the top turret and search, then search again. Wispy white cirrus clouds float dreamily on high whilst below the Adriatic, calm and peaceful, reflects the blue of the sky. To starboard, hidden by haze and distance, lies Yugoslavia. To port I can just make out the flat marshy delta that constitutes the mouth of the River Po.

To relieve the pressure building in my ears I swallow hard and then, as an antidote to boredom, I elevate and depress my guns and check that everything is as it should be with the ammo feed, reflector sight and inter-com.

Top turrets are not the most comfortable of places and as I sit with my head close to the machine guns, I try to relieve an unease that is both mental and physical by tonic sol-fa'ing *"Sentimental Journey"*, a tune I'd adopted for "good luck" when I commenced my second tour of 'ops'.

Immediately after breakfast this morning, we were briefed and despatched to attack Conegliano, our ten Marauder aircraft being the last of the four squadrons of No. 3 Wing S.A.A.F. detailed to bomb the target.

Ahead flies the squadron's first box of four aircraft, closely followed by the second box and *"Nemesis"* leads the third box, which is comprised of three aircraft. She is flanked by "P", piloted by Lt. Cohen and "Y", skippered by Lt. Moolman. The top gunner flying in "P" waves a gloved hand and as I return his friendly gesture I admire, as I have so often in the past, the sleek graceful lines of the B-26, for, despite the flaking drab coat of olive green paint, she still manages to look a streamlined beauty.

Glancing at my watch I see that the time is 11.25 hours, and when I turn my attention once more to the skies around me I note that we have been joined by the four Spitfires detailed to escort us to the target. They are a welcome sight, for recent intelligence has made much of the presence in the area of some sixty or more enemy fighter aircraft, mostly Messerschmitt 109s but with a sprinkling of Focke Wolfe 190s. The pilots of these single engine fighters are said to be German controlled members of the Italian Fascist Republican Air Force.

"*Nemesis*" will now be flying at her optimum bombing height of somewhere between eleven and twelve thousand feet, and it comes as no surprise when bursts of flak appear to starboard. It is heavy stuff and wildly inaccurate but I am immediately reminded of the horror that took place in the skies over Udine less than three months ago. I pray it will stay well away but when a sudden jagged red flash turns into a black cloud I realise that my prayer has gone unanswered.

Lt. Cohen's "P" appears to be in trouble, for the propeller of her starboard engine is no longer rotating. As I watch closely, I see the bomb doors open and the bombs jettisoned. The Marauder then dives away and is soon lost from sight.

I promptly turn my attention to "Y" and find that that aircraft is lagging behind us and losing height.

Neville Pentz requests bomb doors open and, as Dave obeys, further instructions follow. Shortly afterwards it's, 'Steady, steady,' and moments later our bombs are gone.

I report the disappearance of "P", and, with "Y" no longer visible, stress the fact that we are now very much on our own. For good measure I point out that as the flak barrage has ceased fighters may well be waiting to pounce!

'You'd better keep your peepers open then,' laughs Dave.

Bloody hell! Messerschmitts! One, two, three, four, five, six, seven, eight of them.

My God! And there's a F.W 190 with them for good measure!

My stomach loops the loop but training and experience take over as an Me 109G attacks.

I give Dave the required evasive action and when the enemy fighter banks and turns I see grey-green mottled wing tops. A split second later as the aircraft hurtles over my turret I am treated to a close up view of a light blue belly and black crosses, while from the tail a swastika leers at me.

Two of the enemy close for the kill and I am returning their fire when for some reason best known to themselves they break off the engagement.

An Me. attacks from seven o'clock, but as I shout my instructions I realise I am talking to myself for the inter-com has packed up. *Ye Gods! The sky is full of enemy fighters and no way can I communicate with Skipper!*

Dusty's machine guns chatter angrily.

I too fire off about fifty rounds and invite the enemy, in best barrack room language, to do his worst. My heart is pounding now, and although I don't know what adrenalin is I know for sure it has arrived.

Cannon shells hit *"Nemesis"*!

I fight back and yell with savage glee when tracer from my own and Dusty's guns strike home, causing the fighter that has attacked to wobble as it dives away.

Dave is flinging *"Nemesis"* all over the sky in an attempt to make the job of the fighters more difficult, but when hits register on the fuselage only a sudden dive to port saves our bacon.

Another fighter closes from starboard. I open fire and give vent to my feelings by screaming my opinion of aircraft that have dirty-big-black crosses on their fuselage, and evil looking swastikas on their tails. But no one hears my screams, certainly not the pilot of the Messerschmitt.

Suddenly no enemy aircraft are attacking.

I'm puzzled. Why are we flying straight and level, inviting disaster? Does Dave know something I don't? A queer feeling steals over me. Have Dusty and Smithy bailed out? Maybe they are injured or no longer in the land of the living? The latter I feel is a distinct possibility, for no other guns but mine had opened up on the enemy during that last attack.

From dead astern an enemy fighter appears. He's got a nerve! How dare he sit there blasting cannon shells at me? For Christ's sake Dusty open up, give the cheeky sod the squirt he deserves. To my dismay only a frightening silence prevails.

Crash! The Plexiglas of my turret shatters. I duck instinctively. My vision is obscured, something warm is trickling down my cheek. I snatch off a gauntlet, feel at my face and to my horror find blood on my fingers. *Ye gods, I've been hit!* Fear grips me. Is this the end, the chop? If it is I'm not going down without a fight!

'I'll get you, you bastard!' I scream. 'I'll get you if it's the last thing I ever do!'

But no way will I get the fighter that is now attacking "*Nemesis*" for my guns won't fire. I "cock and fire" but to no avail, the Brownings have given up the fight. I check the ammo feed. It appears to be OK. I repeat the "cock and fire" technique but it's no use, the Brownings refuse to function. *Bloody hell fire! No guns! No inter-com! No hope!*

I stare helplessly as yet another fighter hurtles towards me, and feel that I shall be making the grim reaper's acquaintance at any moment. Frightened and helpless I cower behind my useless .5s, but in an instant the certainty of death disappears for the aircraft is not attacking "*Nemesis*", it is itself being attacked and by something that sports lovely great R.A.F. roundels!

Heaven be praised, I am being rescued by a Spitfire. The biters are about to be bitten! A wonderful feeling of relief comes over me but my euphoria soon disappears when I see, to my dismay, that we are flying on one engine.

With my guns useless, inter-com not functioning, one eye out of action and a shattered turret I realise that my usefulness is at an end, so I pull on the catch to release my seat and drop to the fuselage floor.

The sight that greets my one good eye appals me. Smithy is nowhere to be seen, one of the waist guns hangs twisted and mangled over an open hatch, the fuselage resembles a colander and octane, which has escaped from the aircraft's fuel tank, is swilling about the floor. The ammunition tracks leading to the guns in the tail hang suspended in mid-air, and their crazy contortions remind me of a fairground's 'big-dipper'. Little wonder Dusty's firing had ceased so early in the attack.

The aircraft gives a sickening lurch and for one awful moment I teeter parachute-less towards the open starboard hatch. Some two miles below the Adriatic invites me to a watery grave but I manage to cheat death by grabbing the twisted ammo track, before making my way on all fours to the tail.

After an eternity of crawling I reach Dusty and find to my relief that he is alive, unharmed but very dopey, suffering from what I assume to be an excessive inhalation of octane fumes.

I'm helping him out of his confined quarters when a hand tugs at my shoulder, it is blood stained and belongs to Smithy. He opens his mouth, shakes his head and shrugs his shoulders - a set of gestures which perfectly sums up our situation. Lifting the flap of my helmet he informs me that he had, 'gone up front,' when the Spits had come to our rescue. 'Dave's in a bit of a quandary,' he shouts. 'He's no idea how much fuel there is left and, as we're too low to bail out it will be a case of either ditching in the drink, or belly flopping on the sand.' There are more words, one of which sounds like undercarriage, but the rest are drowned by the noise of the slipstream.

'I hope to God he doesn't belly flop!' I cry, pointing to the octane that is soaking into my flying boots. 'One spark and "*Nemesis*" will become a blazing torch.'

Smithy nods. 'One engine's packed up you know, and up front it's a right shambles. The instrument panel is smashed to smithereens, and there's a bloody great hole in the nose.'

'Hadn't we better get the waist hatch covers back on if there's a chance we'll end up in the drink,' I shout.

'That's just what I was thinking.' It is Dusty who is agreeing with my suggestion, and he's becoming more and more "with it" each passing minute.

The three of us are about to manhandle the covers back on when Neville appears. 'Dave's going to put her down on the sand. If the undercarriage proves to be u/s then we'll belly flop. There can't be much fuel left so to hell with those hatch covers chaps, let's take up our crash positions.'

We huddle together against the main bulkhead. I peer through the open hatch and see the sea give way to sand. I estimate that we are now flying at about one hundred feet and are resigning myself to the inevitable when, to my immense relief I hear the undercarriage lock into position. Within seconds "*Nemesis*", our goddess of divine retribution, is down on terra-firma, and when her one good engine coughs and dies she slews to a stop.

'Bloody hell!' cries Dusty, his eyes wide open and staring. 'If Dave hadn't put us down when he did we'd have...' He slits his throat with a finger that has turned into an imaginary knife.

We immediately distance ourselves from the aircraft, fearful that she could still become a blazing torch.

Stinking of cordite, fuel and sweat we inspect each other closely, and giggling like schoolgirls come to the conclusion that we shall all live. "*Nemesis*", however, is a sorry sight. She really has taken a bashing. Her engines are holed, a portion of her tail is missing and my turret looks as if someone has taken a hammer to it. Moving closer to the aircraft Dusty decides to count the cannon-shell holes in the fuselage but - after reaching fifty, and with only half of the aircraft inspected - he abandons the idea.

I then take stock of our surroundings and find that we are on a narrow strip of sand bordered on one side by the Adriatic, and on the other by a rough looking coastal road.

'Any idea where we are?' I ask our navigator. 'Not going to be prisoners of war I hope?'

'I doubt it,' Neville laughs. 'We will soon know though, there's a vehicle approaching.'

My fears prove groundless for the driver of the jeep is an Eighth Army corporal who informs us that his unit is, 'down the road a piece,' and will we take care because the Germans are reputed to have mined the beach in the Cervia area.

'The what area?' asks Dusty, coming to an immediate halt.

'Cervia, sir.'

'Never heard of it.'

'Well sir,' says the corporal, extending an arm. 'Ravenna's up there and Rimini's down there.'

'And where are the Germans?'

'Up there.'

'Phew. That's nice to know!'

More soldiers arrive. They shoo away a number of nosy Eyeties who have gathered close by, set up a guard on the aircraft and arrange transport for us.

After waving a sad farewell to *"Nemesis"* we climb aboard the vehicle provided and set off for our Jesi airstrip. Then, to a man, Dent's crew heap praise on the head of the man who had "brought us back alive".

Dave blushes, waves away our adulation, and thanks us each in turn for our contribution. 'A real crew effort,' he smiles. 'A real crew effort. We owe it to each other that we are alive to tell the tale.' And what a tale, with everyone telling it at the same time.

'When I first saw those fighters...' I say.

'The so-and-so's reduced one of my Brownings to scrap before I...' says Smithy.

'Phew, was I relieved when I saw that strip of sand. I knew it would have to be a once only approach,' sighs Dave. 'That there would be no chance of going round again.'

'He suggested that I fire off a red light to show that we were in trouble,' scoffs Neville, jerking his thumb in Dave's direction. 'My God, imagine what would have happened if I had done, with the aircraft just waiting to blow sky high! I told him he was crazy that no way was I going to send us up in smoke.'

'I didn't know you had passed out,' says Dave, addressing our tail gunner.

'It was those bloody fumes,' claims Dusty. 'But we got a Messyshit didn't we Al? You and I, we got him between us. He went into a steep dive and there was lots of black smoke. When I last saw him he seemed to be spinning down out of control.'

'How long did it all last?' queries Smithy.

'A lifetime!' I say, with feeling.

Dave smiles. 'A real crew effort, a real crew effort.'

'Exactly fifteen minutes,' says Nev, 'from the time we bombed until we reached the coast at Cape Tagliamento.'

'Fifteen years more like,' I insist.

Dave inspects my face. 'Didn't miss your eye by very much Al, whatever it was.'

I return his gaze. 'No, and it didn't miss your hooter by very much either Dave, whatever it was.'

'Hey, just look at my fingers!' Dusty shouts, displaying trembling digits. 'I've developed DTs.'

'You've always had 'em, it's that rot-gut vino you drink,' observes our wireless op, ignoring Dusty's outstretched hands. Then, with a sigh he adds ruefully, 'Good old *"Nemesis"*. I'll never be rude about a Marauder again. If you ever hear me call one a *"Baltimore Whore"* or a *"Martin Murderer"*, feel free to kick me up the arse!'

I laugh as he affects slight contrition, and inform him that he has left out *"Martin Miscarriage"* and *"Flying Fornicator"*.

None of these soubriquets are of our own creation of course, they are nicknames that have been in circulation from the time the B-26 first came off the production lines in 1940, in the good old U.S. of A. Hailed as the most advanced medium bomber in the world the aircraft had proved to be a real headache with its legion of mechanical faults, and within no time at all it had been labelled as 'the aircraft too hazardous to fly'!

Dusty, ever the talker, is at his most voluble during debriefing. After claiming one Me109 "G" destroyed - with a little help from me that is - he has informed everyone that despite all the hazards our bombs had put paid to the railway tracks on the western approach to the marshalling yards at Conegliano.

Smithy too confirms the accuracy of the bombing, confident that the photographs he managed to take of the target will prove him right.

Then, after the I.O. has asked me to present a detailed account in writing of the attacks made upon *"Nemesis"* by the enemy fighters, we are free to retire to the mess. Dave, Dusty and I help ourselves to free issue brandy, and we are happy to raise our glasses when news arrives that Lt. Cohen has force lobbed safely at some distant airstrip, and that the injuries sustained by two of Lt. Moolman's crew are not serious.

The squadron's medical officer decided after the Conegliano affair that Dent and crew were suffering from mild shell-shock, a diagnosis promptly altered to cannon-shell-shock by Dusty. To calm us down we were given some little white pills, and seven days leave.

After "borrowing" a jeep we made for the peace and quiet of Assisi, where everything turned out to be very, very peaceful, and extremely quiet. St. Francis failed to put in an appearance except in Giotto's frescoes, and there were birds galore but not the sort I fancied.

On our return to Jesi yesterday the C.O. informed Dave that for his part in bringing "Nemesis" back from Conegliano - in spite of the serious damage inflicted by enemy flak and fighters - he had recommended that Skipper be awarded an immediate Distinguished Flying Cross. The rest of us didn't even get a pat on the back, and the news I hoped to hear wasn't forthcoming. With thirty-seven "ops" of my second tour completed, I felt that the powers that be might have decided I had done enough. But the faceless ones at the Air Ministry, or D.A.F. H.Q., obviously think otherwise, so here I am about to take off in Marauder "V" Victor for Pont Ebba, a target situated near to the Austrian border.

However, as the wiseacre will have it, "You've gotta laugh", and that's what I did when I looked at the crew list this morning. I've held various ranks in my air-force career but thanks to a slip of the pen, or perhaps a typing finger not pulled out, I had become Lieutenant Alcock, of the South African Air Force!

I glance up at the sky and see it is a glorious blue, a sky just made for Messerschmitts and the odd FW 190 - but not to worry, I have my lucky locket with me and I've taken the trouble to learn the lyrics of *"Sentimental Journey"*.

Nemesis, "Divine Retribution", Cervia, Italy 1945.

Chapter 20

An Itchy Tale

(Early Spring 1945)

A couple of months ago a flight sergeant air-gunner known to most of us as Titch began to show signs of having contracted L.M.F., the dreaded lack of moral fibre.

There were numerous symptoms. Besides consuming vast quantities of vino and free-issue brandy, he chain smoked cigarettes, and the high-pitched whine of self-pity in his incessant chatter had fellow airmen hastening away whenever he opened his mouth. His appearance was slovenly and unmilitary, his chin never saw a razor, and most nights he slept in a ditch near to whichever "vino casa" he'd been thrown out of.

When he wasn't airborne Titch was dancing attendance on the MO, and if he'd claimed to be seeing pink elephants in addition to his fibrositis, noises in the head and nausea, I'm quite sure Doc would have shown no surprise.

At the time I'd felt some sympathy for the chaps who flew with Titch for he could hardly be classed as a reliable crew member. I hadn't given them a lot of thought of late though because I'd contracted prolapsed haemorrhoids.

This unpleasant complaint resulted in a sojourn in Ancona hospital where I was surrounded by servicemen who had just been cured of V.D., were being cured of V.D., had recently been diagnosed as having V.D. or had caught V.D. off some unsuspecting lavatory seat.

With graffiti ruling OK, it was obvious that Kilroy had already been to the hospital for that old favourite – "Is Lenin's tomb a Communist plot?" adorned one of its walls.

Limericks too abounded. One referred to a young lady from the Cape, another to a young man named Hunt, and a girl called Kelly was featured. The latter had a rider, which informed the sitting tenant that if he could read the words without difficulty then he was defecating at an angle of forty-five degrees.

That some of the soon-to-be-released inmates had enjoyed their hospital stay was obvious, judging from the chorus of wolf whistles blown at signorinas as they passed by its open windows. Without doubt some of the chaps were hell-bent on paying a return visit.

With nearly all of their patients suffering from venereal disease I was something of a novelty for the medical staff, and they decided, therefore, that the opportunity to apply surgical instruments should not be missed. But alas, the vagaries of war saw the Eighth Army making one of its "pushes", and - with numerous casualties expected - beds had to be made available. I was, therefore, returned to my squadron with piles intact and a heavy heart, for surgery had seemed preferable to dicing with death in a B-26 Martin Marauder medium bomber.

The first person I see is Titch. Sun bathing on a lizard-infested wall, he has an unrestricted view of the airfield nestling in the valley below.

'What are you up to, small person?'

'I'm waiting for the Squadron's aircraft to return. I've got a grandstand seat. How are the piles?'

'Still there, they didn't operate. It looks like you've been operating though,' I say, pointing to his left arm which is encased in plaster.

'No way, I didn't get this flying on any raid I can assure you.'

'You just like being permanently plastered then,' I joke, alluding to his drinking habits.

'Haven't touched a drop in ages.' he cries, gesticulating with his good arm. 'Not since those silly buggers in the mess decided to do a pretend bombing run. Being on the small side they used me as an enemy fighter. They tossed me up in the air then shot me down with lit matches, chewing gum, fag ends, cigarette lighters and anything else they could lay their hands on! And all the while they were chanting, mostly in Afrikaans. There was some English. "Hold him down you Zulu warrior, hold him down you Zulu chief. Chief! Chief! Chief!" I tell you what they are real head-cases, those Africanders.'

'Afrikaners, Titch, not Africanders. Africanders are humped-back cattle.'

'There's a difference? I blame it all on the free brandy, because when the nutters shot me down for the last time they were so drunk they forgot to catch me. Bloody stupid Africanders!'

'What happened then?'

'I hit the deck and did my wrist in.' A crafty smile creases Titch's features. 'The M.O. says it will probably take weeks for the fracture to mend but as far as I'm concerned there's nothing probable about it, it will take weeks. Months if necessary. I tell you this, I'll never go on another raid. My operational career is well and truly over. This plaster, which I want you to sign by the way, will stay on until the war ends. Tell you what though, it don't 'alf itch.'

'Shake,' I laugh, accepting the pen he offers with the fingers of my right hand, while scratching my backside with the fingers of my left.

B 26 Martin Marauder, 12 Squadron S.A.A.F.

Chapter 21

Hitch-Hike

(Spring 1945)

Rome! When in Rome do as they see done!

And so I will, if I manage to get there, for my seven days leave could hardly have got off to a less auspicious start, with the vehicle that has brought me as far as Fabriano now refusing to go any further.

Something seems to have gone wrong with what Winston Churchill might refer to as its infernal combustion engine, so I'm forced to bid farewell to the stranded vehicle and cheesed-off driver. I mop my brow and stride forth, knowing that I am travelling in the right direction because all roads lead to Rome.

An assortment of vehicles pass me by but none slow to a halt in response to my jerking thumb, and I begin to feel that it's going to be "Shanks's pony" all the way to the Eternal city.

Ahead of me a truly one-horse powered vehicle filled with vegetables moves slowly along the dusty road, its florid Italian driver whipping, punching and threatening the emaciated creature trapped between its shafts.

Typical bloody Eyetie, I think as blows rain down on the defenceless animal. How I'd like to give its master a taste of his own medicine.

I feel that in some way I should be able to come to the animal's aid but the matter is resolved when a large truck skids past and slows, with screaming of tyres and hiss of air brakes, almost to a stop.

Aha! Success at last! But I am mistaken for the driver is not stopping to offer me a lift, he's enjoying himself, and I'm horrified when he expertly swings the rear of his truck to deposit both donkey and cart into the ditch at the side of the road.

Any contempt I'd felt earlier transfers itself to the perpetrator of the ghastly little prank I've just witnessed. The donkey is braying pitifully, and the wheels of the overturned cart spin crazily. I feel sorry for the Eyetie.

He smites the air with his fists and tears run down his cheeks, much to the amusement of a bunch of Yanks who, sitting in the back of the truck, are grinning from ear to ear.

Invective, Italian style, is hurled at me by the driver of the cart, but only because I am a member of the Allied Forces who happens to be in the wrong place at the right time. The man is beside himself with rage, and I fear for my safety, when a car slows to avoid the assorted green stuff littering the highway.

'Any chance of a lift?' I shout my thumb still in the hitch-hike mode.

A rear door opens and a hand beckons.

Without more ado I make good my escape and clamber thankfully into the back of the vehicle, which to my surprise turns out to be a staff car. Glancing at the occupant I find that I have hitched a ride with a Lieutenant-Colonel.

'What on earth is going on?' my saviour asks, as he raps on the glass partition that separates us from the driver.

I attempt to explain, but he's not listening, he's asking me instead if I am bound for Rome - a city whose virtues he then extols in a non-stop travelogue. Capitol Hill, the Forum, the Palatine, the Coliseum and St. Peter's, they all get a mention.

I give him a sidelong glance. He's a cherubic specimen of a man with a beatific smile that would not be out of place in a Botticelli painting. His chubby fingers though are most certainly not high art, and they are gently stroking my left knee.

I raise an enquiring eyebrow but find that the high-ranked one is peering out at the Italian countryside, seemingly unaware that his hand and body have moved appreciably closer to mine. Like me he is dressed in khaki-drill but his knees are pink like his cheeks, and well-rounded like a woman's - the very opposite of my own boney, brown knee-caps.

I ease myself away from the overweight perspiring body but am unable to escape the searching fingers.

Gosh! Is this how young ladies must have felt when, in my teenage years of discovery, I'd inexpertly fondled them as we'd cuddled together in the back row of a cinema? But they were more fortunate than I. They could have clouted me with a handbag and fled but I have no such escape route.

I shudder and think what conclusion a Court Martial would reach when in answer to the question, 'Why did you punch the nice Lieutenant-Colonel in the gonads when he was being so kind as to give you a lift to Rome?' I would have to reply 'Because he was trying to feel me.'

Shades of ignominy, of being cashiered, of spending what was left of the war in a military prison!

The wandering hand climbs higher. Fingers toy with the bottom of my shorts.

I cross my legs in an attempt to protect my virginity. I've heard about these characters but only via the corny jokes that are told and re-told by servicemen and comedians in music halls the world over. Does he walk, I wonder, with his hand on his hip, in the exaggerated way of red nosed comics? One thing's for sure, the accentuated lisp of the mickey-takers is incorrect, for this character's voice is as cultured, charming, and mannish, as his fingers are inquisitive, smooth and searching.

Mopping my brow I heave a sigh when relief comes in an unexpected way and my assailant is himself assailed - by a bout of coughing.

'Which hotel are you staying at in Rome?' he splutters, reaching into his pocket for a handkerchief.

I open my mouth to reply but when alarm bells ring in my brain I am suddenly attacked by a bout of amnesia. 'Er, er, it's a junior officers' hotel, sir, but I can't for the life of me remember its name.'

'Come, come, now. How d'you expect to find the place if you don't know what it's called?' he asks testily.

'Oh, it'll come back to me, sir. I've stayed there before. I've a good idea as to its location.' Damn! Why did I say that? Now he'll insist on taking me there!

With the return of his hanky to his trouser pocket, my molester returns to the attack.

Wild eyed and feeling quite sick I cower in the corner of the car, powerless to put an end to the revolting sexual advances.

A hand steals inside my shorts and moves slowly higher. My God, any moment now he'll be feeling my parts private! I panic, push him aside and rap fiercely on the glass in front of me.

The driver methinks has seen it all before because at the sight of my gesticulating hand he brings the vehicle to an abrupt stop.

I thrust open the door, grab my hold-all, and am hardly out of the car before it speeds away in a cloud of dust. Phew! Talk about escaping from a fate worse than death! The revulsion within me turns to anger. I feel furious because I know there was nothing I could have done to have got even with the revolting little so-and-so.

Standing there, hot and bothered both mentally and physically, I shout obscenities that are every bit as heart felt as the Italian's had been earlier. I salute the settling dust with a victory sign in reverse, a gesture which a captain sporting New Zealand shoulder flashes misinterprets as a request for a lift. We make speedily for Rome in his jeep, and I am truly thankful that the only use he makes of his hand is to change gear.

Chapter 22

Farewells all Round.

(Spring 1945)

The arrival of April has seen me bidding farewell to Dave Dent D.F.C., and on the fourteenth of the month I flew with F/O Dickenson to Argenta, where the target received 90% of our bombs. A similar success was achieved at Consandolo, and on successive days we bombed Medecina, Bonafe and Cento. At Montesanto the Headquarters, Stores and M.T. depot of the 29th Panzer Grenadiers was seriously damaged, but three days later - over Bondeno - we ourselves were mauled by intense, heavy and accurate flak, which resulted in the loss of a Marauder.

On the 23rd of April I was airborne by 06.30 with Lt. Moolman. The target was Guarda Veneta where a ferry was being used by the enemy who was also making use of a pontoon bridge that straddled the river Po. The accuracy of our bombing was matched by the intensity of the flak and Lt. Levin's aircraft, flying number four in our box, was hit in several places. After force landing at Rimini his aircraft was completely burnt out due to contact of the Marauder's wheel rims with the metal runway. His crew escaped but two of them were treated for shrapnel wounds.

That same day I was flying again by 15.30 in Marauder "T", the target this time being a road bridge at Ponte Sandon, near Padova. Our bombing was to depend for accuracy on the "SHORAN" (SHOrt RAnge Navigation) device. After three dummy runs we bombed visually and undershot the target. Needless to say, the raid was a complete failure.

The next day, flying with Lt. Moolman in Marauder "X", we successfully attacked enemy troops waiting for the ferry to cross the river Po at Ro! The flak was fairly accurate, sufficiently so for Lt. Levin's aircraft to be badly damaged yet again.

Was the war over or was it not?

Rumours were rife but on the 2nd of May, 1945, Field Marshal Alexander set our minds at rest. In a special "Order of the Day", he announced that hostilities had ceased.

No more "ops". No more flak. No more enemy fighters.

I didn't know whether to laugh or cry, for the relief I felt was quite overwhelming.

I attended an open air inter-denominational service, and, when the padre offered up a prayer, memories galore crowded my mind.

Later in the day, the inhabitants of Santa Maria de Monsano gathered in the village square to celebrate the end of the war in Europe. 12 Squadron personnel joined in the festivities and wine flowed. Maria, guarded by her mother, looked a picture - a girl to be seen, admired, but definitely not touched. A village council member with fascist leanings was in disgrace, however, and he was certain to be manhandled when his hiding place was discovered!

> **ALLIED FORCE HEADQUARTERS**
>
> *2 May, 1945*
>
> ## SPECIAL ORDER OF THE DAY
>
> ### Soldiers, Sailors and Airmen of the Allied Forces in the Mediterranean Theatre
>
> After nearly two years of hard and continuous fighting which started in Sicily in the summer of 1943, you stand today as the victors of the Italian Campaign.
>
> You have won a victory which has ended in the complete and utter rout of the German armed forces in the Mediterranean. By clearing Italy of the last Nazi aggressor, you have liberated a country of over 40,000,000 people.
>
> Today the remnants of a once proud Army have laid down their arms to you—close on a million men with all their arms, equipment and impedimenta.
>
> You may well be proud of this great and victorious campaign which will long live in history as one of the greatest and most successful ever waged.
>
> No praise is high enough for you sailors, soldiers, airmen and workers of the United Forces in Italy for your magnificent triumph.
>
> My gratitude to you and my admiration is unbounded and only equalled by the pride which is mine in being your Commander-in-Chief.
>
> *H.R. Alexander*
>
> *Field-Marshal,*
> *Supreme Allied Commander,*
> *Mediterranean Theatre.*

"Alex's" Special Order of the Day.

To keep us out of mischief our C.O. laid on formation flying, bombing practice and air firing. On the 14th of May the four S.A.A.F. Squadrons of No. 3 Wing flew to Milan, where we "showed off" for troops of the 6th South African Division.

On the 16th of the month the Squadron flew a low level "cross-country" in tight formation.

I felt rather apprehensive. Was I sticking my neck out? To get the chop now would be nothing short of ridiculous!

Shrugging my shoulders, I climbed aboard the aircraft and thoroughly enjoyed my bird's eye view of Venice, Padova, Bologna and Ferrara.

On the 23rd of May Captain Annez asked me to take part in a formation practice exercise for a forthcoming Desert Air Force display.

I agreed but should have known better, for when the port engine came to a sudden stop so, momentarily, did my heart.

We got down in one piece, however, which proved what Pilot Officer Prune is wont to say in the *"Tee Emm"* magazine: - 'A good landing is one you can walk away from.'

In early June, with my future uncertain, I was posted to Foggia where I "rejoined" the R.A.F. but was destined never to fly in one of their number 40 Squadron *"Liberator"* bombers.

SECOND TOUR

P/O. A.H. ALCOCK.   Sub Form 414

OBSERVER AND AIR GUNNER ON MARAUDER A/C
SUMMARY and ASSESSMENT   Nº 12 SQD. S.A.A.F.
FOR YEAR .... 1944/45 ...

	DAY	NIGHT	GRAND TOTAL
OBSERVER	—	—	....111...... hrs
AIR GUNNER	111.45	—	....45..... mins

Nº of Sorties = 49

1) As a Gunner — ABOVE AVERAGE — G. Lewis Capt
2) As a Bomb Aimer — Gunnery Leader
3) As an Observer —
4) As a Wireless Operator —

REMARKS

Good Operational type.

DATE 10/1/45.

Signature
Designation AH Alcock
                                Lt.-Col.,
O.C. No. 12 SQUADRON, S.A.A.F.

S.A.A.F. "Estimation of Author".

Total number of flights, flying hours and aircraft types 9/6/42 - 13/3/45.

Unit and dates	Aircraft type	Non-ops flights	Non-ops Hours Day	Non-ops Hours Night	Operational flights	Ops Hours Day	Ops Hours Night	Total Hours
No 9 (o) AFU Ser/Oct Llandwrog, N.Wales.	BLENHEIM	20	15.00					15.00
No 28 OTU Dec.42-Mar.43 Wymeswold, Leic.	WELLINGTON	38	49.50	43.05				92.55
No 1656 CU Mar 1943 Lindholme	WHITLEY	3	3.55					3.55
No 1656 CU Lindholme	HALIFAX	4	6.10					6.10
No 1656 CU & 100.12 & 616 squadrons at Wratham & Wickenby 16-4-43 to 18-11-43	LANCASTER	34	39.55	28.35	30	OVER GERMANY	174.20	242.50
No 11 A.G.S ANDREAS. I.o.M 12.44 - 16.11.44	ANSON	122	94.55	1.40				96.35
No 70 O.T.U. KABRIT. EGYPT. 10-7-44 - 20.8.44	MARAUDER	17	34.40	3.05				37.40
24 SQDN. ITALY 25-27 August 1944.	DAKOTA	2	13.40					13.40
No 12 SQDN. S.A.A.F ITALY 29.8.44 - 13/3/45	MARAUDER II				49	OVER ITALY	79	131.55
	TOTAL = 251	279.15	76.35	79		111.45		541.05

Total 'Non-operational' flying = 251 flights
day & night = 355.40 Hours

Total 'Ops' flying = 79 ops day & night = 186.05 Hours

GRAND TOTAL
Number of flights = 330
Flying Hours = 541.05

Total Flying Hours.

Chapter 23

Padre's Pint

(Late Spring 1945)

'You must be a flaming masochist.'

Such is the opinion held of me by a South African pilot when I inform him, after lunch in the mess at Foggia, that I have volunteered for service in the Far East.

'A what?' I ask, feigning ignorance of the word.

'A masochist. A daft twit who takes pleasure in his own suffering.'

'Oh, you mean a person such as yourself.'

'I'm no masochist.'

'Yes you are! Only a masochist would smoke foul smelling "*Springbok*" cigarettes, and drink the filthy stuff that passes for beer.'

'I only smoke them because they're free, and I drink the beer because I can't stand vino.'

'Masochist.'

'Call me what you like but I'm not stupid enough to want to fight those little yellow men. D'you know what they do to you if they take you prisoner?'

'Make you smoke "*Springbok*" cigarettes?'

'Huh!' he scoffs, raising his glass. 'Well here's the best of luck to you, you'll need it! I'm content to stay here until they find me some cushy little number, or the powers that be return me to the "Union".'

The flap to the mess tent swings open and the C.O. enters, followed closely by the adjutant. So close is the latter that some wag is constrained to say 'cut the string' but the remark appears to go un-noticed. Close on the heels of the duo is a tall, extremely thin, captain. In his left hand he holds something that looks suspiciously like a bible.

'Whatever's that? I mean whoever's that?' I ask.

'The new padre. Didn't you see the pantomime that took place at lunch time yesterday?'

'No, I wasn't in the mess. I was busy volunteering to fight the Springboks, er, Japs, sorry.'

'Well watch,' grunts my companion, 'and listen.'

The CO has reached the bar. He orders a brandy and his shadow does the same. The pair then move away leaving the padre standing on his own. Coming smartly to attention the sky-pilot lifts his eyes to heaven, snatches off his dog collar and cries, in tones sepulchral: - 'Off duty, Lord. Barman, give me a f****** pint.'

Chapter 24

The Blanket

(Summer 1945)

The cessation of hostilities in Europe and Japan made me redundant. I was out of work, surplus to requirements, and there were many more like me - aircrew whose services were no longer required. With my de-mob number ensuring that I would be spending at least another year in the R.A.F., the authorities remembered the old adage, "out of sight, out of mind". So they posted me from the dust bowl of Foggia to the magic waters of Sorrento.

It was a harsh life! All play and no work! Up in the morning bright and late. Bathing in glorious sunshine on a private beach, rubbing shoulders and toes with bare foot contessas. Dining and wining in an elegant restaurant and hobnobbing with nouveau poor ladies who, sporting titles, claimed distant relationships with various King Victor Emmanuels.

Alas! How are the mighty fallen? Not too far if the prices reputedly charged by these high-class tarts for the bestowing of their favours was anything to go by.

The idyll proved far too good to last, and three months of luxurious living came to an abrupt end when I was forced to make a choice between working on something connected with War graves, Intelligence or Transport.

I wasn't long in making up my mind. Digging up the dead didn't appeal, I lacked sufficient intelligence to be in Intelligence, so it had to be Transport.

After an interview of sorts I entrained for Milan to become a train conducting officer, a trade which - though it lacks the excitement of operational flying - is considerably less hazardous. And there is an additional bonus, I'm seeing yet more of Europe, but this time it is a worm's-eye view, not a bird's-.

I would be the first to admit that a T.C.O.'s duties require little in the way of grey matter. To literally "own" a train though is the stuff of schoolboy dreams, so much so that when I take one out of the Stazione Centrale, Milano, I feel quite self-important because the whole caboose and caboodle is mine! No matter what the destination, be it Naples, Taranto, Dieppe, Calais or Villach, the clapped-out engine, tender, ancient carriages, hot axle-boxes, windows that won't open, communication cords that don't pull, tea urns, inedible rock buns and Italian style Cornish pasties are mine, all mine. And I mustn't forget the engine driver, the fireman, and the guard, plus my staff of two - an army corporal and a medic.

The servicemen travelling on the train are not my responsibility though, for the most senior officer travelling is O.C. troops and all ranks are subject to his discipline, except me and mine. Many a spattle I've had with waspish, self-important, high-ranking officers, but in the end they have condescended to see eye to eye with me, grudgingly accepting that it is my train they are travelling on.

Troop trains steam continuously in and out of Milan these days, and the reason for all this puffing activity is that, since the war in Europe came to an end, demobilisation has been the name of the game. Service personnel who were called up for the "Duration of the Present Emergency" want out, and as quickly as possible. Most of them will have said countless times over six long years, "Roll on that bloomin' boat", but as the cherished dream comes true the mode of transport is not what they expected for Italian, Swiss and French engines have replaced the ocean greyhound. Other troops who have yet to "get some service in", travel in the reverse direction, and today I am taking several hundred of them to Taranto, down in the heel of Italy.

I stand and gaze out of the window of my compartment but soon return to my seat because the view fills me with little cheer, this Puglia area of Italy being but a barren wilderness where rainfall is insufficient to support agriculture. Water is therefore a scarce commodity but as it is the liquid refreshment on which my puffing billy thrives, the engine is slowing to a halt at this very moment in order to quench its thirst from a water tower situated at the side of the track. Raised voices put an end to my lethargy. Lowering my window I see that a crowd has gathered near the end of the train. An Italian, clutching a blanket to his chest, detaches himself from his fellow countrymen. He moves smartly away but I am able to see that the piece of bedding is not one of the rough variety issued to British servicemen but a much prized G.I. item. Smooth and kind to the skin, these blankets are bestowed by a benevolent Uncle Sam upon his troops, from whom they find their way mysteriously to the black market. High prices are paid to procure such items, and many a senora or signorina is today walking around Italy wearing clothing that originated as U.S. army issue. Suitably altered and dyed of course!

The blanket carrier has not progressed very far before he's confronted by my corporal, a blonde-haired, ruggedly-handsome giant of a man who is brandishing a large stick. An animated conversation ensues, and though I cannot hear what is being said actions suddenly speak louder than words when the stick comes down between the Italian's shoulder blades. The blanket drops to the side of the track, the smitten one makes good his escape and the corporal retrieves the bedding. Soldiers leaning out of their compartment windows cheer mightily at the sight of a thieving Eyetie getting his come-uppance, and they continue to cheer and shout until he's disappeared.

I shrug my shoulders and return to my seat, unable to find any sympathy in my heart for the light fingered thief. Wiping sweat from my brow I make a mental note to congratulate my heavy handed corporal on his vigilance at the first opportunity.

Following an overnight stay in Taranto I have this morning entrained troops whose service abroad is coming to an end. Chugging along at the quite reckless speed of approximately ten miles an hour we have now moved inland and the engine is paying the price of its foolhardiness. Wheezing and lurching it comes to a stop with a bronchitic cough.

'Oh heck, now what?' I poke my head out of the window and see the engine driver bearing down on me. His gesticulations and accompanying shouts leave me in no doubt as to the reason for the sudden halt. The engine has developed a fault, and repairs will have to be undertaken before any further progress can be made.

'Si, si,' I say, resigning myself to a long wait.

As the sun's rays blaze into my compartment I position myself in such a way that my face gets the benefit of its tanning qualities, for I do not intend to be pale faced on my eventual return to Blighty for "demob". I must, after all, show those pallid and unhealthy looking relations of mine that at least one member of the family has hurled back the Hun in a country that was both foreign and hot. I divest myself of my battledress blouse and settle down to read a well fingered, unexpurgated English language version of *"Lady Chatterley's Lover"*, printed in Sweden. The heat is far too oppressive, however, for four letter words, so I close the book and use it as a fan. I mop my brow and place my feet on a folded blanket, the sight of which reminds me that I have yet to congratulate my corporal, something I really must do at the next meal halt.

The walls of the compartment are adorned with tinted photographs of Italian archaeological sites and beauty spots. Age is fast turning them yellow but they still have the power to delight. Capri, Sorrento, a smoking Vesuvius, Pompeian ruins, the Colosseum, and Milan cathedral. The photograph of the last-named having slipped sideways is trying to part company with its frame.

I stand up, take a closer look, and promise myself that one day, when I am filthy rich, I shall return to enjoy these wonderful sights.

An encouraging snort from the engine suggests that progress is being made. I move to the window but regrettably see no tell-tale signs of steam. Local inhabitants have gathered as they invariably do when the train makes one of its frequent unscheduled stops, and the usual bargaining is going on. Silk stockings, pure silk of course, watches, and puppet like toys that are worked by string are being offered for sale to soldiers and airmen who, although their kit bags are full to overflowing, still manage to find room for souvenirs.

A crowd of people has gathered outside the compartment occupied by my staff and as I survey them my stare becomes ever more incredulous. The medic's hands are full of lire and scurrying away is an Italian whose hands are also full, but he's clutching a blanket not paper money. The blanket is not of the rough British variety but of the superior U.S. type, a piece of bedding remarkably similar to the one recently retrieved by my vigilant corporal.

I'm really catching flies now but my mouth only opens to its full extent when I see that two-striped hero emerge from behind the last carriage to re-enact the tragi-comedy of less than twenty four hours ago.

Slowly my mouth closes and the implication of what I have just observed clarifies in my mind. I open my compartment door, drop down onto the track, and make for the staff quarters, where I discover the medic and his partner-in-crime in their counting house. Italian money lies on a handsome looking blanket which covers two pairs of knees, and my sudden arrival sees mouths open even wider than mine had done earlier, and when their owners jump to attention hundreds of lire notes cascade to the floor.

'What in blazes do you think you are up to?' I thunder. 'Just how long has this caper been going on?'

'W, wh, what caper, sir?' stutters the lance-bombardier.

'You know damn well what!' I point at the money, and then at the blanket. 'How many times have you flogged that?'

'Only the once, sir,' the corporal lies.

'Rubbish! I've seen your little game played out twice already on this trip, and from your expertise I'm quite sure you've been doing it for some time. How much money do you take the poor blighters for?'

'Two thousand lire, sir.'

'Two thousand lire! I'm not well versed in con-tricks but I really must congratulate the two of you. Two thousand lire and the same yesterday! Rich pickings indeed! Huh, to think that you've made the equivalent of twenty English pounds! Come on, pick it up and hand it over. I'll have yesterday's takings as well, plus the blanket if you please.'

The medic gives the other a furtive glance. 'We can't, sir,' he says, somewhat sheepishly.

'Can't? What d'you mean, can't?'

'We can't hand over the money we got yesterday because we haven't got it, we've spent it.'

'Don't give me that,' I say, fast losing my temper. 'We were only in Taranto for the one night so how can you have spent it.'

'We picked up a couple of birds,' says the corporal boldly, before adding a reluctant, 'sir'.

'My God! They must be getting really expensive if you had to pay that sort of money. Now smarten yourselves up because when we get to Milan we'll be visiting H.Q. to pay the C.O. a visit. Oh, and one other thing, I suggest you visit the nearest P.A.C., because most of the tarts in Taranto are dosed up to their eyebrows. I'm quite sure both of you will have caught a full house!'

I return to my carriage and wonder how often the crafty couple have flogged the blanket I'm carrying, and how many Italians they've taken for a ride! I've always thought it was the natives one had to be wary of but now I'm not so sure. One thing's for certain though, from now on I won't be so hard on Eyeties.

Clambering aboard I hear a welcome "toot" which indicates that the journey is about to re-commence. I place the lire on one of the compartment seats and cover them with the blanket.

Perspiring freely I remove my shirt which after recent exertions is fit only for the wash tub, and reach for my travel bag.

It's not where I had left it on the rack.

I glance about and to my dismay find that the compartment is empty except for the photographs I'd admired earlier, and as Milan cathedral floats down the truth dawns. I've been robbed! Thieving bloody Eyeties have relieved me of just about everything!

Damn! Damn! Damn! My battledress blouse, gone! Which means that I have lost my wallet, money, pay-book, identity card, train conducting papers and the lucky locket which accompanied me on all my bombing "ops". My treasured photographs! The Waaf I fancied at Waltham, Mum and Dad on holiday, the young lady I had met in Stoke on my embarkation leave, my crew at Jesi. The naughty postcards I bought off an Arab in Suez. A new pair of shoes, a couple of shirts, pyjamas and bedding. My shaving kit, in its handsome leather case, which had been a twenty-first birthday present from Tom, Ginger and the rest of my "Death or Glory" crew. Gone, as they too are gone.

A cold fury wells up inside me. *Ye gods! I'm no better off than the millions of displaced persons who are wandering aimlessly about Europe.* Huh! Come to think of it they probably have more possessions than me, because all I own is a dirty shirt, crumpled shorts, smelly socks, and a pair of tatty brothel creepers! I have no papers and no identity!

Yet, on reflection, I do have something. A smooth G.I. blanket that is worth quite a bit on the black market, and two thousand lire in cash!

Chapter 25

Mammas Mia

(Early Autumn 1945)

"Proceed to Naples and await further instructions." I had received the order with considerable pleasure, for the thought of spending more time in the city appealed to me. But alas, my stay is to be of the briefest, for when I arrived late last night I was told to return to Milan today with thirty women! Further investigation has revealed that the women concerned are Italian, pregnant, and married to British servicemen. My task is to transport them on the first leg of their journey to Britain.

After picking up my staff of two at 6 a.m., I make for the stazione where I am directed to an isolated bay filled with a noisy rabble. Skirting round this vociferous crowd, I find that my train is not made up of the usual uncomfortable coaches, but of "*Wagon-Lits*", which, as my medic succinctly puts it, would have been the perquisite of people, 'with a bob or two,' before the war.

Sorting through my documents, I find that compartments have already been allocated to my "forces sweethearts". I read their names and smile for they sound so incongruous. Luciana Blenkinsop, Silvana Ogglethorpe, Gina Lucia Copeland, Carla Preece, and there are more in similar vein.

I can find no reference to eating arrangements and must assume therefore that we will be stopping at the usual meal halts. A scribbled note informs me that the Italian rail network has been instructed to give the train priority, whatever that means.

06.45. Time to get weaving. I search for my R.T.O. liaison bod but cannot see him in the crowd of people encamped on the platform. There are important persons in top hats, a couple of seemingly high-ranking military men straight out of Italian Opera, and the station-master resplendent in uniform.

Everywhere people are wailing and teeth are being gnashed. Parting is not "such sweet sorrow", it is sheer agony. Sobbing mothers, clad in black, cling to big-bellied hysterical daughters, convinced - I suspect - that they will never see their offspring again. Sisters hug, children tug and babies howl. Fathers weep unashamedly, uncles console and aunts dab at wet eyes with damp kerchiefs. Grandfathers and grandmothers genuflect, a priest mumbles to himself and most everyone fingers what I assume are rosary beads.

'Sorry, I just couldn't find a way through,' apologises the chap I've been waiting for.

'Can we get them aboard? I should have left by now.'

'I doubt it. The girls refuse to leave unless a doctor travels with them. I've never met anything quite like this before. Have you seen your passengers? Most of them are quite large. I don't blame them for wanting a doctor in attendance. And they all have labels, just like the evacuee kids back home did at the start of the war!'

I'm pondering the matter when my medic appears, and the sight of him solves the problem.

'I think I might have the answer,' I say. 'It's a long shot, and I may be biting off more than I can chew, but if it's a doctor they want then they can have one. Get the mothers-to-be on board. If they resist get the police to assist you, I reckon you'll need all the help you can get to part them from their own mothers.'

'I don't get it,' says the medic.

'You will. Give me your arm band.'

23.00. This morning's farewells were of the stuff to break even the sternest of hearts but the girls are quieter now, doing their best to put a brave face on things.

From the depths of his kit bag my lance-corporal medic has conjured up a book that concerns itself with medical emergencies, and chapter five deals with the birth of a baby. Phew! There is certainly more to it than Hollywood movies had led me to believe, much more than just a bowl of hot water and a towel. The diagrams in the book are explicit enough but as we approach Milan I feel that my midwifery skills will not be required, though one false alarm had earlier set my nerves jangling. My fears had been allayed, however, by the medic who, with a twinkle in his eye, assured me that it was only a collision of wind and water.

I must say the girls have behaved quite splendidly, and they have been delighted with the close attention paid to them at all times by their medical man, a charming blue uniformed "dottore" who proudly wears the badge of his profession on the sleeve of his battle-dress blouse - a Red Cross arm band.

Chapter 26

Alano in Milano

(Late Summer 1945)

A knock on the door of the bedroom I occupy - in the grotty hotel that has been made available for the use of train conducting officers based in Milan - disturbs my slumber. Without waiting for a "come in", in walks pyjama clad Taffy, and judging from the look on his face the world is about to end. The smile that usually adorns his visage has been replaced by a look of despair. That he has done something of which he is thoroughly ashamed is quite evident.

I sit up in bed and ask him what on earth is troubling him.

'Oh Al.' His eyes fill with tears. 'Oh Al, last night!'

'What about last night?'

'I er, I had, I er,' he's wild eyed now. 'I went with a woman!'

'You mean?'

He nods his head and avoids my gaze.

I can hardly believe my ears. Taffy the righteous! Taffy the chapel! Religion all day Sunday, choir practice Monday evenings and Men's Bible class every other Wednesday. Taffy, the squeaky clean! Taffy, ever faithful to Megan the girl he married on his embarkation leave. Taffy, fallen by the wayside! I find the news hard to believe because he is due to return to Blighty for "de-mob" in a few weeks' time. Well, well, I would never have countenanced such a fall from grace, never dreamt that he of all people would succumb to the pleasures of the flesh!

'How could I have been so stupid?' he groans, gazing at the threadbare carpet.

He repeats the phrase over and over, and when more self-criticism and castigation follows I feel like I'm a priest at a confessional.

'I have always blamed such weakness in others on alcohol,' he says, 'but I can't offer that as an excuse. I only had a couple of tonic waters at the club.'

Oh Megan, he's failed you my girl, and by gosh he knows it!

He's wringing his hands now, telling me between sighs that he hadn't used anything!

'You did it bareback, d'you mean?' I shake my head in disbelief.

He recoils at the crude expression but nods nevertheless.

I can imagine what he's thinking, that he will have caught just about everything there is to catch. Head buried in his hands, he mumbles words which include "al ricovero" and "cathedral", which lead me to believe that the sinful act had climaxed in an air raid shelter not far from the Piazza del Duomo.

Hardly the place to sin, I think, and not all that far from the Santa Maria delle Grazie and Leonardo's "Last Supper". My mind wanders and I find myself wondering if the last time the shelter had been used was when I'd taken part in the bombing of the city in August 1943, flying from Lincolnshire in Lancaster "H2", LM 321.

Taffy's feeling bitter now, wondering why, if he was going to be unfaithful, he hadn't availed himself of other much more attractive females. The self-styled princess in Sorrento for instance, or the beautiful guide who had temporarily stolen his heart with beguiling glances as she had described the architectural delights in the Sant'Eustorgio.

The bitterness evaporates. Oh woe is he, will he ever be able to look his Megan in the eye again?

Poor Taffy! I gaze helplessly and try to think of something to say that might console him. I'm genuinely sorry because he is without doubt "Mister Nice Guy", a chap who has never harmed anyone apart from an unknown number of the enemy when he was bomb-aimer in a Liberator. I think of telling him that his straying from the straight and narrow - his sowing of one wild oat - was something that he would never do again, that what had happened was just a mental aberration.

He will confess! Honesty will be his best policy. As soon as he sees his Megan his first act will be to make a clean breast of things.

He then tells me he thought he had more sense, that, like me, he knew when to stop when it came to matters sexual.

I suppress a smile and wonder where that fancy notion had come from. Know when to stop indeed! You have to start before you can stop!

He doesn't realise that just two things have prevented me from taking the plunge. One is inexperience, something that makes me scared of being laughed at or humiliated by some knowledgeable tart. The other is fear, a horror of venereal disease that has been with me ever since as a rookie I had been made to see an explicit American "one-reeler", a film deliberately shot by the Yanks in glorious Technicolor in order to ram its message home to their armed forces.

Yet, despite these warnings, I shudder to think how many times I've "lusted after the flesh". Why only a couple of weeks ago I nearly come a cropper.

Would it bring some cheer to Taffy if I was to tell him of that experience? Would it show him that I too was prone to temptation? The baring of my soul would also explain why his sleep had been broken recently in the middle of the night by a female voice wailing, 'Alano'. Cries eventually silenced by a chorus of rude words from half a dozen, sleep-disturbed train conducting officers.

'I'm no angel Taff, believe you me. Why only recently when I went for a stroll in the Giardini Publici my thoughts turned immediately to sex, for the place was full of couples embracing and pretty pram pushing young females. Thinking naughty thoughts I went to the Galleria which was full of fashionably dressed lovelies, and by the time I reached the Officers' club I was most definitely in the mood for love.

'Two of our chaps were just leaving with shapely young ladies clinging to them like limpets. 'You on your own?' the chap they call "Bunch of Hair" asked me, and, when I nodded, his pal "Puffing Bailey" suggested that I go with them to the girls' apartment.

'Not wanting to play gooseberry I shook my head, excusing myself on the grounds that I was bound for Villach early the following morning.

"Oh, come on," "Bunch" insisted. "I'm sure Anna here has got a sister, haven't you my beauty?"

'I doubt if his female companion understood one word of what he'd said but she nodded her head nevertheless.

'I hesitated but when it occurred to me that the sister might look like Anna I agreed to accompany them.

'Misgivings began to set in though long before I climbed the stairs to the apartment, and when the door closed behind me and the others disappeared I knew that I'd been taken for a ride for standing before me was not Anna's sister! Anna's grandmother, more like! A woman with a moustache boasting more hairs than my own.

'Thanks very much Bunch and Puffing I thought, you've certainly lived up to your reputation as practical jokers.'

I pause for breath and glance at Taffy. He looks miles away, which probably means I'm overdoing things and boring him stiff. Oh well, never mind, I can only hope I'm keeping his mind off his troubles.

293

'I was standing looking at the woman wondering what to do next when she held out her hand. Hardly knowing what I was doing I handed her my cap which she placed on a peg. Then, pushing me onto a bed, she tried to kiss me.

'I panicked. I had to get away, but how?

'She opened her mouth but to my intense relief it was to ask a question. "Komay see key arma?" the words sounded like, so I knew that she was asking me my name.

'"Alan," I said, rather feebly.

'"Alano."

'"No, Alan."

'"Alano, si."

'I certainly didn't ask her what her name was because I didn't want to know. I was only interested in one thing, how to get out of her clutches. After murmuring "Alano" to herself her lips sought mine and her fingers started fiddling with my flies. What the woman didn't realise was that she would never get my thing to stand to attention.

'The unwanted attacks on my mouth had left my lips dry, and she must have noticed that I was continually licking them because all of a sudden she said something like "bayray".

'"Si!" I cried, hoping that I had understood her, and that she would bring me a beer.

'She continued to talk, however, and when several references were made to a "Joe", I realised that Yanks had met "Anna's grandmother" before me, which was yet another reason for avoiding her embraces.

'Rolling off me, she ran her fingers through my hair, then disappeared into what I assumed was a kitchen.

'This was my chance. It was now or never! The moment she disappeared from view I tiptoed to the door, thanked the Lord for well-oiled hinges, and made good my escape.

'Once outside I realised that I hadn't got a clue where I was! I remembered passing close to the Castello Sforzesco shortly before we'd reached the apartment, and figured that if I turned right I'd be travelling in the proper direction. And right proved to be right, for within minutes the imposing pile had loomed into view. Hastening on, I got to wondering if the lady I had so unceremoniously dumped would try to follow me. I had no idea but in order to avoid a possible scene in a public place - for I knew that hell hath no fury like a signora scorned - I broke into a trot. Placing my hand on my head to hold down my field service cap I found to my dismay that it was not there, that I had left it hanging on a peg in Anna's grandmother's apartment!

'On the other side of the street a woman was making her way towards the castello. Being uncertain of my whereabouts I hurried over to ask her for directions but my polite, "Buona sera, signora," sent her scurrying away like a scared rabbit. "Scusi," I said to a man who had been walking some distance behind the woman. "Dove albergo Esperia er, er." You would hardly credit it but I couldn't recall the other half of our hotel's name, and when it eventually came to me the chap was long gone.'

Taffy is silent now, more composed. He gives me a wan smile which I take to be one of encouragement, so I plunge once more into my tale.

'"Parla Inglese?" I asked of another man.

'He shook his head at first and muttered what sounded like, "Non ho capito," but then showed a flicker of understanding when I blurted out "Stazione."

'"Stazione Centrale? Stazione Genova? Stazione Nord?"

'"Stazione Centrale."

295

'"Si, si." And with that he turned himself into a sort of whirling dervish. Pointing, gesticulating, raising a leg, he showed me the way to go home. "Vias" poured from his lips - Pontaccio, San Marco, della Moscova. Then he seemed to change his mind and I was given a new set of streets - Turati, Piazza della Republica, and finally the via I so much wanted to hear - Via V. Pisani.

'"Yes, yes, grazie, si, si, that's the street, Pisani, just down the road from Stazione Centrale. Grazie tante."

'"Prego, prego."

'"Arrivederla."

'"Buona sera."

'"Mille grazie."

'"Prego, prego."

'Minutes later I was back here in the hotel with my door locked and the light out. I climbed into bed and was congratulating myself on my escape when I heard a distant female voice shouting, "Alano!' 'Alano!" So she had followed me. She must have got the address off "Bunch of Hair" and "Puffing Bailey", who had decided to cause me further embarrassment.

'"Alano!' Alano!"

'Gosh but her voice had sounded eerie. As it echoed through the hotel I trembled, felt really scared, almost as if I'd committed a crime. All I could do was whisper, "Go away woman, please go away." After what seemed an eternity she did just that but not until she had brought down the wrath of yourself, and the rest of the erstwhile sleeping T.C.O.s, on her head.'

Taffy's half smiling now. There's precious little joy in it but it's an improvement on the earlier tears. He has perked up to such an extent that he is thinking about food!

'Breakfast? Yeah, OK,' I agree. "I'm peckish too. Let's bribe Luigi into giving us three eggs with our bacon. A couple of fags work wonders with him!'

Shaven and reasonably well groomed the two of us avoid the early morning maniacs who are fast turning the Piazza Duca d'Aosta into a race track, and enter the Excelsior, which, though reserved for senior ranks, graciously provides food for we train conducting officers. "Try and look invisible", had been the advice given to us on our first visit, and not wishing to tread on superior corns we have kept out of the lounges and taken our food in a remote corner of the elegant dining room.

Luigi, our favourite waiter, is doing us proud as I knew he would. We tuck into ham and eggs, munch toast, and partake of the delicious Excelsior coffee.

'I take it you have given "Bunch of Hair" and that mate of his a mouthful?'

'No, they've kept out of sight since it happened. Which reminds me I haven't told you the best bit. When I crept downstairs early the following morning to go to Villach you'll never guess what was hanging from the hat rack?'

'Your forage cap, of course, courtesy of Anna's great grandma.'

'Got it in one!'

After breakfast I make an effort to complete the letter to my parents that I commenced yesterday. Now let me see. I've told them about my visit to Lake Como, and that Gracie Fields is to entertain servicemen at La Scala, an opera house which the Eyeties claim is the finest in the world. I've mentioned that I may soon be learning to ski having been invited by some of the chaps to go with them to Cortina d' Ampezzo in the Dolomites, and that I have purchased a camera.

What else has happened? Not much. I don't think I'll tell them about my visit to the Piazza Loretto to view the spot where Mussolini and his lady friend Clara Petacci were hung upside down by partisans, and I doubt very much if I will be telling them of my encounter with the bearded lady of Milano!

Chapter 27

The Swiss Lieutenant's Woman

(Spring 1946)

The Lieutenant has been more relaxed of late but today I sense that some of his earlier diffidence has returned. He has nevertheless thrown up the usual polite salute, and apologised for having to escort me and my train full of demob happy troops once again through Switzerland.

'As you know we have to make a show of our neutrality,' he says, before presenting me with a small gift as a token of his friendship. It is a bottle of water and he is apologising yet again, this time because he thinks the contents will be too warm to be savoured properly.

'Thanks very much. I'm sure it will be delicious.'

'In the summertime, in our Alpine villages, such water when ice cold will quench the most insistent thirst.'

Good grief, he sounds like a travelogue as he fidgets, averts his gaze and lapses into silence.

I glance out of the compartment window as the train fairly hurtles through sunny Sierre, and realise that my glum companion would normally have mentioned his fiancée half a dozen times by now - for if anyone is head over heels in love it is the lieutenant. He does on occasion of course speak of other things. His family, his high hopes for the post-war world, his interest in the modelling of clay and the making of pots, but in the end he always returns to the love of his life.

The train slows through Sion. Glancing upwards I admire the twin fortresses that crown its rocky peaks and wait for news of the wonderful Yvette but the lieutenant remains depressingly silent.

Come on my friend, if you have something to say, or to ask, then please get it off your chest.

We will shortly be passing through Martigny and he hasn't as yet sought the usual assurance from me that when I myself am discharged from the R.A.F., I will speak to a manufacturer in the "Potteries" about the possibility of having a clay bust of his sweetheart "cooked" - as he so quaintly puts it.

The tension mounts. I see Chillon castle reflected in the waters of Lake Geneva and feel I could cut the atmosphere in the compartment with the blade of a Swiss army knife. Relief eventually comes, however, when the loudspeakers at Lausanne station blare out their customary recorded welcome to the, 'gallant men of the British army!'

I follow the lieutenant into a station restaurant redolent with the smell of cigars and coffee, where I sign documentation relevant to the passage of the train through Switzerland.

Wolf whistles accompany my return to the compartment. This shrill cacophony is not for my benefit, however, it is directed by the uncouth but gallant men of the British army towards a number of Swiss lasses who are handing out chocolate and baskets of fruit.

On a previous occasion I was introduced to one of these young ladies, Francoise by name, and she's here again - pretty as a picture in her cantonal costume. 'I am to go soon to England,' she says, 'for I have been accepted as an au pair by a Lord you see.'

'Good Lord,' I joke. 'What Lord?'

But his name escapes her, and she's not even sure where his ancestral pile is located. Surrey she thinks, or Sussex maybe. After presenting me with a bar of chocolate she bestows the lightest of kisses on my cheek, and makes me promise that I will meet her in London when she first comes to England.

Um, if she's going to be that liberal with her affection, I will most certainly keep my word.

With the necessary formalities completed the train glides smoothly out of the station to the farewell strains of martial music, leaving behind a collection of rather forlorn-looking, empty-handed young ladies.

The lieutenant shifts uncomfortably in his seat. That he wants to ask me something is now so obvious I feel I must do my utmost to encourage him.

'How is Yvette?'

'Oh, she is wonderful, wonderful, and though the two of you have yet to meet she sends you her best wishes.' He pauses for a moment and then blurts out. 'We are to marry shortly you know.'

'No, I didn't know. Congratulations.' I reach over and shake his hand.

'Yvette and I would like very much if you could come to the wedding.'

'That's very kind of you both, but with my demobilisation from the R.A.F. due any time now I'm unable to make definite plans for the future.'

He nods, then blurts out. 'I, I, want to ask a favour of you.'

Ah, at last!

'It is to do with my getting married.' He bites his lip. 'Oh dear, I fear this might embarrass you as much as it does me.'

'This is my fifth year in the R.A.F.,' I laugh. 'I can assure you that I've quite forgotten how to blush!'

'Well, because of the war, we have become short of many things in Switzerland.'

'Not bars of milk chocolate and baskets of fresh fruit, judging from the amount you so kindly give to the gallant members of the British forces.'

'No.' He shakes his head. 'Oh dear, this really is most difficult.'

'We shall reach the frontier before long Lieutenant and you will be leaving me. What is it you want?'

'I was wondering if you could find, er, get that is, er, any, er, rubbers for me? You see they are in very short supply here in my country and as I am marrying my darling Yvette as I told you, I was wondering if...?'

'Frenchies?' I interrupt.

'Pardon?'

'French letters.'

'Oh, is that what you call them?'

'They have several names. Condoms, contraceptives, sheaths, johnnies. I think Sam Pepys called them 'armour'.'

'Who?'

'Never mind. Now let me see. There are several prophylactic aid centres in Milan and I could visit them all I suppose but I've no idea how many they would let me have. Do you suppose they would object if I asked them for a gross?'

'A gross?'

'Sorry, I was thinking of a rather weak joke I heard recently. A chap, taking his lady friend to Brighton for a dirty week-end, goes to the chemist for a gross of, er, you-know-whats. On the Monday he returns to the shop and complains bitterly that his week-end had been ruined because they had only sold him one hundred and forty three.'

The Lieutenant is not amused. 'Gross?' he queries.

'Yeah. Twelve dozen.'

'I do not understand your English jokes.'

'I'm not surprised, it's the way I tell them.'

'I would certainly appreciate it very much though if you would make enquiries.'

'Sure. I'll see what I can do.'

But what I really need to know is just how many of the things he wants. It is a delicate matter, even an educated guess could prove to be well wide of the mark. I have no desire to cause further embarrassment so I can hardly ask him how many times a night he, a madly in love young Swiss lieutenant, expects to roger his new missus.

'I shall of course pay for the articles.'

'Oh no, I won't want any money. The medical authorities in Milan are always stressing the danger of unprotected sex but those gallant British servicemen of ours pay no heed, and as a consequence V.D is quite rampant. In an attempt to combat the menace contraceptives have been made available, at no cost, to members of the armed forces. So, if I do manage to get my hands on any, you can rest assured they will not cost you anything. Come to think of it, they can be a wedding present for you and Yvette.'

The lieutenant thanks me courteously but I feel that in spite of what I have said he will repay me in some way.

I'm home, home at last, back home in dear old England, with several weeks of paid "de-mob" leave to enjoy before I return to my civilian job.

After an emotional reunion with my family I present them with their 'presents'. For dad, a handsome watch and extending wooden book-ends. Hand woven linen and a cuckoo-clock for Mum. Fancy hankies and a musical box in the shape of a Swiss chalet for my sister, and for my brother-in-law a pipe, tobacco jar, cigars and cigarettes. Lastly, for all of them to enjoy, several bars of chocolate.

Father, taking me aside, thanks me profusely. 'You've brought some very nice things,' he says. 'I'm sure none of us expected so much. They must have cost you a small fortune.'

'Oh, I don't know.' I reply, but I do really.

A gross of French, er, er, you-know-whats.

HEY, DON'T YOU REMEMBER?
You called me Al

Appendices and Glossary

Appendix 1

Papal Blessing - The Aftermath

The rear half of Martin Marauder "S" Sugar had fallen to earth in a field near to Cusignacco, a village situated a few kilometres south west of Udine. An Italian family named Vidiamar who lived in the village were first on the scene. They examined the wreckage of the stricken aircraft and discovered the bodies of three airmen. Two of the bodies had suffered severe burns and the features of the third man, who was larger in stature than the others, were so burned as to be unrecognisable. After completing their inspection the Vidiamars returned to their house taking with them parts of the wreckage as 'mementos'.

The forward part of "S" Sugar lay near to the tiny hamlet of Gerbasutia on land owned by Giovanni Jureti, and it was he who discovered three bodies in the cockpit and the aircraft's two engines lying close by. He also found two more badly burned bodies but further inspection was prevented by the arrival of German soldiers who removed items from the pockets of the airmen. Jureti then heard a name read out which sounded like "Brichard". After the departure of the soldiers the Italian came across two legs which he promptly buried. He also discovered a Browning .5 machine gun and, while he was examining it, he was joined by a number of locals, one of whom took a photograph of the wreckage. An animated discussion then ensued and the conclusion was reached that the aircraft had collided with another in mid-air and then fallen to earth.

An Italian called Del Zotto went to the field where he had seen the other Marauder aircraft crash and on arrival he counted five bodies. Two of the airmen appeared to have fallen out of the wreckage with their parachutes half opened and Del Zotto was puzzled to see that their clothing differed in colour, one uniform being blue, the other khaki. He was soon joined by soldiers from a nearby anti-aircraft battery who removed all papers and valuables from the bodies. Civilians too arrived on the scene and after dismantling parts of the aircraft they scurried away with various bits and pieces in the direction of their homes.

Two female members of the Italian Red Cross gazed in horror as the two Marauder aircraft, both apparently out of control, dived into a field in the vicinity of Cusignacco. One of the ladies was Ida Vignando, whose husband was a prisoner of war in Germany, the other was Lucia Basandella. They hastened to the burning wreckage of one of the aircraft where they found that two of the flyers, Lieutenant Funkey and Sergeant Haynes, appeared to be still alive. Neither of the men was conscious, however, and within five minutes of the nurses arrival both were dead.

A mixed group of Italian fascists and German soldiers arrived and after ordering the ladies not to assist in any way they removed documents, money, watches, rings and a cigarette lighter. The ladies ignored the order and as they continued to search they found a badly mutilated body which was minus a left leg, right side of face and right upper arm. These remains were those of Lieutenant Van Rensburg. Ida Vignando then discovered the body of Lieutenant Paola and came across part of a "Mae West" marked "Sgt. Hipwell", a piece of material with the initials "J. B." written on it and two twelve squadron officers' mess tickets. At this juncture a senior official in the Italian Red Cross arrived and ordered the two nurses to leave the area immediately, insisting that they were to have nothing more to do with the affair.

The twelve bodies of the dead airmen were left unburied in the field at Cusignacco despite offers by the two Italian Red Cross nurses to bury them. The German Commandant of Udine, a Major reputed to be ruthless in all his actions, visited the scene where he abused and kicked the remains and would do nothing about interference by dogs. A few days later, on the fourth of January, 1945, the bodies were removed to a mortuary. The Germans were very crude in this action and it was left to the nurses to arrange the bodies in the coffins provided. The twelve airmen were then buried at San Vito in the military section of the civil cemetery, and with the Italian authorities being under the impression that the crews were American the burials were recorded as "In Memorandi dodeci Aviatori Americani". The priest in charge later offered to have concrete slabs with marble plaques erected, and when this offer was accepted he was asked to inscribe them as "Aviatori Sudafricane. S.A.A.F. morti 29 dicembre 1944".

In Memorandi

Marauder Aircraft "S"   Pilot. Lt. C. J. P. Brichard. 2nd Pilot. Lt. P. J. Van Rensburg. Observer [Navigator]. Lt. D. John. Top Gunner. W/O. A. Ramsay. WT/AG. W/O. A. A. Jordan. Tail Gunner. W/O. J. W. Thompson.

Marauder Aircraft "R"   Pilot. Lt. H. T. Funkey. 2nd Pilot. Sgt. A. J. Morley. Observer [Navigator]. Lt. J. J. Paola. Top Gunner. W/O. D. P. Huskisson. WT/AG. Sgt. P. O. Haynes. Tail Gunner. Sgt. J. H. Hipwell.

Marauder aircraft "V" Victor, piloted by Major Braithwaite, suffered severe damage over Udine but the six crew members were able to parachute to safety. Lt. Anderson, the wireless operator, who had sprained an ankle on landing, was picked up by Italian partisans operating in the Buttrio area who took him by bicycle to a "safe house" in Caminetto. He had been there about eight hours when a German search party discovered him and as he was being taken prisoner, six of the partisans were led away to be shot for having befriended him. Anderson was taken to Udine where he was re-united with his crew who had all been captured. They were interrogated at some length by the Germans, with a Dr Lassel of Udine acting as interpreter.

The conclusion of the war brought release for the Major and his crew from a P.O.W. camp but there was no freedom for Dr Lassel, he being put under immediate house arrest. Lt. Luttig, the German commander of the Buttrio section, who had been captured and detained at Gemona, was at a loss for words when asked for an explanation of what he had done with the million lire he had received from each partisan in exchange for their freedom.

The lady doctor in the municipality was later accused of being obstructionist. With her authority she could have insisted on an earlier burial of the dead aircrew but she would do nothing, being anxious only to please the Germans.

The ruthless German commander at Udine was reported to the Allied War Crimes Commission for his acts of brutality.

Appendix II

R.I.P.

I flew with the airmen listed below on night operations over Germany and Italy in 1943. They were all killed in action.

S/L D. C. Anset D.F.C. and Pilot Officer J. Walker, with whom I flew on fifteen operations flying in Lancaster ED 749 from Waltham [Grimsby]. They transferred to 156 Pathfinder Squadron in July 1943.

They failed to return from Berlin having taken off from Warboys on 22 November, 1943 at 16.55 hours. They have no known graves and their names are recorded on the R.A.F. Memorial at Runnymede.

F/L S. C. P. Godfrey D.F.C., who had been my navigator at 100 squadron, Waltham, also transferred to 156 squadron.

He failed to return from Frankfurt, 4th/5th October, 1943 and is buried in Durnbach War Cemetery.

The following, flying in Lancaster JA 864, UM "D2", 626 Squadron, based at Wickenby, failed to return from Berlin, 2nd/3rd December, 1943.

They are buried in Berlin War Cemetery. Plot 5, Row E: -

S/L George Alan Roden D.F.C, aged 25. Pilot. Grave No. 2.

Sgt. Thomas R. Jackson. Bomb Aimer. Grave No. 5.

Sgt. Leslie C. J. Street, aged 34. Navigator. Grave No. 4.

Sgt. Henri Antonius Van Hal, aged 20. Flt. Eng. Grave No. 3.

The other two members of my crew, Sgt. Harold W. Whitmore, Mid-upper Gunner, and Sgt. George H. Brittle, Wireless Operator, have no known graves, and their names are recorded on the R.A.F. Memorial at Runnymede.

I never flew with Sergeant A. G. Luke, who had the misfortune to fly in my place on 2nd/3rd December, 1943.

He is buried in Berlin War Cemetery, Plot 5, Row E, Grave No.1

The Author photographed in May 1989 beside the graves of his long dead crew in the Berlin War Cemetery.

Gunnery Combat Report

12 Squadron. S.A.A.F.
3rd. March, 1945.
Target: CONEGLIANO. [Railway Marshalling Yards]

No. 3 Box. Lead Aircraft. 'N'.

Report of Attack by Enemy Fighters

Top Gunner: Pilot Officer Alcock.

No. of enemy a/c in attack	Rounds fired	Results and remarks
One	50	Fire diverted enemy a/c. Hits observed.
One	50	Tail obstructed view. Intercom u/s.
One	150	Observed hits, dense black smoke. Enemy aircraft damaged.
Two	80	Feinted attack, fire diverted enemy.
One	50	Fire diverted attack. No hits observed.
One	-	Turret and guns damaged by enemy a/c.
One	-	Attacking aircraft jumped by Spitfire(s).

Tail Gunner: Pilot Officer Menear.

No. of enemy a/c in attack	Rounds fired	Results and remarks
One	25	Returned fire.
One	130	Hits registered on enemy a/c which dived away trailing black smoke.
One	35	Fire diverted attack.

Waist Gunner: Lt. Smith.

Dropped pamphlets. No rounds fired, both guns damaged.

Glossary

A.C. Plonk	Aircraftman, 2nd class
A.C.W.	Aircraftwoman. A rank in the W.A.A.F.
Ammo	Ammunition
A.T.C.	Air Training Corps
A.T.S.	Auxiliary Territorial Service
Bail out	To land using a parachute
Belly flop	Wheels-up landing
Blonde job	A fair haired female
Blood wagon	Ambulance
Bob	A shilling
Bod	A person
Bullseye	A Bomber Command night exercise
Cheesed off	Fed-up
Chocks away	Let's get started
Chute	A parachute
Circuits & bumps	Practice take offs & landings
Civvy street	Civilian life
Clapped out	Worn out
Close the hanger doors	Stop talking 'shop'
C.O.	Commanding Officer
Conservatory	Perspex cabin of an aircraft
Cookie	4,000lb blast bomb
Corkscrew	A manoeuvre to evade enemy night fighter attack

DAF	Desert Air Force
D.F.C.	Distinguished Flying Cross
D.F.M.	Distinguished Flying Medal
D.n.c.o.	Duty not carried out
Erk	An aircraftman
Elsan	Chemical toilet
Fizzer	A charge
Flak	Anti-aircraft gunfire: (Flieger Abwehr Kanonen)
Flg Off, (F/O)	Flying Officer
Flying Fort	Boeing Fortress Bomber, B 17
Flicks	Movies/Pictures
Flight	Flight Sergeant
Flt Lt., F/L, Flight Louie	Flight Lieutenant
Gen	Information
Get cracking	Make a move
Gong	Medal
Gremlin	Mischievous creature
GY	Grimsby
H2S	Scanning radar reflecting ground detail
H.C.U	Heavy Conversion Unit
Halibag, (Hallybag)	Halifax heavy bomber
I.O.	Intelligence Officer
ITMA	"It's that Man Again." A BBC comedy programme
Jankers	Punishment
Kites	Aircraft

L.A.C.W.	Leading Aircraftwoman. A rank in the W.A.A.F.
Limping Annie	Avro Anson aeroplane
L.M.F.	Lack of Moral Fibre. An R.A.F. designation for those who refused to fly, or cracked under the strain of duty. They were stripped of their rank and humiliated in front of their Command.
Mae West	Inflatable life jacket
M.O.	Medical Officer
N.A.A.F.I.	Navy, Army and Air Force Institutes. Providers of canteens.
N.C.O.	Non-commissioned officer
Nissen hut	Pre-fabricated hut with a corrugated iron semi-circular arching roof.
Oboe	Navigation aid
O.T.U.	Operational Training Unit
Op	Operation
P.A.C.	Prophylactic Aid Centre
pfc	American Army Private First Class
P.F.F.	Path Finder Force
P.R.U.	Photographic Reconnaissance ("Recce") Unit
Plt Off, (P/O) P.O.	Pilot Officer
P/O Prune	The dimwit featured in *"Tee Emm"*
Pit	Bed
R.T.O.	Railway Transport Officer
Scarecrow	German device to simulate exploding aircraft

Scrambled Egg(s)	Gold braid on service cap
Sgt. Sarge	Sergeant
S.P	Service Police
Skipper	Captain of an aircraft
Sparks	Wireless Operator
Split-arse cap	Field service cap
S/L	Squadron Leader
SHQ	Station Headquarters
S.W.O.	Station Warrant Officer
Tail-end Charlie	Rear gunner
T.I.	Target Indicator
Tee Emm	Training manual for aircrew
Thin blue band	The sleeve and shoulder insignia of an R.A.F. Pilot Officer
U/S	Unserviceable
Wakey-wakey pill	An anti-fatigue pill, allocated for use on long-range bombing missions
W.A.A.F.	Women's Auxiliary Air Force
Waaf	A member of Women's Auxiliary Air Force
W.O.	Warrant Officer
W/op.	Wireless Operator
White flash	Worn in the cap to show that an airman has been accepted for aircrew training
Wimpey	Wellington bomber
Window	Strips of foil used to confuse enemy radar
Wingco/Winco	Wing Commander
Wop-ag	Wireless operator-Air gunner

Overheard on an air test.

THE END

Printed in Great Britain
by Amazon.co.uk, Ltd.,
Marston Gate.